Industrial Organization
and the Digital Economy

Industrial Organization and the Digital Economy

edited by Gerhard Illing and
Martin Peitz

The MIT Press
Cambridge, Massachusetts
London, England

MIT Press books may be purchased at special quantity discounts for business or sales promotional use. For information, please email special_sales@mitpress.mit.edu or write to Special Sales Department, The MIT Press, 55 Hayward Street, Cambridge, MA 02142.

This book was set in Palatino on 3B2 by Asco Typesetters, Hong Kong and was printed and bound in the United States of America.

Library of Congress Cataloging-in-Publication Data

Industrial organization and the digital economy / edited by Gerhard Illing and Martin Peitz.
    p.   cm.
Includes bibliographical references and index.
ISBN-13: 978-0-262-09041-4 (alk. paper)
ISBN-10: 0-262-09041-4 (alk. paper)
1. High technology industries—Management. 2. Industrial organization. 3. Information technology—Management—Case studies. 4. Electronic commerce—Management—Case studies. I. Illing, Gerhard. II. Peitz, Martin.

HD62.37.I53   2006
658.8'72—dc22   2006041782

10   9   8   7   6   5   4   3   2   1

Contents

Industrial Organization
and the Digital Economy

1 Industrial Organization and the Digital Economy

Gerhard Illing and Martin Peitz

The digital economy has been in the public interest limelight since the 1990s. As a consequence of the digitalization of written work, music, games, and movies, these information goods can be moved almost without cost from one party to another. This has given rise to new business models and strategies used by firms operating in these markets. The rise of the Internet (and more recently broadband access) has had a dramatic impact on how real markets work: since transaction costs have fallen for physical goods also, more and more trade now takes place online—think of the success of eBay and Amazon as intermediaries and of Dell as an online seller.

Rapid innovations in computing capacity and upgrades of telephone and cable networks and wireless transmission have made it possible to transmit larger files faster so that software products, recorded music, and movies can be distributed via the Internet. Product information (including in the form of digital images) is also immediately accessible, increasing the flow of information. Software programs and other information goods, as well as the information that is distributed over the Internet, constitute the software side of the digital economy.

In this new economy, many things happen that seem to contradict standard economic wisdom: Platforms for software (such as Microsoft) subsidize other software producers that need this platform to offer software running on that platform. A famous pop artist (Robbie Williams) publicly invites his audience to download his music for free, right at the music industry's annual trade fair where executives are discussing how to contain the prospect of falling record sales due to the spread of piracy.[1] New Internet journals provide the latest news worldwide without charging consumers. Famous journalists, known as fervent protectors of their own copyright, start to post their reports (blogs) on the Internet without any protection. Many clever young software engineers seem to be addicted to publicly sharing the development of new software products. Is standard economic theory in conflict with the digital economy? Do we need a new paradigm for industrial organization of this economy? This book is an attempt to provide a better understanding of the software side of the digital economy.

1.1 Overview of the Book

The digital economy is evolving rapidly, leading to dramatic changes in the structure of many industrial sectors. To understand what is going on and where this process is heading, we first need a deep understanding of the facts of this rapid change. At the same time, we also need a sound theoretical base. This volume makes important contributions to both aspects of industrial organization (IO) in the digital economy.[2]

Theory should be guided by facts, and facts need theory for understanding. The book as a whole, as well as its individual chapters, tries to cross-fertilize facts and theory. Chapters 2 through 5 extensively present factual knowledge of the digital economy. The remaining chapters concentrate on the theoretical modeling of various IO aspects of the digital economy.

This book focuses on software and music as the two industries of information goods that have experienced the most significant recent change and so have dominated the public debate. Since the digital economy has given rise to electronic intermediation, the book also considers the impact of electronic commerce and intermediation on the markets for physical goods.[3]

Chapters 2 and 3 present stylized facts on the software industry. Chapter 2 provides an empirical analysis to measure the innovation value of software patents. Chapter 3 contains a number of case studies on the business models of software platforms. Chapters 4 and 5 concentrate on the music industry. Chapter 4 is a broad guide to music in the digital economy; chapter 5 discusses the evidence concerning the impact of file sharing on sales for recorded music. Chapters 6 through 8 present theoretical contributions to the understanding of firm strategies related to digital goods. Chapter 6 analyzes versioning strategies, chapter 7 product announcement strategies, and chapter 8 protection strategies. Finally, chapters 9 and 10 focus on electronic commerce. Chapter 9 contains a collection of facts and some theoretical analysis on the adoption of electronic commerce. Chapter 10 provides new theoretical perspectives based on insights from the literature on two-sided markets.

1.2   The Industrial Organization of the Digital Economy

Does the industrial organization literature have anything new to say about the digital economy? Or is this all old wine in new bottles? The industrial organization literature provides a general framework; many of its important theoretical and empirical insights over the past thirty years are directly applicable to the digital economy. Nevertheless, the digital economy poses new challenges for the theory of industrial organization: industries of the digital economy work quite differently from old industries, so new questions arise. Some old insights must be revised and seen from a different angle. Key issues are the following:

1. Two-sided markets   These markets are characterized by indirect network effects between the different sides of the markets. In a buyer-seller context the buyer side cares about the number and possibly the composition of sellers, and the seller side has the same concerns about buyers. If a single firm operates the platform, then this firm affects the interaction between buyers and sellers with its pricing decisions and has to take the indirect network effects into account.

2. Intellectual property rights   The economics of patents and copyright must be reconsidered in the case of information goods that can be exchanged easily. In that context, end-user piracy is a phenomenon that applies only to information goods and has become more important in the presence of fast Internet connections and file-sharing technology.

3. Marketing and selling techniques   New marketing and selling techniques arise for information goods and for goods that are sold over the Internet.

4. Electronic commerce and the power of consumers and intermediaries   Electronic commerce involves more active consumers engaging in searches, and intermediaries pricing the buyer and seller side.

1.2.1   Two-Sided Markets
Industries trading products such as software and games operate quite differently from old industries: firms at multiple layers determine the

success of a software or game "system." In contrast, products in the old industry, if consumed jointly, usually are sold jointly and thus more often controlled by one firm (for example, consider the automobile industry). Related to this is that consumers in the digital economy customize their system; for example, they buy a game platform and select their favorite games. Clearly, customization also plays a role in other parts of the old economy. But in the old economy, different components of a "platform" are often compatible—one can put clothes in any washing machine, dishes in any dishwasher, etc. Hence, in the latter examples, purchasing decisions can be separated.

In the case of game systems (similar to software and music systems), consumers must decide jointly on the platform and applications. Because of incompatibility, games, software, and songs cannot be moved from one system to the other, nor can they be sold easily in a second-hand market. This implies that consumers are locked into a certain standard, and this standard is in some cases proprietary (for example, iTunes and game platforms). Examples from the digital economy have led to an emerging literature on two-sided markets. Even though other examples for such two-sided markets may be found outside the digital economy, this literature is closely linked to phenomena observed in the digital economy. Note also that this includes electronic commerce, that is, markets with electronic intermediaries that often distribute physical products.

In this book, two chapters are devoted to such systems in the digital economy. In chapter 3, David S. Evans, Andrei Hagiu, and Richard Schmalensee provide a case-based analysis of the economic role of software platforms. They present case studies of personal computers, video games, personal digital assistants, smart mobile phones, and digital content devices and explain several aspects of these businesses including pricing structures and degrees of integration. These observations are of high relevance in the emerging literature of two-sided markets.[4]

In chapter 10, Bruno Jullien discusses electronic intermediation from the perspective of two-sided markets. He builds a simple model of intermediation, which requires the matching of trading partners—say buyers and sellers. In this framework he presents a survey of the insights that emerge in the two-sided market literature and discusses some new aspects. The first part of the chapter is dedicated to monopoly intermediation and contrasts efficient pricing to monopoly pricing. The second part is concerned with the nature of competition between intermediaries. Jullien addresses important issues such as competitive cross-subsidies, multihoming, and tying.

1.2.2 Intellectual Property Rights

Intellectual property right issues have received renewed attention in the context of the digital economy. Here, one can distinguish between patents and copyright. Patents play an important role in the software industry. An important patent issue is the measurement of patent value, as analyzed in chapter 2. With respect to copyright, the current debate is dominated by the analysis of a particular industry, namely the music industry, because music industry representatives have made a big issue of the impact of electronic transfer of music files over file-sharing systems. However, lessons learned from that industry are likely to have a wider impact because other industries have similar characteristics. In this book chapters 4 and 5 deal directly with digital music and file sharing. Chapter 2 addresses intellectual property right issues from a broader, theoretical perspective.

For a long time, economists have been asking whether incentive schemes like the patent system provide proper incentives for firms to invest in research and development. Recently, the digital economy put new emphasis on this question. Such an analysis requires a good measure of the value of innovations and patents. This quantification is not an easy task, especially in the digital economy, which is characterized by knowledge industries such as computer software. Yet quantification is especially important in the digital economy, where technology has changed rapidly, the number of patents has grown exponentially, and patenting has become an important strategy of firms.

Economists have used primarily patent citation data as a proxy for the value of the underlying innovation and knowledge flows. In chapter 2, Chaim Fershtman and Neil Gandal propose a refined measure of patent citations for software patents that weighs citations by the importance of the citing patent in such a way that the resulting weights are both endogenous and consistent. They then compare this *consistent weighted ranking* system (CWR) to the traditional measure of patent counts. Their empirical analysis suggests that the CWR measure is better in measuring patent value for the data they consider than simply the number of citations considered by others. They also uncover that there may be strategic reasons for citing patents.

In chapter 4, Martin Peitz and Patrick Waelbroeck present a fact-based guide to digital music. They contrast the traditional way of selling recorded music to new ways with the Internet and compression technologies. As an alternative channel for disseminating music, file-sharing systems have played an important role recently. In their analysis of the music industry and file-sharing (or P2P) networks, they present industry and survey data, complemented by case studies of reactions to the rise of file-sharing networks. To understand these trends, they present survey evidence on consumer behavior in the digital world. They also provide some background on copyright issues and digital rights management.

In chapter 5, Stan J. Liebowitz gives a detailed account of the empirical evidence on the impact of file sharing on music sales. He reviews some of the theoretical analyses on end-user copying and concludes that there are few a priori reasons to expect that file sharing could increase or be neutral to music sales. According to his examination of recent empirical studies, the overall evidence supports the view that file sharing has hurt music sales. Liebowitz provides a critical reflection on methodological issues, implementation, and interpretation of the econometric estimations.

In chapter 8, Amit Gayer and Oz Shy provide a theoretical analysis of end-user copying and copyright enforcement. In particular, they question whether file sharing is inflicting significant harm on the recording industry. They argue that because of network effects an increase in end-user copying under certain conditions may actually make producers better off. They also point to a potential conflict between the creators of copyrighted works and the publishers because musicians or other creators often sell complementary products such as merchandise and concert tickets that strongly benefit from a wide distribution of recorded music, whereas the record companies typically benefit only from sales of recorded music.

1.2.3   Marketing and Selling Techniques

The digital economy has revived interest in sophisticated price discrimination, advertising, and protection techniques. In the case of digital goods, firms have the option to modify their products and offer them in different versions. They may want to preannounce their products in the case of network effects. In addition, firms can decide on protection of information goods through technological and legal measures.

In chapter 6, Paul Belleflamme provides a theoretical analysis of versioning practices (or second-degree price discrimination) for information goods. He presents simple and concise models that elaborate on the strategic tools available to a firm with market power. In particular, he analyzes bundling, functional degradation, and conditioning prices on purchase history. These versioning tools are important strategic choices by firms operating in the digital economy.

In chapter 7, Jay Pil Choi, Eirik Gaard Kristiansen, and Jae Nahm give a theoretical analysis of a business practice prevalent among software developers: preannouncing new products. They give several explanations for the phenomenon. These preannouncements may be aimed at competitors or at consumers. The authors analyze in detail when such announcements are credible. In particular, software developers may acquire a reputation for being honest.

With chapter 8, Amit Gayer and Oz Shy also contribute to our understanding of the impact of copy protection on market outcomes. In particular, they show that in the presence of network effects a firm may not be interested in a severe punishment of copyright infringements.

1.2.4 Electronic Commerce and the Power of Consumers and Intermediaries

Not only firms use more sophisticated strategies; consumers may also change their behavior. An obvious example is that of search engines that allow consumers to find the lowest price for a certain product. Hence it is not at all clear whether firms or consumers will benefit more from the rise of exchanges for digital goods and more generally of electronic intermediaries for physical goods. In this context, electronic intermediaries must decide on their pricing strategies with respect to consumers and sellers. Two chapters of this book focus on electronic commerce and electronic intermediation.

In chapter 9, Emin M. Dinlersoz and Pedro Pereira discuss facts and develop theory about the adoption of electronic commerce by retailers. To explain these facts they construct a theoretical model focusing on market characteristics such as differences in firms' technologies, degrees of consumer loyalty, and preferences of consumers across the traditional versus the virtual market. The model generates results about the timing of decisions and the pricing in the market.

Chapter 10 by Bruno Jullien contributes to our understanding of electronic commerce from the angle of the two-sided market literature. In particular, he focuses on price-setting by electronic intermediaries. Electronic intermediaries control trade on the trading platforms and decide which prices to set for the different sides that participate on the platform.

1.3 Further Issues and Looking Ahead

This book connects with additional industrial organization aspects of the digital economy. Some of them are just beginning to be analyzed in economic research, and they certainly deserve further investigation. Here we discuss a few of them. The methods and industry studies presented in this book, in particular the analyses of two-sided markets, provide an especially promising starting point for this future research.

The open-source movement has provided an innovative solution to the allocation of property rights. People and firms involved in the movement contribute for free to the development of a digital product, for example, the software platform Linux. People contributing to a digital product such as Linux are providing a "community service." Such community services are not restricted to programmers' efforts for certain software products but include contributions to information goods such as online encyclopedias. It is interesting to note about these cases that the ascent of the Internet and the associated free community services lead to a substitution of nonmarket transactions for market transactions.

By contrast, other community services lead to new market transactions. For example, markets now operate that did not exist before the Internet and the business models that rely on community services. A good example is eBay, which provides a platform to buy and sell almost any kind of good and service.

The success of eBay rests in part on the trust trading partners have in each other, even though they are unlikely to ever trade with one another again. In particular, trading partners must trust the other side to carry out transactions as promised (that is, buyer makes payment and seller ships the good according to the agreed terms). This trust is achieved through a reputation system in which market participants voluntarily evaluate their trading partners. Market participants on each side try to build up and maintain their reputation because the other side of the market can condition its behavior based on the reputation. This is particularly relevant for sellers. Sellers with a good reputation command a higher price than sellers with a bad reputation, and so the reputation system works as a disciplining device. Note that because of high transaction costs some items would be traded in the absence of eBay; others would still be traded, but there would be a less efficient match of buyer and product.

The analysis of reputation on the Internet is a fascinating issue. It has the potential to provide a low-cost solution to an otherwise severe asymmetric information problem. Overall, the Internet may make consumers more active and better informed. Lemons likely will be detected quickly and information spread rapidly. In this sense, electronic intermediaries become mainly certifying intermediaries where the intermediary simply aggregates the evaluation efforts of the market participants. To the extent that reputation cannot be moved between platforms, the reputation system is clearly an important source of network effects and is likely to lead to a highly concentrated industry (as in the case of eBay). The framework of two-sided markets as advanced in this book appears to be highly useful for the analysis of reputation effects in the digital economy.

Apart from solving asymmetric information problems, the easy accessibility of information on the Internet can lead to different selling strategies for information goods. In particular, rental and subscription services become attractive. Examples are digital music and video on demand. Note that buy-versus-rent decisions are also relevant for physical goods; however, such decisions likely will become more frequent in the digital economy. Similarly, the Internet allows for more sophisticated price and nonprice strategies, which are analyzed in various chapters of this book.

The increase of easily accessible information on the Internet and the reduction of transaction costs for trade have led to a substantial increase in the product variety that is available to average consumers, provided they have access to the Internet. Currently, we observe that new technological advances try to partly reverse this trend by introducing features that help to prevent information sharing and restrict the flexibility of use of information goods. Serious efforts toward an evaluation of the welfare effects of these changes are of critical importance for policy recommendations, including the evaluation of government interventions on the hardware side, such as the regulation of broadband.

In sum, this book improves our understanding of the microeconomics and industrial organization at work in the digital economy. We hope that it will stimulate further research in this promising field.

Notes

1. See *Economist*, Stepping up the war against piracy, January 30, 2003. Remarkably, Robbie Williams made this statement after he signed a deal in 2002 in which he gave his record label a share of money from touring, sponsorship, and DVD sales as well as from CDs, in return for big cash payments.

2. Preliminary versions of most of these contributions have been presented at a CESifo conference in Munich in summer 2004, published in *CESifo Economic Studies*.

3. A reader mainly interested in the software industry should definitely read chapters 2, 3, 6, 7, and 8. The music industry is analyzed in chapters 4, 5, 6, and 8. Chapters 9 and 10 cover electronic commerce and intermediation.

4. In chapter 4, Martin Peitz and Patrick Waelbroeck provide complementary information in the case of music platforms.

2

Software Patents

Chaim Fershtman and Neil Gandal

2.1 Introduction

The importance of innovation in the digital economy to the U.S. and world economies probably cannot be overstated.[1] As Scotchmer (2004) remarks, "Patents are the gold standard of intellectual property protection. With other forms of protection (like copyright), if a third party duplicates the protected innovation independently, he or she can use it. The absence of this independent-invention defense makes patent law uniquely powerful."[2] This is especially true in the case of software and other digital products, since reverse engineering is often feasible.[3]

In recent years, economists have begun asking whether incentive schemes like the patent system provide proper incentives for firms to invest in pathbreaking research and development. Important topics include the optimal length of the patent, the patent scope, and whether software firms are excessively patenting.[4]

Such an analysis requires a good measure of the value of innovations and patents. This quantification is not an easy task, especially in the digital economy, which is characterized by knowledge industries such as computer software. Yet such quantification is especially important in the digital economy, where technology changes rapidly and the number of patents grows exponentially.[5] Patents are often essential for the rise of new business models, such as software platforms. See Evans, Hagiu, and Schmalensee (chapter 3 in this book).

Information on the value of patents is important for firms and universities that actively license their intellectual property (patent) portfolios.[6] Knowledge of valuations likely would help facilitate the licensing of intellectual property, which is important for advancing R&D.

Economists and researchers have used primarily patents and patent citation data as a proxy for the value of the underlying innovation and knowledge flows. Intuitively the measure makes sense because in theory major innovations are important building blocks for subsequent innovations and hence likely would be highly cited. Nevertheless, evidence regarding whether patent citations are a good measure of the underlying value of the innovation is mixed.

Seminal work by Hall, Jaffe, and Trajtenberg (2001) put data on all patents issued in the United States between 1963 and 1999 on the National Bureau of Economic Research (NBER) website.[7] These data, which include all pair-wise patent citations between 1976 and 1999, are publicly available in a convenient format.

A small number of recent studies have examined whether patent citations are correlated with nonpatent measures of value. Lanjouw and Schankerman (2004) find that a measure based on multiple factors including patent citations has statistically significant explanatory power in predicting whether a patent will be litigated. Shane (2002) finds that for MIT patents there is a positive correlation between the number of patent citations and the probability that the patent will be licensed.

Hall, Jaffe, and Trajtenberg (2000) find that "citation weighed patent stocks" are more highly correlated with firm market value than patent stocks themselves. Nevertheless, they also find that R&D stock is more highly correlated with firm market value than either patent- or citation-weighted patent stocks. In a study of university patents, Sampat and Ziedonis (2002) find that while citations are a good predictor of whether a patent will be licensed (a result similar to that of Shane 2002), they are not a good predictor of revenues earned from licensing; that is, the number of patent citations may not be a good measure of the underlying value of the innovation.

Preliminary research by Campbell-Kelly and Valduriez (2004) suggests that the fifty most highly cited software patents are all incremental improvements in technology, rather than major innovations. This research is particularly interesting because the classifications (incremental innovation, dramatic innovation) are based on the authors' expertise and a detailed technical analysis of the patents themselves. Hence the evidence as to whether citations are a good measure of economic value is mixed.

In this chapter, we examine a consistent measure of patent citations for the computer software industry. While research has shown that citations are a better measure of innovation than pure patent counts, it is probably important to "weigh" the citations as well. Consider the analogy to academic citations.[8] Citations from important papers may be more beneficial in helping determine the value of the paper than a citation from a paper published in a less important journal. The same logic may be true for patents as well and thus citations should be weighed by the source of the citation. Is the citing patent itself an important or unimportant patent? If the citing patent has a lot of citations itself, its citation should be more heavily weighted than a citing patent that has very few citations.

We employ a measure that weighs patent citations by the importance of the citing patent—denoted by the *consistent weighted ranking* (CWR) scheme.[9] This measure is consistent in the sense that citation weights used in constructing the ranking are identical to the final ranking produced by our method. Our measure is quite different than counting the number of citations.

Our empirical work suggests that the CWR measure may be better in measuring patent value for these data than simply counting the number of citations. Our empirical work also suggests that there may be strategic reasons for citing patents. This may be an important strategy in the digital economy, where often the most important asset of the firm is the patent(s) that it holds.[10]

In the following section, we explain the intuition behind the CWR. In section 2.3, we describe the formal methodology. In section 2.4 we construct a ranking of software patents using the CWR and compare these rankings to rankings based on the number of citations. In section 2.5 we examine the performance of the CWR and the number of citations using properties of the patents themselves. Section 2.6 provides brief conclusions.

2.2   Intuition for the CWR

To better understand the construction of CWR, consider the following example with six patents. The citations across patents are described by table 2.1.

The second row of the table shows the patents that cite patent one, while the second column shows the patents cited by patent one, etc. The total number of citations appears in the "citations received" column.

Both the second patent and the sixth patent are cited twice. However, if we weigh the citing patent by the number of citations it received, the weighted citations index in the CWR first iteration column shows that

Table 2.1
Citations by each patent

Patent	Citing patent 1	Citing patent 2	Citing patent 3	Citing patent 4	Citing patent 5	Citing patent 6	Citations received	Initial weights	CWR first iteration	CWR final rating
1	0	1	1	1	0	0	3	3	2	3.00
2	0	0	0	0	1	1	2	2	3	2.79
3	0	0	0	0	0	0	0	0	0	1.00
4	0	0	0	0	0	0	0	0	0	1.00
5	0	0	0	1	0	0	1	1	0	1.42
6	1	0	0	0	1	0	2	2	4	2.86

patent six is more important than patent two. This, of course, is just a single iteration of weights. The outcome of this iteration is another set of weights. To calculate the CWR, we require consistency, which means that the weights used in calculating the weighted index must be identical to the resulting index itself. To perform this task we need to continue iterating until a fixed point is reached, or to use an algorithm that identifies such a fixed point given the matrix of citations.

Using such an algorithm, the final weights (and hence ratings) are shown in the final column of table 2.1 and patent six indeed has a higher rating than patent two. Also notice that the rankings between patent one and patents two and six are much closer, reflecting the fact that although patent one has 50 percent more citations, it is cited by relatively unimportant patents.

2.3 Our Formal Ranking Methodology

In this section, we present a system of indices for each patent that will capture not only the number of patents that cited it, but also the importance of the citing patents. To achieve a ranking we will search for a vector of ratings $z = \{z_i\}_{i=1}^{N}$, which assigns each patent i with a respective rating z_i. All the ratings (values of indices in z) will be interdependent. Hence we need to create a system of equations in which all ratings are determined simultaneously.

As we show below, to ensure existence of a solution to the system of equations, we must limit the range of possible z_i values, in particular $z_i \in [l, h]$ while l and h are exogenously determined. Moreover, to avoid the trivial fixed point for which $\forall_i.z_i = 0$, we require that l be positive.

2.3.1 The General Formula
We start with a simple equation:

$$z_i = l + b \sum_{j \neq i} z_j a_{i,j}, \tag{2.1}$$

where $a_{i,j}$ equals one if patent or article i is cited by patent j and b is a coefficient designed to ensure that $l \leq z_i \leq h$.[11]

We will let b be determined endogenously in a way that ensures the highest rating will be infinitesimally close to h. The lowest rating will inevitably be close to l. If a patent is not cited then it receives a rating of l regardless of the value of b.[12] The following condition must hold for the highest rated patent,

$$l + b \sum_{j \neq highest} z_j a_{highest, j} = h$$

$\Rightarrow$ (2.2)

$$b(l, h, z, a_{highest}) = \frac{h - l}{\displaystyle\sum_{j \neq highest} z_j a_{highest, j}},$$

where *highest* is the index of the highest rated patent.

After defining b we can define (2.1) as the condition for the index. Note that for every pair i, j, $a_{i,j}$ are given. The number of equations equals the number of patents. Hence we have a system of linear equations that can be solved and yield a fixed point.

After solving for the index z (as a function of b), we can update b so that (b, z) where $b(l, h, z, a_{highest})$ fulfills condition (2.2) and $z(l, b, X)$[13] is determined by the system of equations resulting from condition (2.1).

We stress that although l and h are parameters chosen to determine the spread of the ratings, they might influence the final ranking as well. As we choose a higher l, and a lower h, $(h - l)$ becomes lower and the differences in ratings decrease. In this case the ranking becomes similar to the old fashion ranking—merely counting the citations.

2.3.2   A Simpler Formula

If one is ready to relax the demand for the maximum spread possible within the ratings' range, and for the existence of only one possible ranking for every given l and h, a simpler formula can be employed. Condition (2.2) can be replaced with

$$l + b \sum_{j \neq i} h \cdot a_{highest, j} = h$$

$\Rightarrow$ (2.3)

$$b(l, h, a_{highest}) = \frac{h - l}{h \cdot \displaystyle\sum_{j \neq i} a_{highest}}.$$

Note that in this new condition b is not a function of z.[14] This clearly simplifies the calculations. Condition (2.3) ensures that no patent receives a rating of more than h, although it does not imply that any will reach h. From combining (2.1) and (2.3) we get

$$z_i = 1 + \left[\frac{h-1}{h \cdot \sum_{j \neq i} a_{highest}} \right] \sum_{j \neq i} z_j a_{i,j}. \tag{2.4}$$

Hence we again have a system of linear equations that can be solved to yield the fixed point.

2.4   Data and Construction of CWR for Software Patents

Our data include information on patents classified under International Patent Classification (IPC) G06F and granted between 1976 and 2000—a total of 76,920 patents. The data include information on "who" cites "whom." This yields a matrix of $76,920 \times 76,920$ where each entry is either a zero or a one. This matrix is the input we use in our CWR calculations and it enables us to build the CWR at the level of the patent.[15]

We limited the data to IPC G06F in an effort to obtain an objective sample of software patents. The classification G06F refers to "electric digital data processing."[16] The subclassifications under G06F are shown in the appendix.[17] Other definitions of software patents are, of course, possible. Indeed one can classify patent classes endogenously by other patents that they cite. Since we focus on the most highly cited software patents, it is likely that our results are robust to any reasonable classification scheme.

There are 76,290 software patents in the G06F class. Of these, 57,382 either cited at least one of the software patents in the G06F class or received a citation from at least one of the software patents in the G06F class. We refer to this as the relevant *group*.

On average, the total number of citations per patent is quite skewed. Excluding own citations (by the same firm), the mean number of citations per patent is 7.9, but the median is only 3. Further, 75 percent of the patents received 10 citations or less.

In the case of citations from patents within the group, the number of citations per patent is even more skewed. Only 35,556 patents receive citations from other patents in our group. The mean number of citations per patent is 4.4, but the median is 1. Of the patents, 75 percent received 5 citations or less. Using the 57,382 patents, we compute the following measures:[18]

Table 2.2a
Correlations among measures (full group, 57,382 observations)

	All	NS	IG	CWR
All	1.00			
NS	0.98	1.00		
IG	0.84	0.83	1.00	
CWR	0.80	0.79	**0.95**	1.00

Table 2.2b
Correlation among measures (6,821 patents with more than 10 forward citations within the group)

	All	NS	IG	CWR
All	1.00			
NS	0.97	1.00		
IG	0.83	0.83	1.00	
CWR	0.75	0.75	**0.89**	1.00

• All. All forward citations including citations from the firm that holds the patent.

• No self (NS). All forward citations from patents held by other firms.

• In group (IG). All forward citations from patents in the G0F6 class.

• CWR. Our ranking index.

We are primarily interested in the comparison between the IG and CWR rankings. We report the other results for the sake of completeness. When we consider the full group, we obtain the correlations in table 2.2a between the raw measures.

Table 2.2a shows that the correlation between the IG and CWR measures is quite high (0.95). This is primarily because many of the patents do not receive even a single citation. For all of these patents, IG equals zero and the CWR measure takes on the minimum possible value. Hence it makes sense to restrict attention to patents that receive more than just a few forward citations from other patents in the group.

Table 2.2b shows the correlation between measures and patent ranks for all 6,821 patents that received 10 or more forward citations from other patents in the group. The correlation between IG and CWR is lower for these patents (0.89) than for the full group.

Table 2.2c
Correlation among measures (103 patents with 70 or more forward citations within the group)

	All	NS	IG	CWR
All	1.00			
NS	0.98	1.00		
IG	0.92	0.92	1.00	
CWR	0.75	0.72	**0.77**	1.00

In table 2.2c, we examine the correlation between measures and patent ranks for the 103 patents that received 70 or more forward citations from other patents in the class. Note that the correlation between IG and CWR is quite a bit lower for these highly cited patents (0.77) than for larger groups of patents.[19]

The top thirty patents according to IG citations are shown in table 2.3. The table shows that, with the exception of CWR, all measures are virtually identical in the case of the top ten patents. We are interested primarily in IG and CWR rankings. Table 2.3 shows that these measures are quite different, even for the thirty most highly cited patents within the group. Table 2.4 shows the top thirty patents according to the CWR measure. This table includes the IG rating as well.

The top patent in both the CWR and IG measures is a software management system patent owned by Xerox that automatically collects and recompiles component software objects over a computer network. The software management system periodically updates the component software objects using a system editor and can handle inputs from different users from different locations.[20] This patent, issued in 1985, cites only one other patent.

The second-highest-rated patent according to the IG measure (third according to CWR) is a power manager inside of a laptop computer. It includes a software program that monitors and controls the distribution of power to the various units in the computer in order to conserve the battery. The patent was issued in 1992 and cites seventeen other U.S. patents.

The second-highest-rated patent according to the CWR measure (eighth according to IG) is a multiprocessor system that interconnects two or more separate processors. The redundant multiprocessor system allows online maintenance of one part of the system while the rest of the system is functional. It also includes a distributed power supply

Table 2.3
Patents with the most in group citations in the G06F classification in order of IG rank

Year	Assignee	Patent	Forward Citation Measures				Rank			
			All	NS	IG	CWR	IG	CWR	NS	All
1985	Xerox	4558413	267	263	252	3313	1	1	1	1
1992	Apple	5167024	252	247	226	1957	2	3	2	2
1993	Nexgen Microsystems	5226126	218	218	188	1440	3	20	3	3
1989	Hitachi, Ltd.	4858105	196	188	186	1435	4	22	8	8
1993	Eastman Kodak	5181162	198	198	171	1662	5	7	4	6
1991	Xerox	5008853	208	193	170	1638	6	8	7	5
1989	Cornell Univ.	4807115	197	197	167	1429	7	23	5	7
1980	Tandem Computers	4228496	218	194	164	2692	8	2	6	4
1993	NexGen Microsystems	5226130	176	176	161	1570	9	12	9	9
1992	AT&T	5093914	175	175	161	1251	9	30	10	10
1992	HP	5133075	166	164	150	1541	11	13	16	18
1992	Schlumberger Technology	5119475	157	157	143	1436	12	21	17	20
1989	Apollo Computer	4809170	146	145	140	1523	13	14	24	27
1989	Tektronix, Inc.	4821220	150	150	134	1587	14	10	20	24
1989	Tektronix, Inc.	4885717	148	148	134	1572	14	11	22	26
1990	HP	4953080	151	146	134	1455	14	16	23	23
1977	Siemens	4044338	134	134	127	946	17	90	33	41
1985	AT&T	4555775	172	170	120	1782	18	4	13	14
1989	Tektronix, Inc.	4853843	122	122	118	1475	19	15	42	51
1991	Intel	5075848	124	124	112	1246	20	32	40	48
1992	IBM	5151987	133	123	110	1133	21	43	41	43

1996	Sun Microsystems	5530852	136	125	109	881	22	126	38	39
1991	Xerox	5072412	137	120	108	1077	23	57	45	37
1978	Cray Research	4128880	141	112	105	1613	24	9	55	31
1987	Signetics	4669043	110	108	105	1445	24	19	64	72
1990	Fairchild Semiconductor	4928223	106	106	105	878	26	128	70	82
1982	Intel	4325120	121	115	104	1764	27	5	51	54
1987	Intel	4674089	123	112	102	1453	28	17	56	49
1981	Intel	4257095	107	107	102	1057	28	61	65	76
1992	Tektronix	5136705	109	109	98	1054	30	62	61	74

Table 2.4
Patents with the highest CWR measure in the G06F classification in order of CWR rank

Year	Assignee	Patent	IG rank	CWR rank
1985	Xerox Corporation	4558413	1	1
1980	Tandem Computers	4228496	8	2
1992	Apple Computer, Inc.	5167024	2	3
1985	AT&T Bell Laboratories	4555775	18	4
1982	Intel Corporation	4325120	27	5
1978	Codex Corporation	4096571	33	6
1993	Eastman Kodak Company	5181162	5	7
1991	Xerox Corporation	5008853	6	8
1978	Cray Research, Inc.	4128880	24	9
1989	Tektronix, Inc.	4885717	14	10
1990	Hewlett-Packard Company	4953080	14	11
1992	AT&T Bell Laboratories	5093914	9	12
1992	Hewlett-Packard Company	5133075	11	13
1989	Apollo Computer, Inc.	4809170	13	14
1989	Tektronix, Inc.	4853843	19	15
1989	Tektronix, Inc.	4821220	14	16
1981	Intel Corporation	4257095	29	17
1987	Measurex Corporation	4635189	55	18
1987	Signetics Corporation	4669043	25	19
1993	NexGen Microsystems	5226126	3	20
1992	Schlumberger Technology	5119475	12	21
1989	Hitachi, Ltd.	4858105	4	22
1989	Cornell Research	4807115	7	23
1985	Texas Instruments	4562535	36	24
1978	Bolt Beranek and Newman	4130865	128	25
1986	IBM	4594655	69	26
1984	IBM	4442487	84	27
1980	IBM	4200927	117	28
1978	Bunker Ramo Corporation	4075691	39	29
1993	NexGen Microsystems	5226130	9	30

system that ensures that each device controller has two separate power supplies and can function even if one of the power supplies shuts down. The patent was issued in 1980 and cites thirteen other U.S. patents.

2.5   A Formal Analysis Using the CWR and IG Measures

The difference between the IG citation and CWR rankings raises the question of whether one of the measures better captures the value of a patent. In this section, we examine whether observable characteristics of the patents can explain the number of citations and the CWR measure. We employ characteristics from the NBER patent database (such as the number of claims and the year in which the patent was granted) as well as characteristics from work by Campbell-Kelly and Valduriez (2004). These characteristics—scope and technical depth—are especially interesting because they are based on a scientific examination of the patents by researchers familiar with the technologies described by these patents.[21] Campbell-Kelly and Valduriez (2004) determined these characteristics for the fifty most-cited patents.[22]

Our analysis in this section employs the following variables:

• Claims. The number of claims made by the patent.

• Scope. A dummy variable that takes on the value one if the scope of the patent is broad, and zero if the scope is narrow.

• Depth. A dummy variable that takes on the value one if the technical depth is high, and zero if the technical depth is medium or low.[23]

• Year1976. The difference between the year in which the patent was granted and 1976, the first year for which the patent data are available.

Descriptive statistics are available in table 2.5.

Table 2.6 shows the correlation matrix between the dependent and independent variables. The CWR and IG are quite highly correlated. Scope and Claims have a correlation coefficient of 0.47, while Depth and Claims have a much smaller correlation coefficient (0.25); Scope and Depth are virtually uncorrelated (-0.12).

The first column in table 2.7 shows a regression of the CWR measure (not the ranking) on the four variables described above. The second column in the table shows a regression of IG citations on the same variables. The third and fourth regressions in the table repeat the analysis using the natural logarithm of the dependent variables from the

Table 2.5
Descriptive statistics (49 observations)

Variable	Mean	Minimum	Maximum	Standard deviation
CWR rating	868.26	143.06	3313.50	611.61
IG citations	77.91	1	252	52.50
CWR ranking	1296.98	1	12956	2529.31
IG ranking	972.47	1	12926	2383.53
Claims	28.35	6	85	18.54
Scope	0.37	0	1	0.49
Depth	0.63	0	1	0.49
Year 1976	15.16	5	20	3.90

Table 2.6
Correlations between dependent and independent variables (49 observations)

	CWR	IG	Claims	Depth	Scope
CWR	1.00				
IG	0.96	1.00			
Claims	−0.33	−0.33	1.00		
Depth	0.25	0.23	0.25	1.00	
Scope	−0.35	−0.32	0.47	−0.12	1.00
Year	−0.37	−0.22	0.08	−0.11	0.09

Table 2.7
Regression results

Independent variables	Dependent variable			
	CWR rating	IG	log(CWR)	log(IG)
Constant	1716.59 (5.11)	120.19 (3.93)	7.24 (17.35)	4.62 (6.64)
Claims/ log(claims)	−10.10 (−2.05)	−0.93 (−2.07)	−0.22 (−1.22)	−0.23 (−1.04)
Depth	343.39 (2.05)	30.46 (1.99)	0.47 (2.20)	0.58 (2.28)
Scope	−183.17 (−1.01)	−13.11 (−0.79)	−0.23 (−0.98)	−0.16 (−0.57)
Year 1976	−46.94 (−2.39)	−2.00 (−1.12)	−0.042 (−1.68)	−0.0086 (−0.29)
Adjusted R^2	0.27	0.18	0.19	0.08
Number of observations	49	49	49	49

regressions in columns one and two, respectively, and the natural logarithm of claims. The main results in table 2.7 are as follows:

Observation 2.1   More claims lead to lower CWR rankings and fewer IG citations. This may reflect a strategic incentive on behalf of the citing firm.

The possible strategic incentive is that if the citing firm cites a patent with many claims in its patent application, it may be less likely to receive a patent or it may take a longer time for a patent to be issued. Hence, other things being equal, the citing firm would not want to cite patents with many claims.

This effect is statistically significant in the first two regressions in table 2.7. This strategic incentive may be especially important in the digital economy, since often a patent is the most important asset that a firm holds. To the best of our knowledge, there is no theoretical or empirical work on strategic citations.

Observation 2.2   Patents described in greater technical depth receive higher CWR ratings and more IG citations.

This result is statistically significant in all four of the regressions in table 2.7. It suggests a nonstrategic *information effect*. Other things being equal, these patents are clear and relatively easy to understand. Hence they receive more citations.

Observation 2.3   Patents with broader scope have lower CWR rankings and fewer IG citations. This again may reflect a strategic incentive on behalf of the citing firm.

This effect seems similar to the effect described in observation 2.1. If a very broad patent is cited, the citing firm may be less likely to receive a patent or it may take a longer time for a patent to be issued. Hence, other things being equal, the citing firm would not want to cite patents with broad scope.

This effect is not statistically significant, however, in any of the four regressions in table 2.7. Nevertheless, it raises the possibility concerning a strategic incentive that may be important for firms competing in the digital economy.

Observation 2.4   The CWR measure may be better in capturing patent value for these data than the number of citations.

The adjusted R-squared values in table 2.7 are higher in the CWR regressions than in the corresponding IG citation regressions. If the variables in the regressions in table 2.7 are truly characteristics that explain patent value, this result suggests that the CWR measure may be better in capturing patent value for these data than the number of citations. Of course, the empirical analysis in this section is suggestive at best, since it is based on such a small number of observations.[24]

2.6   Further Discussion

Our chapter constructs a new metric of patent valuation for software patents. If the independent variables in the regressions in table 2.7 are truly characteristics that explain patent valuation, our results suggest that the CWR measure may be better in measuring patent value for these data than simply the number of citations. Additional research is, of course, necessary to examine this issue in greater detail.

Our analysis also suggests that a citation may be due in part to strategic reasons, since firms in oligopolistic industries may have incentives to cite (or not cite) particular patents. This may be especially true in the digital economy, where often the sole asset of a firm is the patent(s) that it holds. To the best of our knowledge no empirical work has been done on the strategic patenting issue.[25]

Appendix: Subclassifications under G06F

3/   Input arrangements for transferring data to be processed into a form capable of being handled by the computer

5/   Methods or arrangements for data conversion without changing the order or content of the data handled

7/   Methods or arrangements for processing data by operating upon the order or content of the data handled

9/   Arrangements for program control

11/   Error detection, error correction, monitoring

12/   Accessing, addressing, or allocating within memory systems or architectures

13/   Interconnection of, or transfer of information or other signals between, memories, input/output devices, or central processing units

15/   Digital computers in general

Notes

1. We are especially grateful to Martin Peitz, and also thank Josh Lerner and Mark Schankerman for helpful comments. We are also grateful to Michael Campbell-Kelly and Patrick Valduriez for providing us with their data. Financial support from NERA is gratefully acknowledged. Any opinions expressed are those of the authors.

2. Scotchmer (2004), p. 66.

3. This does not imply that copyright protection is unimportant in protecting innovations. Most software firms obtain both copyright and patent protection. In the music industry, copyright protection is the essential form of intellectual property, since digital music can be reproduced easily at very low cost. As Peitz and Waelbroeck discuss in chapter 4 in this book providing a detailed analysis of the digital music industry, Napster, a firm that allowed users to exchange music files, was found guilty of copyright infringement and had to shut down. Gayer and Shy (chapter 8 in this book) also examine copyright issues for products like digital music.

4. For a summary of early empirical work, see Griliches (1990); for a summary of recent empirical work, see Jaffe and Trajtenberg (2002). For a summary of the theoretical work, see Scotchmer (1991, 2004).

5. See Kortum and Lerner (1999).

6. Gotro (2002) notes that IBM earned approximately $1 billion from licensing its patents in 2000, while Qualcomm earned more than $700 million from patent licenses in the same year. In 1998, three universities (California, Stanford, and Columbia) each earned more than $60 million in licensing revenues in 1998.

7. See http://www.nber.org/patents.

8. See Palacios-Huerta and Volij (2004) for an axiomatic approach of defining a consistent rating scheme for academic journals.

9. See also Fershtman and Gandal (2004) for a consistent ranking method for sports teams.

10. Other potentially important strategies in the digital economy include the pre-announcement of products (Choi, Kristiansen, and Nahm, chapter 7 in this book) and versioning (Belleflamme, chapter 6 in this book).

11. In the example in section 2.2, $l = 1$, $h = 3$, and $b = 0.42$.

12. We determine b in that way, to achieve the maximum spread within the ratings' range, and ensure that there is only one ranking possible for every given l and h. A simpler way of determining b, which relaxes these demands, and therefore requires a simpler computer algorithm is described in section 2.3.1.

13. X is a matrix of 1 and 0 and defines which patent cites another patent.

14. *Highest* refers to the patent or article with the most citations.

15. In the analysis in this section, we use the simpler formula described in section 2.3.1, with $l = 100$, $h = 300$.

16. International Patent Classification, World International Property Organization website at http://www.wipo.int/classifications/en/index.html?wipo_content_frame=/classifications/en/ipc/index.html.

17. For a more detailed description of subclassifications under G06F, see the World International Property Organization website at http://www.wipo.int/classifications/fulltext/new_ipc/index.htm.

18. Patents that did not receive any citations have a CWR ranking equal to the minimum value of the ranking index (100 in this case).

19. In the case of ranks, the correlation between IG and WCR is 0.57.

20. For abstracts for the patents discussed in this section, see www.uspto.gov.

21. We are grateful to Campbell-Kelly and Valduriez for providing us with these data.

22. In particular, the fifty patents include the forty-one most cited patents (not including citations from the same firm) and nine patents granted since 1990 with the highest number of forward citations within three years from the year the patent was granted. They chose the sample in this manner in order that several more recent patents would be in their data set. See Campbell-Kelly and Valduriez (2004) for details. One of the nine patents granted since 1990 has no forward citations within the group. Thus, the CWR and IG rankings are not defined and there are forty-nine observations.

23. Campbell-Kelly and Valduriez (2004) also determine whether the disclosure level is high or low. This variable was not significant in any of the regressions.

24. The number of observations is limited by the Campbell-Kelly and Valduriez (2004) study.

25. Other research suggests that patent examiners and patent lawyers play a nontrivial role in determining which patents are cited. See Cockburn, Kortum, and Stern (2002).

References

Campbell-Kelly, M., and P. Valduriez (2004), "A Technical Critique of Fifty Software Patents," mimeo.

Cockburn, I., S. Kortum, and S. Stern (2002), "Are All Patent Examiners Equal? The Impact of Examiner Characteristics on Patent Statistics and Litigation Outcomes," NBER Working Paper 8980.

Fershtman, C., and N. Gandal (2005), "A Consistent Weighted Ranking Scheme: An Application to College Football Rankings," Tel Aviv University mimeo.

Gotro, J. (2002), "Unleash Your Intellectual Property Potential," available at http://www.circuitree.com/CDA/ArticleInformation/features/BNP__Features__Item/0,2133,81218,00.html.

Griliches, Z. (1990), "Patent Statistics as Economic Indicators: A Survey," *Journal of Economic Literature* XXVIII: 1661–1707.

Hall, B., A. Jaffe, and M. Trajtenberg (2000), "Market Value and Patent Citations: A First Look," NBER Working Paper W7741.

Hall, B., A. Jaffe, and M. Trajtenberg (2001), "The NBER Patent Citation Data File: Lessons, Insights and Methodological Tools," NBER Working Paper 8498.

Jaffe, A., and M. Trajtenberg (2002), *Patents, Citations, and Innovations: A Window on the Knowledge Economy*, The MIT Press, Cambridge, MA.

Lanjouw, J., and M. Schankerman (2004), "Patent Quality and Research Productivity: Measuring Innovation with Multiple Indicators," *The Economic Journal* 114: 441–465.

Kortum, S., and J. Lerner (1999), "Stronger Protection or Technological Revolution: What is Behind the Recent Surge in Patenting?" *Research Policy* 28: 1–22.

Palacios-Huerta, I., and O. Volij (2004), "The Measure of Intellectual Influence," *Econometrica*, 72: 963–977.

Sampat, B., and A. Ziedonis (2002), "Cite Seeing: Patent Citations and the Economic Value of Patents," mimeo.

Scotchmer, S. (1991), "Standing on the Shoulders of Giants: Cumulative Research and the Patent Law," *Journal of Economic Perspectives* 5: 29–41.

Scotchmer, S. (2004), *Innovations and Incentives*, The MIT Press, Cambridge, MA.

Shane, S. (2002), "Selling University Technology: Patterns from MIT," *Management Science*, 48(1): 122–137.

3 Software Platforms

David S. Evans, Andrei Hagiu,
and Richard Schmalensee

3.1 Introduction

DoCoMo in Japan offers a mobile information service called "i-mode."
Based on a mobile telephone handset, it enables users to access content
from some 93,000 websites and to run a wide variety of software applications on DoCoMo's mobile telephone network. The iPod is a digital
music player sold by Apple. It is designed to play music downloaded
from Apple's iTunes service using Apple's iTunes media player (which
is built on top of Apple's QuickTime media player).

The iPod and i-mode are two examples of economically important
products based in part on computer systems. Every component of
computer systems plays a critical role in these businesses. The characteristics of the software platform, however, can be the key to the
viability of a computer system, facilitating the creation of software
applications and increasing the value to consumers of the integrated
system. Moreover, the degree to which software platforms are integrated with other components affects many aspects of the organization
and evolution of computer systems.

Some software platforms are integrated tightly with the hardware
platform—for example, Apple Macintosh for personal computers
and Sony PlayStation for video games. Others are not—for example,
Windows for personal computers and Symbian for mobile phones—
and, as a result, have facilitated competition among suppliers of the
hardware platform. Integration between the software platform and
software applications has also varied. In the early development of video games, manufacturers made the game platform as well as the
games; today, most platform vendors license their platforms to independent game developers who generate the bulk of applications. Here,

we analyze the business dynamics of industries based on computer systems, with special attention to the software platform.

Computer systems are often organized as "multi-sided platform markets" (Rochet and Tirole 2004). A business is based on a multi-sided platform if it serves two or more distinct types of customers who depend on each other in some important way, and whose joint participation makes the platform valuable to each. Windows is an example of a three-sided platform. Rochet and Tirole (2004) use a more formal version of this requirement: for them, a necessary and sufficient condition for a market to be two-sided is that the volume of transactions be sensitive to the distribution of total costs between the two sides. This implies that a platform can improve upon the market outcome through a pricing structure that rebalances costs between the two sides by internalizing (to a certain extent) the indirect externalities.

In the case of software platforms, the platform provides services to application developers, hardware manufacturers, and end-users. Each group needs the others to participate if the platform is to generate market value. The emerging economics literature on multi-sided platform markets provides interesting observations into pricing and business strategies, offering insights into the workings of industries based on computer systems.

It is worth noting, though, that some markets organized around multi-sided platforms could be viable as traditional one-sided markets. (Contrast this with, for example, the payment card industry, where it is simply implausible to imagine the integration of the two sides of the business—payers and payees—into a traditional, single-sided market.) Firms can choose to integrate vertically into the supply of a component rather than relying on the market. For example, Apple's iPod could be operated as a multi-sided market platform, but Apple has decided to build its business model around a fully integrated single-sided product. Apple produces the hardware and software platforms; it operates its own content-provision service and licenses the content from music publishers. Some of its competitors have decided to take a multi-sided approach, creating portals through which consumers buy music or other content from third parties and music devices that combine separately produced hardware and software platforms.

Our survey is organized around case studies of five industries based on computer systems: personal computers, video games, personal digital assistants, smart mobile phones, and digital content devices. We first present some principles for analyzing business models in these

Table 3.1
Overview of computer systems

Platform	Examples	Complements	Examples
Computers	Windows, MacOS, Solaris, Multos	Applications Hardware platform Hardware peripherals	Acrobat, Quicken, Star Office, Dell, iMac, TV-tuner card, CD-ROM
Video games	Playstation, Nintendo, Xbox	Games Hardware platform Hardware peripherals	Mario Bros., Halo, Playstation 2, joystick, steering wheel, memory card
Personal digital assistants	PalmOS, Windows CE	Applications Hardware platform Hardware peripherals	Address book, Graffiti, Handspring, Pilot, Sony Clie, GPS, memory card
Smart mobile phones	Symbian, Windows CE	Operators Applications Handsets Peripherals	Vodafone, 3, Orange, organizers, games, Nokia, Ericsson, Samsung, hands-free car kit, wireless headset, phone cover
Digital content devices	iPod, Sony Network Walkman, Creative Zen Micro	Downloadable music Hardware platform Hardware peripherals Media players	iTunes, Dell Pocket DJ, Bose speakers for iPods, QuickTime, RealPlayer

industries. We then describe the organization and evolution of each of these five industries. Finally, we draw some broad conclusions from the case studies, and leave some puzzles for future research.

Table 3.1 presents an overview of the computer systems that we consider in the remainder of this chapter.

3.2   Economic and Technical Background

A number of forces drive the proliferation of industries that rely on computer systems. Microprocessors have become cheaper, smaller, and more powerful, while memory devices have become much less expensive (Hennessy and Patterson 1996). Today, many products come with built-in computer systems complete with microprocessors and operating systems, which in some cases are more powerful than the PCs of less than a decade ago. Typical Pocket PCs available today have processor speeds between 266 and 400 MHz. It was not until 1997 that Intel released a chip with a clock speed of 233 MHz and not until 1999 that they released a chip of 450 MHz. (These numbers are not directly comparable due to the differing architectures of the systems.) Often, these computer systems are integrated with the product and are designed to perform a specific set of tasks. The computer systems embedded in cars, often called engine controllers, provide a familiar example.

In the markets in which we are interested, the computer system is the core of the product and can support a multi-sided market by becoming a focal point for the development of complementary products. Smart cards with built-in chips, like the American Express Blue card, are examples. Payment card systems have designed these cards to encourage the development of applications that can run on them. While these cards are not yet widely used in the United States, most cards in Europe will be based on computer chips by the end of this decade.

Industries based mainly on computer systems are quite diverse. Nonetheless, they share economic and technical features, which we summarize in the remainder of this section.

3.2.1 Some Technical Observations

The microprocessor is at the core of a modern computer system. PCs center on a microprocessor, a central processing unit that carries out instructions, performs computations, and issues commands to the peripheral devices connected to the system. Microprocessors control the logic of digital devices ranging from climate control systems in office buildings to handheld global-positioning appliances. The operating system is equally important to the working of the system. It consists of software code that instructs the microprocessor to perform specified tasks, notably controlling and exchanging information with hardware. The operating system also enables software developers to write applications that use the operating system instructions to interact with the microprocessor rather than directly interacting with it themselves. Operating systems that provide services to application developers are software platforms; in some cases, software known as *middleware* provides these services to developers while relying on an operating system to control the hardware.

Memory is another important category. A variety of mechanical and solid-state devices can store anything that can be reduced to digital information, and then make this information available to the microprocessor and operating system.

Software technology has evolved to facilitate the writing of new code for both applications programs and operating systems. This technology consists of "high-level" languages such as C++. Programs written in these languages can then be "compiled" into binary code that gives the microprocessor the digital 0/1 instructions it understands. Important innovations in computer systems involve developing languages and tools that help programmers write applications efficiently.

Software platforms contain modules of code that perform various tasks. (These modules may be in separate files or "linked" together in a single file for distribution.) These modules provide services used by other parts of the operating system or by software applications. Access to these services is provided through applications program interfaces (APIs).

APIs are similar conceptually to a statistical command like regress (x,Y), where the underlying code performs the specified algebraic manipulation on (x,Y) and returns results. In the case of regression (x,Y) denotes data on a dependent variable (x) and on one or more independent variables (Y). The statistical command returns estimates of the effect of the independent variables on the dependent variable and various statistical test results such as t-stats, R-squares, and so forth. The user does not see the specific algorithms used to invert matrices or to calculate distribution functions. Like the user of a statistical command, the user of an API typically does not see the code underlying the command. The user inputs arguments or data; the code processes the data and returns results.

In some cases, application developers must use APIs to work on a hardware platform with a particular microprocessor. In most cases, though, application developers use APIs to avoid the tedious process of writing code to perform routine functions. Software platforms also serve as interfaces for hardware manufacturers, allowing them to finesse the writing code specific to the myriad potential permutations in the way systems are configured. For example, some hardware, including some external DVD drives like the MCE "Superdrive" that connects to a computer through an industry-standard interface, is designed to work only with a single software platform. This is the case with the Macintosh; the Mac computer OS shields the drive from the computer's graphics and sound cards, so that a user plugging the drive into a Mac need not worry that the drive will not function.[1] Other peripherals, such as the CanoScan 8000F scanner, use an industry-standard interface to allow the user to connect it to multiple platforms, for which Canon has written code to permit such connections.

Most operating systems facilitate writing and running applications on the underlying hardware, and therefore function as software platforms. However, software platforms do not always provide basic hardware-related operating system services. When they do not, they are called *middleware* because they sit logically between the operating system and the applications. For example, Java Virtual Machines and the Java class libraries provide a platform for applications to run on a variety of hardware and operating systems. To take another example, the Nokia Series 60 is a middleware platform that Nokia uses for its phones to provide services to developers; it works with the Symbian operating system controlling the phone hardware.

Two other observations are worth making here. First, the development of many of the key components of computer systems requires large investments in research and development, and embodies significant intellectual capital. An important source of protection for software comes from the fact that the code is typically released only in binary form, which can be read only by microprocessors. The underlying source code, written in a higher-level language, is kept secret to prevent the theft of ideas. (Software is also subject to copyright protection and certain aspects of software may be protected also by patents.)

Second, there are extensive scale economies when creating some of the key components. That is true for microprocessors, where the substantial fixed costs include both the construction of specialized plants for fabricating chips and the R&D embodied in the design and testing of the chip. The same holds true for software, where virtually all the costs come in writing, testing, and debugging the code. What little incremental cost there is consists almost entirely of outlays for marketing and distribution; the cost of physically reproducing copies of the software is minimal (Campbell-Kelly 2003).

Figure 3.1 shows the relationship between software platforms and various components. The platform components on the lefthand side consist of hardware (including the device that contains the microprocessor) and applications. These components all have interfaces (denoted by the dots on the left side of the platform) with the software platform that provides support. The circles within the software platform box illustrate the portions of code to which the interfaces provide access (and these in fact may be interlinked).

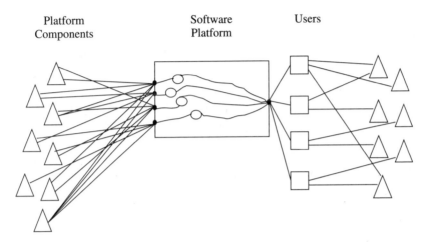

Figure 3.1
Relationship between software platforms and components

Users connect to the platform. They in turn have components they are able to use because they are supported by the platform. The components on the left and right side are the same. Indeed one can think of wrapping the left and right sides on themselves to show the virtual circle that is created by the platform.

3.2.2   Bundling Components

Computer systems are comprised of many components. Firms combine these components to create products that ultimately are sold or licensed to end-users. The contours of these products—what is included or excluded from the bundle of components—are determined by business and design decisions. (See chapter 6 in this book by Belleflamme for discussion of product bundling.)

The microprocessor, memory, and other components are combined typically to create a hardware platform such as a PalmOne Zire PDA, a Nokia mobile phone handset, or an Xbox game console. Hardware components not included in the physical product are termed peripherals and include items such as headphones, pointing devices, and printers. Sometimes one model of a product will integrate a specific component, while another will not—for example, a pointing device virtually always is integrated into a laptop computer but rarely into desktop models.

With time, many peripherals become integrated into the hardware platform. Consider the case of the math coprocessor, which facilitates number crunching. Prior to the release of Intel's 486 chip, Intel's micro-processors did not include a math coprocessor; customers who wanted a coprocessor purchased it separately from one of several vendors at substantial cost. Today, one cannot buy an Intel $\times 86$ processor without a built-in math coprocessor.

Similar economic and technological forces are at work in software. Operating systems, software platforms, and applications consist of code that accomplishes specific tasks. Where those tasks are accomplished is a matter of business and design decisions. And those decisions may vary among competing products as well as between generations of the same product. Many tasks that were once performed by stand-alone applications have been integrated into other applications (for example, spell checkers, which originally were sold separately from word processors) or into the software platform itself. Early operating systems, for example, did not include built-in calculators.

A variety of economic considerations go into the decisions of what to include in a product:

1. The benefits and costs of offering separate products As shown by Evans and Salinger (2005), firms tend to bundle components together when the fixed costs of offering them separately are high relative to demand. Thus if there are fixed costs of offering math coprocessors separately and most consumers want these together with their microprocessor, it is more efficient to provide them together.

2. Integration and coordination benefits The value of the whole may exceed the combined value of the parts. Thus businesses may be able to make more competitive products by integrating components. Most hardware platforms sold to end-users are, in fact, assembled from components purchased from a variety of vendors.

3. Demand aggregation When there are fixed costs of producing and distributing products, but low marginal costs in adding components, it may be possible to lower costs and reduce variation in reservation prices by combining components that appeal to different groups of customers. Hardware and software typically include many features that most consumers never use. However, by including these features vendors expand the number of consumers who find the product valuable at the offered price.

These considerations are not unique to computer systems. They apply to everything from newspapers (a bundle of news, arts, lifestyle, and sports content) to cereals (consider bran flakes plus raisins), to cars (few come these days without air conditioners and rear window defrosters).

3.2.3   Complementarities and Network Effects

System components are generally complements. Moreover, in many cases, systems are characterized by indirect network effects linked to the presence of components. That is, an increase in the number of users for one component often makes that component more valuable as a complement to other components.

For example, as Sony's Internet-based game center for the Play-Station 2 draws more users, more PlayStation 2 owners will want to buy games supported by the Internet service and more consumers will prefer PlayStation 2 consoles to competitors' models. Likewise an increase in the variety of components (printers for personal computers, for example) often increases the value of other components to end-users.

There also may be direct network effects. An increase in the number of users for a platform makes the platform more valuable to each user—typically because a common platform enables people to work together and share information. It is easier to work with people who use the same platform—Apple, Linux, or Windows, for example—than with people who use a different platform.

3.2.4   Multi-Sided Market Considerations

The literature on multi-sided markets considers situations in which a platform can internalize externalities among several distinct customer groups. The primary means for accomplishing this is to set prices in a way that balances the demand of the multiple customer groups (that is, multiple sides of the market) in order to maximize the value of the platform. A robust conclusion of this literature is that, because the price structure serves to internalize externalities, the price levels for each side do not track traditional price-marginal cost relationships. Instead, optimal pricing turns on the demand structures and marginal costs of the several sides. Prices on one side may be less than marginal cost—even less than zero (see Armstrong 2004, Evans 2003, and Rochet and Tirole 2003).

Four types of multi-sided market platform businesses have been identified in the literature. *Match-makers* aid members of one or both sides in their quest for a match on the other side (real-estate brokers, business-to-business (B to B) websites, and stock exchanges). See chapter 10 in this book by Jullien for further discussion of matchmaking businesses. *Audience-makers* bring advertisers and audiences together, matching buyers and sellers (yellow page directories, television, newspapers, magazines, and Internet portals). *Transaction-based businesses* meter transactions between the two sides of a market (monetary media such as credit cards or traveler's checks and advanced-generation mobile phone networks).

The fourth type, *shared-input platforms,* include the hardware and software platforms discussed in this chapter. Participants on at least one side need to obtain access to another side to provide value to participants on at least one other side. Thus software developers need to obtain access to the APIs and other features of the software platform in order to write applications for end-users. Likewise, software platform designers and hardware peripheral manufacturers need access to the functionality of the hardware platform to develop products for that platform (see Hagiu 2004).

Many of the firms in the computer-based industries examined here are organized as multi-sided platforms. However, unlike some other cases, the decision to organize computer-based businesses this way seems to be dictated by the same considerations that determine whether a firm follows a vertically integrated or disintegrated business model. For example, advertising-supported media cannot integrate vertically into advertising, exchanges cannot realistically integrate vertically into the sell-side, and transaction-based platforms cannot become sellers. Nor is there a way of providing a general-purpose payment card without a two-sided model.

But there is a way of running a computer–system-based business in which the firm supplies, and perhaps bundles, all components. In fact, many computer-based businesses have adopted this vertically integrated model instead of creating multi-sided markets. "Multisidedness" is therefore considerably more dependent on the particulars of technology and market environment in the computer-based industries than it is in many other platform-based businesses. Most importantly, it is a strategic decision.

Before we go to the case studies, it may be helpful to consider figure 3.2, which shows the components of computer systems. Consider the left side of the figure. The computer system can be thought of as a stack that consists of the hardware (most importantly the device that includes the microprocessor), the software platform (which may con-

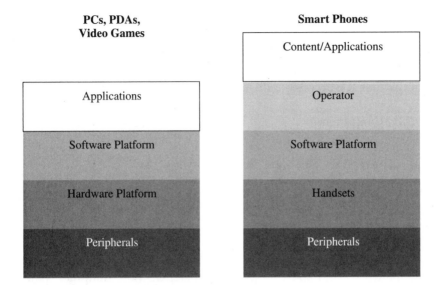

Figure 3.2
Components of computer systems

sist of middleware in addition to the operating system), applications that work with the software platform, and hardware peripherals that work with the hardware platform.

Mobile telephones follow a somewhat different model shown on the right side. There is a network operator that generally stands between the software platform and the content and applications. A developer or content provider generally cannot access the mobile phone (which bundles the hardware and software platform) without the permission of the mobile operator. The same is true for smart cards, a technology that is not considered in this chapter, in which case the application provider needs to get access through the card issuer (for example, American Express or a bank that issues MasterCard or Visa cards).

3.3 Computer–System-Based Industries

This section surveys five diverse computer-based industries. To avoid getting lost in a mass of detail, we focus on two issues related to the degree firms have chosen to organize themselves as multi-sided platforms. The first is the structural dynamics of the industry, including how the degree of vertical integration varies over time. The second is pricing strategies and their use in exploiting network effects. A particular focus here is on businesses that have adopted multi-sided market models and on how they have used pricing to "get all sides on board" and to maximize the value of their systems. We devote the greatest attention to the computer industry itself, and then compare its development with other industries based on computer systems.

3.3.1 Computers

Several sorts of computers have emerged since the first commercial machines were introduced in 1951. It is useful to distinguish mainframes, minicomputers, personal computers, workstations, and server computers. These sectors have followed diverse dynamics and employed different business models over time. We begin with an overview of the hardware and software platform relationships, and then focus on personal computers.

Vendors of many sorts of computer systems have chosen to provide the hardware and software platform together. Most computer mainframe and minicomputer companies have produced their own operating systems, which are optimized for the computer hardware, and have bundled these operating systems with the hardware platform. In these circumstances, software applications can run only on the specific hardware and software platform combination. IBM, for example, developed several operating systems for the computers it introduced in the 1950s and 1960s, beginning with the GM-NAA I/O System for its 704 mainframe in 1956. It developed OS/360 for its System/360, which was the leading mainframe-computing platform for many years after its introduction in the late 1960s. Recently, IBM attempted to standardize its various mainframes on the open-source Linux OS. (There are other dimensions to decisions on vertical integration not discussed, for example, the relationship between the computer manufacturer and the suppliers of components such as microprocessors.)

Some thought the Unix operating system, introduced by Bell Labs, would provide an operating system that worked across different hardware platforms. However, the computer manufacturers using Unix found there were advantages to modifying the OS to optimize its performance with the underlying hardware.

When personal computers first were introduced in the late 1970s, producers generally followed the traditional vertical integration model: firms provided both the hardware and software platforms. That is how Apple did it—not to mention Tandy, Commodore, Texas Instruments, Coleco, Atari, Timex, and Sinclair (Campbell-Kelly 2003). Some vendors relied on the CP/M operating system, licensed from Digital Research. But CP/M had to be modified for each hardware platform, and applications that ran on one CP/M system generally did not work on others.

When IBM entered the industry in 1981, the company planned to make its hardware platform work with several operating systems. These operating systems included PC-DOS developed by and licensed from Microsoft, CP/M licensed from Digital Research, and the UCSD p-System licensed from Softech. (When IBM released its personal computer, MS-DOS, rebranded PC-DOS when purchased through IBM, it was the only complete, fast-running OS available for its hardware. The UCSD p-System was available, but ran very slowly. CP/M-86 did not become available until 1982, and had the added drawback of a hefty price tag—$240, compared to DOS at just $40 when introduced in 1981.) The personal computer marketplace soon became a battle between the Apple and IBM platforms.

Beginning in the 1980s, several companies, including Sun and Hewlett-Packard, produced workstations designed to perform more processing-intensive tasks than most personal computers. These workstations had operating systems based on the UNIX or OpenVMS operating systems, but were tightly coupled with a specific hardware platform. Vendors typically bundled their hardware and software platforms, much like Apple has done in PCs. Microsoft introduced a version of Windows for workstations in the early 1990s that ran on the increasingly powerful Intel platform.

More recently, the development of networked personal computers led to the creation of an industry providing "server computers," which performed various specialized tasks on the network.

Two business models have coexisted in the workstation and server industries for a number of years. Some manufacturers, including Sun, provide integrated hardware and software platforms. Several others, notably Microsoft and Novell, license software platforms that can be used with Intel-compatible hardware platforms manufactured by others.

The choice of business models appears to have had a dramatic effect on the evolution of the personal computer industry. Apple bundled its proprietary hardware platform with its proprietary software platform. IBM did not. The company offered several compatible operating systems developed by third-party vendors and permitted vendors to license these operating systems to other hardware vendors.

IBM tried to thwart the cloning of its hardware platform, but it did not succeed. Microsoft widely licensed the operating system it had developed for the IBM PC, which ultimately led to intense competition among purveyors of the hardware platform. Despite some experiments with licensing its operating system, Apple continued to follow an integrated strategy. (From 1994 to 1997, Apple licensed its operating system to manufacturers of Apple clones. It stopped because the licensing revenue gains did not begin to cover the engineering costs.)

With the benefit of hindsight, one tends to think that Apple's strategy was foolish and Microsoft's strategy was brilliant. At the time, however, both strategies had advantages and disadvantages that left it unclear which strategy would prevail. Apple could coordinate the hardware and software platform, realize possible benefits from integrating them tightly, and ensure the quality and reliability of the combined system. Microsoft, for its part, could benefit from hardware competition and perhaps from specializing in what it knew best— writing software. But the company could not test any single hardware and operating system combination as intensively as Apple could, and thus it could not do as much to ensure overall system quality and reliability.

The Apple-versus-Microsoft competition is well-trod territory. We consider it here only from the perspective of multi-sided markets theory. Microsoft followed a four-sided strategy in which it tried to bring hardware platform manufacturers, application developers, peripheral manufacturers, and end-users on board its platform. Apple initially followed a two-sided strategy in which it marketed to end-users, integrated the hardware platform and peripherals, and tried (though with less gusto than Microsoft) to enlist application developers as partners. Apple's strategy subsequently became three-sided as it loosened its grip on printers and other peripherals.

We begin by examining how Microsoft and Apple dealt with the applications side, and then turn to how Microsoft has dealt with computer manufacturers.

Software Applications From the beginning, the fortunes of the Apple and IBM platforms depended on their ability to win over independent applications developers as well as end-users. Both platforms took off in part because of "killer apps"—novel applications that enable a task that previously was impossible or too expensive, and thereby drive the adoption of a new technology. Apple sales for personal and business use increased rapidly with the introduction of VisiCalc, the first commercial spreadsheet program, which originally was available exclusively for the Apple II. Likewise, IBM PC sales took off once the Lotus 1-2-3 spreadsheet application was released.

We have found no evidence that these platform providers (Apple, IBM, and Microsoft) actively encouraged the creation of the killer apps. Moreover, it appears the software platforms at the time played much less important roles in providing services to applications than they did later in the history of the personal computer business. Visi-Calc for the Apple II and Lotus 1-2-3 for the IBM PC sometimes found it even more efficient to use its own code rather than code embodied in the operating system to perform routine tasks. But in later years, Microsoft and Apple realized that, with so much riding on the quality of applications available, it made sense to make it as attractive as possible to write software for their platforms.

Most importantly, both Microsoft and Apple expanded the set of APIs providing services to developers. This was apparent especially at Microsoft as it moved its software platform from DOS to Windows. According to Bill Gates, Windows XP exposes more than 6,000 APIs for developers through its Win 32 API set. Apple has also created an extensive set of APIs for the convenience of its developers. Indeed it has split these APIs into Cocoa, a set of high-level functions that developers can use to write complex applications using very little code, and Carbon, a class of fine-grain procedural APIs.[2]

Both launched programs for "evangelizing" their respective software platforms among developers, with Apple taking the lead in the early 1980s. According to Guy Kawasaki, the greatest Apple software evangelist,

The secondary effects of getting people to believe, who then got more people to believe, is something that was stumbled upon. In my recollection, I was never told, "OK, you go get XYZ to write software, and they in turn will get more customers to buy your software and to buy Macs." That's what happened, but that was not the plan.[3]

In 1984, shortly after Apple's introduction of the evangelist role, Microsoft formed the Developer Relations Group (DRG) to drum up support from third-party application developers for the first release of Windows. DRG's mission was to "Drive the success of Microsoft's strategic platforms by creating a critical mass of third-party applications." By 1995, DRG had more than eighty-five employees in the United

States and many more in the rest of the world. Their evangelism process is well defined, and is broken into four steps that focus on choosing which technologies to evangelize and working one-on-one to support early adopters.

Both platforms now provide benefits to software developers at little cost. In fact both platforms have developer networks that offer online assistance at no cost through their developer websites. Members of these networks receive newsletters, documentation, software seeds, system software, and software development kits. (Microsoft's Microsoft Developer Network [MSDN] began in 1993. Apple's Developer Connection [ADC] began in 1998.)

According to a 1995 Microsoft report, the company has long been committed to supporting third-party development:

Microsoft has its roots in developer support. The company was founded to develop languages and tools for PC application developers. As developers themselves, Microsoft's early employees understood the difficulties of supporting product on the multiplicity of operating systems that existed in the late 1970s and early 1980s. One of their key interests in MS-DOS was to try to create a broadly popular platform that would greatly simplify their own development process. In recognizing that, the company also realized that it needed to marshal other developers and hardware vendors to create a critical mass of support for MS-DOS.[4]

As of 1995, Microsoft was spending about $65 million annually to support software developers, and had about 400 technical support engineers on staff. By 1998, Microsoft was spending more than $250 million annually on developer-related activities that included research, events, marketing assistance, training programs, product support, and publications. In January 1999, Paul Maritz, the Group Vice President of Platforms and Applications at Microsoft, testified that Microsoft was planning to spend $630 million to help software developers write applications, and that 2,000 of Microsoft's 27,000 employees work full time helping developers.[5]

It is obvious that Apple and Microsoft would benefit from stimulating the production of applications. It is less obvious that the profit-maximizing strategy involved giving away developer services. The application developers, after all, were getting something of value from the software platforms: by writing for these platforms, they could market their applications to businesses and individuals using Apple- or IBM-compatible computers. By 1990, Microsoft had 71 million users worldwide and Apple had 5 million users worldwide.[6] Therefore, both

Apple and Microsoft could, in theory, have charged for access to their APIs and for the other platform services for developers, once they had established a substantial user base. And, in fact, that is just what makers of video game platforms did.

In addition to persuading third parties to write applications, Apple and Microsoft created applications for their own software platforms. (This is not surprising for Microsoft since a major part of its business was writing applications. It supplied some of the biggest selling applications for the Mac—Word and Excel—well before these applications became successful on Windows.) As of 1999, Microsoft applications represented about 20 percent of the sales of applications for its own platform, while Apple had a 10-percent share of applications for its platform.[7]

Hardware   Apple and Microsoft differed in how they treated the hardware platform. Apple began as an integrated hardware and platform company. Its first computer, the Apple I, was introduced in 1976 and came with a firmware resident system monitor that allowed the user to display, write, debug, and run programs. Except for a brief flirtation with licensing clone manufacturers in the mid-1990s, Apple has always bundled its hardware and software platforms.

Bill Gates sent a now famous letter to Apple's CEO John Sculley and Apple Products President Jean-Louis Gassée in 1985 in which he argued that Apple should license its operating system software to other manufacturers. Gates advised Apple to consider licensing the Mac OS in order to "create a standard," stating that the "significant investment (especially independent support) in a 'standard personal computer' results in incredible momentum for its architecture."[8] Gates's counsel was not altruistic. Microsoft had a financial interest in the success of Apple because, as noted, it was a major supplier of applications for the Apple platform. At this time Microsoft's future success in software platforms was far from ensured and one could view Gates's plea as an effort to hedge Microsoft's bets on its application and software business.

Many observers argue that Apple's failure to follow his advice contributed to Apple's loss of the market share to the open Microsoft platform. It is hard to know for sure. After all, much of the appeal of Apple computers is the seamless integration of its hardware and software, and a three-sided model might not have done as well. We might scoff at Apple's sales compared to Microsoft's, but it is the only one of the entrants in the late 1970s and early 1980s to survive this long. Integration may have been a smart differentiator.

Microsoft started as a software company focused on programming languages and began working with operating systems only when it was commissioned by IBM to do so. In its agreement with IBM, Microsoft reserved the right to license the operating system to other companies. Soon after the IBM PC had established itself as a serious contender in the emerging personal computer industry, Microsoft started working with other computer manufacturers who were developing IBM clones. It is generally accepted that the ensuing competition with IBM helped reduce the price of IBM-compatible PCs, thus increasing total PC output and expanding the demand for Microsoft's operating systems.

In some respects, Microsoft is the tail that wags the proverbial PC dog. Computer manufacturers—known as original equipment manufacturers (OEMs)—install copies of MS-DOS (and later Windows) on their computers before shipping them to end-users, and end-users are made aware that their PCs have Microsoft operating systems installed. For the end-user, the operating system is a visible, distinct, and important element of the overall system, an element with which they interact directly. Disk drives also have been important over time, but they generally have been viewed as simply commodity inputs used to build the hardware platform. One can view Intel's "Intel Inside" marketing campaign as an attempt to transform its microprocessors from inputs that are used by manufacturers to products that manufacturers distribute to consumers.

Manufacturers pay license fees to Microsoft based on the number of personal computers they ship installed with Microsoft operating systems. As in any manufacturer-distributor relationship, these license fees are based largely on the ultimate demand by end-users for Microsoft's operating systems; for the computer manufacturers, Microsoft's operating systems are a cost that is passed on in whole or in part to end-users. It is important, however, to distinguish here between OEMs as Windows licensees and OEMs as the third side of the market. In the computer market, it just happens that, in addition to building the hardware, OEMs are also the major distribution channel for Windows. The payments from OEMs to Microsoft are exclusively for the Windows license and are passed on to end-users; they do not reflect the services that Microsoft offers OEMs to help build the hardware.

The relationship between Microsoft and the computer manufacturers is a bit more complex than the preceding discussion suggests. Microsoft, Intel, and the major computer vendors have worked with each other (and often with peripheral manufacturers) to prepare new products; in the early days in particular, the process was driven by advances in microprocessors. Microsoft worked with the computer manufacturers to ensure that its operating system worked well with the next generation of hardware and that the next generation of hardware made use of features that Microsoft was developing for its operating systems. Over time, Microsoft has created pricing incentives for the inclusion of hardware features that made Microsoft's operating systems more useful.

Microsoft provided services to computer manufacturers and makers of peripherals in several ways. In the early days of DOS, any developer who wanted its application to work with, say, a large set of printers already in use had to customize its application for each printer. If there are N applications and M peripherals in use, in order for every program to interact with every peripheral, $N * M$ drivers would have to be written.

With the transition to Windows, however, application programs needed only to include a single general Windows driver for each type of peripheral (printer, scanner, etc.) and device manufacturers needed only write Windows drivers to make use of their device's features; the operating system linked them together.[9] As a result of this development with Windows, for every program to communicate with every device, only $N + M$ drivers had to be written. Microsoft continued to put much effort into making it easier for manufacturers of peripheral equipment to write for their operating system. For example, when Windows 95 was released, the platform supported more than 800 different printers right out of the box (Mace 1995).

Another example of Microsoft's contribution to the development of hardware peripherals is its collaboration in the development of the CD-ROM. In 1986, prior to having a CD-ROM product in the works, Gates insisted that Microsoft associate itself with CD technology by holding a CD-ROM conference (Manes and Andrews 1994). The conference was a success, and Gates decided to make it an annual event. Gates recognized that to fully exploit the technology, Microsoft would need to acquire new skills. He was not convinced that a viable business was possible in this arena. In fact Gates told a colleague that he was willing to invest $200 million to research if a profitable market existed for the CD technology (Stross 1996).

To jumpstart the industry, according to Stross (1996), Microsoft worked with representatives from Sony, Phillips, Digital Research, Apple, and others to accelerate the establishment of a single-file format. Microsoft also evangelized the "religion of CD-ROM" by convincing hardware companies to offer personal computers with preinstalled and configured CD-ROM drives in addition to add-on external drives.

Apple has followed a very different path with respect to peripherals. Because the IBM PC is an open platform with no single vendor controlling the standard, anybody can produce peripherals to work with any PC. By contrast, Apple exercised significant control over its system. The company manufactured and sold it own peripherals—opening the platform to others, the thinking went, would cut into Apple revenues. As a result, Apple was usually late to include industry-standard ports and mostly relied on its own peripherals.[10] For example, the market for third-party Mac monitors did not exist until 1987. Even today, many Macintosh computers house the monitor and the computer core in a single unit.[11] Apple recently released the iMac G5, which contains many peripherals within its two-inch thick display. Apple advertises that "The entire computer, including a G5-based logic board, slot-loading optical drive, hard disk, speakers, and even the power supply—dwells inside the enchanting display." Note, too, that the very first Mac was designed to make expansion as difficult as possible. It included a physical bar above its few ports to make expansion awkward. What is more, the cover was difficult to remove—the better to discourage users from opening it.[12]

Even after Apple opened the Macintosh to third-party peripheral manufacturers, it retained a significant advantage for its own equipment through the tight integration of the Macintosh with Apple-made peripherals. For example, at the end of the 1980s, Apple remained virtually the only supplier of printers for the Macintosh platform; not surprisingly, 95 percent of the printers attached to Macintoshes were made by Apple.[13]

Pricing Structures   Multi-sided market theory is built on the premise that pricing is a critical element in any strategy to maximize platform value. Microsoft's pricing structure is such that it has earned virtually all of its revenue from end-users—either directly through the retail channel, or indirectly through computer manufacturers who pass on the licensing charges to end-users. Microsoft has given away access to its APIs as well as to other valuable services for writing applications, and thus earned only minor revenue from licensing software tools. It has also given away valuable services to computer manufacturers and hardware peripheral manufacturers. Apple has adopted a similar pricing structure, though as noted before, it has integrated vertically the production of hardware.

3.3.2 Video Games

The video game industry has been remarkably dynamic since its birth, starting with Pong in 1975. Comparing its evolution with that of computers provides useful insights concerning choices of structure and business models.

3.3.2.1 Evolution of Business Models Video game consoles were introduced in the 1970s as devices that played a single game that was hardwired into the console's circuitry. The most successful ones were versions of already popular arcade games, such as Atari's Home Pong (1975) and Coleco's Telestar (1976). With the release of Fairchild's Channel F game console in 1976, a new business model emerged. Channel F did not hardwire games, but rather played games stored in interchangeable cartridges. Atari expanded on Fairchild's approach with the release of the Video Computer System (VCS) in 1977 (Kent 2001). Neither Fairchild nor Atari moved quickly to write contracts for new games with independent developers, but they did establish the technological separation of the hardware platform and the game software.

A new dimension of the business model started taking shape in 1979. Some Atari programmers defected to found Activision, the first independent software company in the home video game market. The company's initial goal was to create games for the VCS model 2600. Activision soon released its first games and was an overnight success. That encouraged other startups in independent game production, which represented a turning point for the industry. From then on, a manufacturer entering the console market had to attract both gamers and developers to the platform to ensure its success.

Today's platform business model originated with the introduction of Nintendo's Nintendo Entertainment System (NES) in the mid-1980s. Nintendo actively pursued licensing agreements with game publishers to support the NES, and was the first console maker to introduce a security chip that locked out unlicensed games. Both practices have been adopted since by virtually all console manufacturers.

Just as computer operating systems must attract applications software and users to succeed, video game platforms must attract game publishers and gamers: in this sense, both markets are two-sided. Platform competition in the video game industry is extremely fierce: a new round of competition takes place every four to five years when new models are released; the two most successful platforms typically end up with more than 80 percent of the market, and one platform generally achieves clear dominance (Clements and Ohashi 2004). Moreover, 50 percent of console sales come within three months of the introduction of a new model, and fully 80 percent within nine months (Coughlan 2000). Thus a platform either succeeds or flops quickly, and platform owners understand that having a solid library of games available at launch is necessary for success.

3.3.2.2 Attracting Game Developers It is interesting to compare the personal computer application industry and the game publishing industry. Both were created to exploit the popularity of the early platforms in their respective industries, the Apple II and the Atari VCS. Moreover, killer applications have played important roles in both industries. It is noteworthy, however, that unlike killer apps for PCs, virtually all killer games have been produced by console makers themselves—Pong (Atari), Mario Bros. and Pokemon (Nintendo), and Sonic the Hedgehog (Sega). Note, too, that although the video game industry had become two-sided by the 1985 release of NES in the United States, first-party (or inhouse) games continued to account for a large share of total games developed for consoles as late as 1995. In that year, Nintendo was still developing 57 percent of Nintendo 64 software inhouse, according to Coughlan (2001).

The first console to break with this tradition was Sony's PlayStation, for which only 23 percent of the games were developed inhouse. In fact even among these games produced inhouse, a large part came from recently acquired publishing companies such as Psygnosis, creator of the hit game *Lemmings*. Neither the original PlayStation nor its successor, PlayStation 2, could boast of any killer game in the sense Sonic and Mario had been killer games for Genesis and NES, respectively. Instead, PlayStation achieved supremacy by attracting the support of game companies that developed a wide variety of popular offerings.

Key to PlayStation's popularity with game developers were Sony's excellent development tools, which earned its platform a reputation for being very easy to program in comparison to Nintendo's Nintendo 64 and Sega's Saturn. Furthermore, Sony made life easier for developers by opting to store games on CD-ROMs, while Nintendo continued using cartridges. CD-ROMs were substantially cheaper to make in quantity than cartridges, and the medium allowed for much faster adjustments in production to meet changes in demand. (At the time it cost about $1.50 to press a 640-megabyte CD and about $12 to manufacture an 8-megabyte cartridge. See Campbell-Kelly 2003). These two factors enabled Sony to earn the same per-unit profit as Nintendo while charging substantially lower licensing fees, according to Kent (2001).

The importance of developer support in the video game industry, as in the computer industry, became clear when Microsoft launched the Xbox console in 2001. The company announced two programs, the Independent Developer Program and the Incubator Program, to encourage smaller developers by providing free software tools and waiving normal prepublishing requirements. Furthermore, Microsoft had extensive meetings with developers before the hardware specs for the console were set, and incorporated many of the developers' suggestions into the final design. Microsoft also made it easier for developers with PC experience to develop games for the Xbox by relying on DirectX (a collection of Windows APIs that serves as the foundation for most PC games) in the design of the console.

3.3.2.3 Hardware In contrast with personal computers, the hardware platform has remained tightly integrated with the software platform in the video game industry. Console makers design their own operating systems to take advantage of technological advances in hardware. The most recent consoles contain operating systems whose functionality extends beyond simple support for video games. For example, the recently released PlayStation X (PSX) includes a DVD player and Internet connectivity.[14]

3.3.2.4 Pricing Structures Perhaps the most interesting contrast between the personal computer industry and game console manufacturers is the pricing structure. The pricing model that emerged with the NES in the mid-1980s, and is still prevalent today, is based on selling the console to end-users at or below the marginal cost of production.

For example, Nintendo sold the original NES for $249 and charged 20 percent plus $14 per game sold; Nintendo 64 was sold at $250 with $20 or more per-game royalties. When first released, Sony's Play-Station 2, Nintendo's GameCube and Microsoft's Xbox all sold for around $200–300 and charged $7 to $10 royalties per game to independent game publishers. In each case, competition and falling component prices prompted console makers to cut hardware prices. In 1996, Sony Computer's PlayStation and Sega's Saturn, all priced around $300–$400, were sold at a loss of between $50 and $80 per unit. In September 2003, Microsoft had dropped the price of the Xbox to $179, for a loss of around $100 per console.

Console makers then rely on revenue from games produced inhouse, along with royalties from games sold by independent developers, to recover fixed development costs.[15] That is, users pay a direct access fee for the right to access the platform—but a fee that is less than the marginal cost of serving users. (We define an access fee to be one that is independent of usage. Virtually all mass-market software products, including games, applications, and software platforms, have been licensed in perpetuity based on a one-time fee, which is therefore an access fee. There have been discussions in the industry about moving to more usage-based fees.)

Developers pay no access fees. Their access is, in fact, subsidized through the provision of numerous development tools at little or no cost. But they are charged usage fees in the form of royalties that depend on the number of end-users who buy their games. (This is true if we define a unitary interaction between users and game developers as the purchase of a game. One could alternatively consider that a unitary interaction occurs each time a game is played by a user. In this case the royalties are positive access fees for users, since according to this definition they do not depend on the intensity of usage of the console, that is, on how often users play games.)

This pricing model is the exact opposite of the model used by computer software platforms—a fact that is all the more remarkable since video game consoles are technologically equivalent to computer operating systems integrated with a hardware platform.

3.3.3 Personal Digital Assistants
Personal Digital Assistants (PDAs) provide users with electronic applications such as address books, calendars, schedule organizers, memo-writing capabilities, etc. Like computers, PDAs are based on a software

platform—the best-known and most widely used being the Palm OS. Palm's history and business strategies are well documented elsewhere (see Gawer and Cusumano 2002). We therefore focus on elements directly relevant to software platforms.

3.3.3.1 Evolution of Business Models   The Palm Pilot, introduced in 1996, was not the first PDA. It was the first to achieve widespread popularity, however: after selling over 1 million units by the end of 1997, Palm reached cumulative sales of over 3 million by 1998, and 28 million by 2002.

The first Palm was a fully integrated device for consumers, combining hardware, an operating system, and a major application. Its early success seems to have been linked to ease-of-use, low price, good handwriting recognition, and PC connectivity. Subsequently, Palm's popularity with users attracted a large community of developers of complementary software and hardware, which Palm actively encouraged and has become known as the Palm Economy. Today Palm has more than 400,000 registered software developers as of April 2005.[16]

Thus, much like video game consoles and PCs, Palm evolved from a one-sided consumer product into a two-sided market platform. The process took just two years, compared to ten years for video games and nearly three decades for the computer industry. Of course, this difference has a lot to do with the relative stages of advancement in hardware technology at the time each of these industries was created. It is arguably much easier to create a software platform today than it was in the 1960s.

The next step in Palm's platform strategy was to license the Palm operating system to manufacturers of other consumer devices, most importantly cell phones. In 1998, Palm decided to license the Palm OS to competing handheld manufacturers. The goal was to expand the user base of its operating system platform, whose dominance had begun to come under pressure from Microsoft's Pocket PC OS. Thus, although Palm allowed the cloning of its hardware platform, it kept the development of the software platform inhouse.

In 2003, Palm split into PalmSource, its operating system division that continues to license the Palm OS to a broad range of handheld devices (including smart phones), and PalmOne, the hardware division, which at the same time acquired rival hardware maker Handspring.

3.3.3.2 Complements: Applications and Hardware Add-ons Graffiti, Palm's hand-recognition application, is generally regarded as the killer application that drove adoption of the Pilot, much like VisiCalc drove the success of the Apple II. It made PDAs popular because it gave users an easy and appealing way to enter data into their address books, to write short memos, etc.

However, Graffiti was produced inhouse, like virtually all early applications for the Palm. Although Palm's founders were fully aware of its potential to become a software platform at the outset, the Pilot was conceived initially as a vertically integrated consumer device. This strategy reflected lessons learned from the early failures in the PDA business, such as the Apple Newton and Palm's own Zoomer, and the initial difficulties encountered in attracting independent developers.

Palm held its first developer conference in late 1997.[17] Since then, it has been involved aggressively in the development of the Palm Economy, with efforts in this direction very similar to Microsoft's. Like any computer operating system vendor, Palm realized that more software and hardware complements make devices running the Palm OS more attractive, and therefore allow Palm to sell more copies of the operating system.

Palm helped its developer community stabilize interface standards, and facilitated business and technical exchanges among them. For example, Palm worked with five other firms to found the SyncML Initiative, aimed at developing a standard open protocol for data synchronization. The company also regularly offered Palm OS development classes and encouraged other activities among its community of users through developer portals (see Gawer and Cusumano 2002).

Palm also provided business resources to developers, including joint development, marketing, and bundling. The most important resources offered were its software development forums, which helped third-party developers start their own businesses. Palm even created a $50 million–venture capital unit called Palm Ventures to support businesses focusing on Palm OS applications. Today, PalmGear, the leading Internet provider of software and hardware products for the Palm OS platform, offers more than 22,000 applications.[18]

3.3.3.3 Hardware Platform Initially, Palm sold a fully integrated consumer device. But after recognizing that most of the value of its platform resided in the operating system, it chose to license the operating system to manufacturers of other hardware, including competing

PDA makers—among them Handspring, Sony, IBM, Qualcomm, and Supra. One key reason for doing so was to expand the market for the Palm operating system in the face of increasing competition from devices based on Windows CE, Microsoft's version of Windows for handheld devices. In other words, the company decided that the competitive threat at the software-platform level was more serious than the loss of competitive advantage in hardware.

3.3.3.4 Pricing Structure   Given the similarity of the relationship between Palm and the Palm Economy to the one between Microsoft and the PC applications industry, it is perhaps not surprising that the Microsoft and Palm platform pricing structures are virtually identical. Software and hardware developers are charged little or nothing for support from Palm, and there are no variable fees parallel to the royalties collected in the video game industry.[19] (One could, however, argue that the venture capital support to developers possesses a variable fee dimension if, for example, Palm retains an equity position in the newly created ventures. This would mean that it capitalizes on successful complements, much like video game console makers capitalize on successful games through royalties. We were unable to find any detailed data regarding the funding deals made by Palm Ventures, but we suspect that net revenues from venture capital deals are small compared to revenues from licensing the Palm OS.) Palm's revenues come from licensing its operating system to device vendors and from direct sale of its own devices. (As mentioned, this was true until 2003. After the split, PalmSource became the operating system licensor and PalmOne the hardware vendor as one of many other PalmSource licensees.)

3.3.4 Smart Mobile Phones

The market for smart phones has exploded during the past two years; indeed, in 2003, sales of smart phones overtook those of PDAs. Smart phones are the most sophisticated category of wireless devices, possessing advanced capabilities and data services (calendars, address books, computer-like applications, wireless access to content, etc.), as well as mobile phone capacities. The leading software platform for smart phones is the Symbian operating system.

3.3.4.1 Evolution of the Business Model   Symbian was established as an independent software licensing company in June 1998 by Motorola, Ericsson, Nokia, and Psion (a PDA vendor), with the goal of creating a common operating system for wireless information devices based on Psion's EPOC 32 OS. Subsequently, Nokia, Matsushita (owner of the Panasonic brand), Sanyo, Sony, Fujitsu, Siemens; Samsung all became Symbian licensees; some of them also became Symbian shareholders. The majority of Symbian's shareholders are among the top ten handset vendors.

3.3.4.2 Applications Initially, most Symbian applications were developed inhouse and distributed to its hardware licensees, or directly developed and installed by the hardware licensees themselves. Symbian provides its licensees with customizable user interfaces, which allow them to differentiate their products, as well as support for color displays and advanced Internet connectivity. Handset manufacturers integrate the Symbian OS with their hardware and sometimes their own applications, and then market their mobile phones through network operators such as Vodafone and T-Mobile.

However, as mobile phone capabilities developed, a market for third-party applications for smart phones emerged and expanded spectacularly, with products ranging from productivity applications (communication, data, and file management) to entertainment (games and media players). The number of Symbian applications offered by third-party vendors rose from 1,323 to 2,954 between 2003 and 2004.[20] Noteworthy examples include Access's NetFront browser, RealNetworks's RealPlayer Mobile, and Macromedia's Flash Player for Symbian OS.

Symbian seems to have succeeded in creating a Symbian Economy similar to the Palm Economy. The company very actively supports this economy. Through its website, Symbian offers SDKs, programming languages (Java, C++, OPL, and Visual Basic), development tools, APIs, and documentation to independent developers. It also holds industrywide events and even organizes application contests. In addition, Symbian relies heavily on joint efforts for making improvements to its platform, setting up a partnership initiative in 2002 "to promote the creation of innovative software and hardware technology solutions."[21] It also develops and licenses products with and from software companies including Oracle (wireless access to data residing in Oracle databases), IBM (wireless enterprise applications for users of Symbian-based smart phones and communicators), Sybase (SQL anywhere and UltraLite deployment technology for smart phones), Metrowerks (CodeWarrior software development tools), InfoMatrix (file format converters for MS Office email attachments), Opera Software (Opera browser), RealNetworks (RealPlayer Mobile), and ARM (Jazelle technology software).

3.3.4.3 Hardware What sets Symbian apart from all other software platforms is its status as a joint venture of competing mobile phone handset manufacturers. No such entity exists in any other industry. In fact it is interesting to note the stark contrast in platform strategy compared to Windows CE, Symbian's main competitor in the market for smart phone operating systems. Microsoft's approach has been to partner with low-cost original design manufacturers (ODMs) to produce Windows-powered, network-operator–specific phones, thereby bypassing the brand name handset makers. For example, France's Orange operator sells phones built by HTC, one of many Taiwanese ODMs, and uses Windows CE as the software platform.[22]

For Microsoft, the idea is to commodify the hardware and make the industry revolve around a proprietary software platform controlled by the operating system vendor and the telecom network operator. That, of course, is similar to the way the PC industry has evolved, with the operator playing a similar role to that of the microprocessor manufacturer (for example, Intel) in PCs. This platform has three sides: users, application developers, and hardware makers. In contrast, leading hardware makers would like to see the software commodified instead—which is why Symbian champions open standards—and have the industry revolve around hardware platforms that share an open software platform not controlled by any one firm. This platform would be two-sided: users and application developers. The model resembles the PC industry before the emergence of the IBM PC and DOS, with CP/M as a more or less open software platform that hardware manufacturers could customize and integrate with their machines.

3.3.4.4 Pricing Structure Symbian's pricing structure is very similar to the ones adopted by PalmSource and the software platforms in the computer industry. Symbian invests considerable effort and financial resources in developer support, but application developers pay little if anything in return. Symbian then receives royalties on each Symbian OS-based phone shipped by hardware licensees, as well as consulting fees for helping licensees implement the Symbian OS. (From Symbian OS v7.0 onward, the royalty has been set at $7.25 per unit for the first

2 million units shipped by a licensee and $5 per unit thereafter.) Thus, there are no usage fees, negative access fees for developers, or, assuming royalties charged to hardware licensees get passed on to consumers, positive access fees for end-users.

3.3.5 Digital Content Devices

As the Internet and wireless telecommunications networks have become faster and capable of transmitting larger chunks of data, the market for digital content has expanded greatly. Access to digital content—including music, multimedia clips, and games—is controlled by software platforms, which provide the technology that enables users to "consume" the content.

At this early stage of development, different digital content platforms have adopted different business models. In particular, Apple's iPod is a one-sided consumer product, while NTT DoCoMo's i-mode is a two-sided platform, and RealNetworks' RealPlayer is a mix of the two. Here we consider these digital content platforms, focusing on the first two.

3.3.5.1 Description Apple's iPod is a portable digital device for listening to music stored in Apple's Advanced Audio Coding (AAC) digital format. The iPods can hold around 7,500–15,000 songs, which users can purchase and download via the Internet at Apple's online music store, iTunes. (See chapter 4 by Peitz and Waelbroeck for further discussion of iTunes and other music platforms.)

A "third-generation" mobile-phone service, i-mode, was introduced by NTT DoCoMo in 1999 (as a 2.5 generation mobile phone). Still the market leader in Japan, it is an always-on wireless service. This service allows consumers equipped with i-mode–powered handsets to exchange emails and access a wide variety of content—including news, personal finance, games, and ringtones—through i-mode's portal.

3.3.5.2 Content Provision Perhaps the most interesting difference between the iPod and the i-mode is their relationship with content providers. The iTunes music store, an online shop run by Apple, provides music for iPod. Consumers buy songs for 99 cents individually (or entire albums for $9.99), which they download onto their computer, manage using the iTunes software and iTunes or QuickTime media player, and transfer to the iPod portable device. (Songs come wrapped in Apple's digital rights management [DRM] technology. This limits the use of the files to Apple's iTunes and QuickTime media players on only five authorized PCs). Rights to distribute the approximately one billion songs available on iTunes have been purchased by Apple from record labels, which receive a percentage of revenues for songs downloaded. Thus Apple's iPod/iTunes business model is no different from traditional retailers, which acquire supplies before selling them to consumers.

By contrast, no content that users can access through the i-mode portal is owned in any sense by DoCoMo. The company simply provides a digital interface through which users and content providers interact. This business model is two-sided, as the value of the service to users depends on the variety of content available (that is, the number of content providers signed up), and the value to content providers depends on the number of subscribers to i-mode. It is noteworthy that two-sidedness was one of the major strategic differences between i-mode and another failed attempt in the third-generation market, Vizzavi, which relied exclusively on its own content.

Today the i-mode service has more than 93,000 official (that is, directly accessible through the i-mode portal) and nonofficial sites. Two of the main reasons behind i-mode's success in attracting content providers were the choice of the c-HTML language over wireless application protocol (WAP), which greatly reduced costs for providers who already had websites, and an advanced billing system, which enabled content providers to charge small monthly fees to users.

3.3.5.3 Hardware Apple's iPod/iTunes business model is vertically integrated, with Apple providing both the software (QuickTime and iTunes) and the hardware (iPod). By contrast, handsets designed specifically for i-mode are supplied by a number of manufacturers with close relationships to DoCoMo—in particular Matsushita (owner of the Panasonic brand), NEC, Fujitsu, and Sharp.

3.3.5.4 Pricing Structure As discussed, Apple's iPod/iTunes business model is one-sided; There is nothing unusual about it. Like any other merchant, Apple "buys" music from record labels and "resells" it to users, along with the iPod device. According to most analysts, Apple barely breaks even on the music part of the business, making its money on the hardware-and-software bundle.

The i-mode pricing structure issue is more interesting. DoCoMo does not charge fixed fees to content providers to make their content accessible through i-mode, even though reportedly there are hundreds of new providers queuing up every month for this privilege. It charges relatively modest subscription fees to users (including significant handset subsidies), but uses its sophisticated billing system to charge them variable fees based on their intensity of content usage. (Indeed the system does not charge based on the time spent on the network—it is an always-on service—but rather based on the amount of data transferred.) Furthermore, it offers content providers the option of joint billing (which makes life easier for everyone since consumers receive a single unified bill) in exchange for 9 percent of the content revenues.

3.4   Regularities and Puzzles

The five computer-based industries surveyed here have notable similarities, as well as striking differences that give rise to interesting puzzles—some of which we highlight in this concluding section.

3.4.1   Integration and Multi-sidedness

Observation 3.1   Within individual industries, there are significant differences in the extent of vertical integration across companies and over time.

The less vertical integration, generally the greater the extent of multi-sidedness, the greater the complexity of the task of "getting all sides on board," and the more industries rely upon the market to lower cost and improve quality. However, greater integration provides greater control over the total system as experienced by the end-user.

Figure 3.3 shows the evolution of integration in four of the five industries (digital content devices are too new for consideration here).

Observation 3.2   Across and within industries there has been a broad tendency toward less vertical integration over time, reflecting the development of markets that can be relied upon for low-cost, high-quality complementary products.

For example, the early video game console manufacturers wrote their own games and operating systems—nobody else was going to do it. A robust industry of game developers has since emerged, and console vendors have found it useful to rely more on the market to supply desired games. They have moved from offering a one-sided consumer product to a two-sided platform. (An important qualification

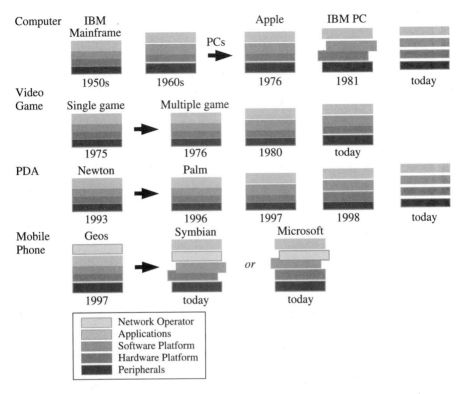

Figure 3.3
Evolution of integration

is that there also has been a broad tendency toward the technological integration of features—both software and hardware—with their respective platforms.)

Similarly, in the absence of a capable set of outside suppliers, Palm initially wrote all the applications for its PDA and sold a software platform/hardware platform/applications bundle as a consumer product. As outside applications suppliers developed, Palm moved to a two-sided strategy relying in part on the efforts of suppliers. Currently, the Palm Economy also includes independent suppliers of hardware platforms and peripherals, and PalmSource was spun off to focus tightly on its software platform, the Palm OS.

Computers offer the most extreme example of this sort of evolution. Early users of mainframe computers bought the hardware platform, operating system, applications, and peripherals from the same firm. As the mainframe computer industry matured after the introduction of the IBM System/360, independent vendors of applications and peripherals emerged. By the time the IBM PC was introduced in 1981, there were numerous independent software applications vendors. Today, Microsoft's Windows software platform plays a central role in personal computers. But Microsoft is not integrated with hardware platforms; it is one of many vendors of applications programs and, to a very minor extent, peripherals (mice, keyboards) that work with the Windows platform.

Observation 3.3 Some important differences in industry integration reflect differences in business strategies, which in turn reflect different perceptions of competitive advantage and/or market trends.

The differences between Apple and Microsoft are now classic. Apple's greater integration facilitated delivery of quality and reliability, and eased the task of coordinating changes in hardware and operating systems. Microsoft's reliance on a competitive market for hardware led to both hardware innovation and low hardware prices—and, with hindsight, this seems to have been the better business strategy. As the creator of the leading handset manufacturers, Symbian's strategy aims toward a smart phone industry with a cheap, open software platform and differentiated hardware platforms. By contrast, software platform vendor Microsoft aims to create a PC-like smart phone industry in which relatively undifferentiated hardware platforms all use a proprietary software platform. In setting up iPod, Apple made a choice to distribute only content it owned, while NTT DoCoMo chose to own none of the content flowing through its i-mode system. Purely as a technical matter, each could have made the other choice.

3.4.2 Pricing Strategies

Table 3.2 summarizes the pricing strategies followed by the software platforms we have considered. We do not consider digital content devices, which have heterogeneous strategies and are at an early stage in their market development.

Observation 3.4 Most vendors of multi-sided platforms seem to earn the bulk of their profits from only one side.

This in itself is something of a puzzle. The pattern characterizes all the industries we have discussed here. In PCs and PDAs, all the money is earned from end-users. Neither Palm, Apple, nor Microsoft (in either sector) charges applications writers or peripherals manufacturers for

Table 3.2
Software platforms pricing structure

Software platform	Complements		Users	
	Access	Usage	Access	Usage
PC operating systems	≤ 0	$= 0$	> 0	$= 0$
Personal digital assistants	≤ 0	$= 0$	> 0	$= 0$
Smart mobile phones (except DoCoMo)	≤ 0	$= 0$	> 0	> 0
DoCoMo	≤ 0	> 0	≤ 0	$= 0$
Video games	≤ 0	> 0	≤ 0	$= 0$

the right to access its software platform. In fact all expend resources to facilitate access. Microsoft profits by licensing its operating systems to end-users through hardware manufacturers; Apple profits by selling hardware-and-software bundles to end-users. The two companies created from the original Palm Computing collectively employ both channels.

As we note, pricing strategies in the video game industry are dramatically different. Video game platforms are sold to end-users as integrated bundles of hardware and operating systems, but these sales yield little or no profit. As with personal computers, video game platform vendors subsidize access by applications (that is, game) developers. In stark contrast to personal computers, however, game developers pay platform vendors fees for use of the platform in the form of royalties for each game sold.

When pricing strategies differ so sharply between industries using broadly similar technologies and integration strategies, but are nearly identical within those industries, it seems clear that industry-level cost and/or demand differences (rather than, say, firm-level differences or strategic choices) are playing the lead role in shaping strategies. As noted, however, the literature does not yet contain a rigorous explanation of the differences in pricing between PCs and PDAs on the one hand, and videogames on the other. This is perhaps the most interesting puzzle we have encountered in this research.

Differences in pricing strategies within the other industries discussed here seem to reflect mainly strategic choices. Symbian's owners want to make money by selling smart phone handsets, not by licensing the Symbian OS, while Microsoft wants to make money licensing its operating system. At the end of the day, of course, end-users purchase hardware-and-software bundles, and neither Symbian nor Microsoft intends to earn revenues from applications developers. Apple makes money on the iPod device (a hardware-and-software bundle), not on the music it buys and resells to iPod owners. NTT DoCoMo makes money on the network traffic generated by i-mode services, not by charging high prices for i-mode handsets or by levying access or usage fees on content developers. In these last two cases, alternative pricing strategies would be possible and, arguably, plausible—though they may not be optimal.

3.4.3 Bundling and Feature Accretion

Observation 3.5 Driven by advances in hardware technology, hardware and software platforms (as well as applications programs) have steadily added features and functionality.

While this process has been most visible in PC operating systems, thanks to antitrust cases brought against Microsoft in the United States and elsewhere, it is not obviously the most dramatic. Mobile phones, once capable only of placing and receiving voice telephone calls, have become smart phones with cameras, Internet browsers, instant messaging capabilities, and a host of other features and functions. Today's PDAs are much more capable than the Apple Newton or even the first Palm Pilot. This advance has been supported by increasingly complex and capable operating systems and applications programs, which in turn are made possible by increases in the power of the handheld platform. Video game platforms now include the ability to play DVDs and access the Internet. The market for PC modems has almost vanished, since modems are built into most new PCs—often along with Ethernet ports and wireless networking capability.

As discussed at the outset, there is little mystery about what is going on here. Increases in hardware power make it possible for software to do more without undue sacrifice in speed. The earliest PCs were too slow to support a graphical user interface, for instance, while current models do so with ease. As disk storage has become cheaper, the cost of adding new features to an operating system or an applications program has fallen rapidly, and new features broaden product appeal. Many end-users agree that software is too complex. But there is much less agreement on what features should be dropped, and most users acknowledge that they simply ignore features they do not find valuable. Similarly, antitrust authorities who view product integration with suspicion are standing in the path of what seem to be strong, broad technology-driven trends.

3.5   Concluding Observations

As a general matter, forecasting the evolution of technology is hazard-ous business. Many technological wonders confidently forecast a few decades ago have yet to appear on the market, while our everyday lives have been profoundly affected by innovations like email and GPS navigation that entered the world of commerce with little fanfare. Still, it is hard not to be confident that computer-based industries will grow in importance over the next few decades at least. Hardware perfor-mance is almost certain to rise even as machinery size falls, most in-formation and entertainment can be reduced to digital content, and software is arguably the most flexible of creative media.

This is good news for consumers—and, we would argue, for econo-mists. The computer-based industries discussed here exhibit fasci-nating, rapidly changing patterns of product design, integration, and pricing. Many firms pursue interesting multi-sided platform strategies. As these industries evolve and others like them emerge, there will be much for economists to study, and important lessons for us and anti-trust authorities to learn.

Notes

1. "MCE Desktop Series External 8× DVD±R/RW FireWire/USB 2.0 'SuperDrive'", http://www.mcetech.com/sd8fwusb2-d.html (downloaded July 5, 2004).

2. Apple's developer connection website, "An Introduction to Mac OS X Development Technologies," June 1, 2004, http://developer.apple.com/macosx/introdevtech.html (downloaded September 3, 2004).

3. McConnel and Huba (2003).

4. Microsoft (1995).

5. Direct Testimony of Paul Maritz, January 20, 1999, in U.S. v. Microsoft and State of New York, et al. v. Microsoft, Civil Action Nos. 98–1232 and 98–1233 (TPJ), http://www.courttv.com/archive/trials/microsoft/legaldocs/maritz_full.html (downloaded September 2, 2004).

6. IDC (1993).

7. IDC (2000).

8. Linzmayer (1999).

9. "Review Microsoft Windows Software Development Kit," *Byte*, June 1, 1987.

10. IDC (1988, p. 2).

11. "Where did the computer go? The all-new iMac G5," http://www.apple.com/imac/ (downloaded September 10, 2004).

12. Kunkel (1997).

13. IDC (1988, pp. 16–17).

14. "The Complete Home Entertainer," *The Economist*, February 27, 2004.

15. C. Thomas Veilleux, "Costly Battle for Share in Video-Game Arena," *HFN*, June 3, 1996, p. 4; Wachovia Securities, "Company Note—MSFT: Hit By Double Whammy— Nintendo and HPQ Announcements," September 24, 2003, p. 2.

16. Palmsource, "Developers," http://www.palmsource.com/uk/palmos/developer .html (downloaded August 19, 2004).

17. Palm Computing Press Release, "3Com Rolls Out New Developer Program to Bring Internet Content to the Palm VII™ Connected Organizer," December 2, 1998, http:// www.palmone.com/us/company/pr/1998/devpr.html (downloaded June 21, 2004).

18. PalmGear, "Education and Enterprise," http://www.palmgear.com/index.cfm ?fuseaction=software.enterprise&SID=E35F1560–CF18–AC90–8352FED820EF5049&Part nerREF (downloaded September 14, 2004).

19. PalmGear, "Education and Enterprise," http://www.palmgear.com/index.cfm ?fuseaction=software.enterprise&SID=E35F1560–CF18–AC90–8352FED820EF5049&Part nerREF (downloaded September 14, 2004).

20. "Symbian Announces Q3 2004 Results," Symbian Press Release, November 11, 2004, http://www.symbian.com/news/pr/2004/pr041111.html (downloaded April 29, 2005).

21. Symbian Press Release, "Symbian opens its source code to third party software and hardware developers," April 23, 2002, http://www.symbian.com/press–office/2002/ pr020423.html (downloaded August 4, 2003).

22. See "The Third Way," *The Economist*, September 18, 2003.

References

Armstrong, Mark (2002), "Competition in Two-Sided Markets," Nuffield College, Oxford University, Working Paper.

Armstrong, Mark (2004), "Two-Sided Markets: Economic Theory and Policy Implications," mimeo.

Bakos, Yannos, and Eric Brynjolfsson (1999), "Bundling Information Goods: Pricing, Profits, and Efficiency," *Management Science*, vol. 45, pp. 1613–1630.

Baye, Michael R., and John Morgan (2001), "Information Gatekeepers on the Internet and the Competitiveness of Homogeneous Product Markets," *American Economic Review*, vol. 91, pp. 454–474.

Caillaud, Bernard, and Bruno Jullien (2003), "Chicken and Egg: Competition among Intermediation Service Providers," *RAND Journal of Economics*, vol. 34, pp. 521–552.

Campbell-Kelly, Martin (2003), "From Airline Reservations to Sonic the Hedgehog: A History of the Software Industry," (The MIT Press: Cambridge, MA).

Carlton, Jim (1998), "Apple," (HarperBusiness: New York, NY).

Carrol, Paul (1994) "Big Blues: The Unmaking of IBM," (Crown Publishers: New York, NY).

Clements, Matthew, and Hiroshi Ohashi (2004), "Indirect Network Effects and the Product Cycle: Video Games in the U.S. 1994–2002," mimeo, University of Tokyo.

Coughlan, Peter J. (2000), "Note on Home Video Game Technology and Industry Structure," (Harvard Business School: Boston, MA), p. 12.

Coughlan, Peter J. (2001), "Competitive Dynamics in Home Video Games (K): PlayStation vs. Nintendo 64," (Harvard Business School: Boston, MA).

Davis, Steven J., Jack MacCrisken, and Kevin M. Murphy (2001), "Economic Perspectives on Software Design—PC Operating Systems and Platforms," in *Microsoft, Antitrust and the New Economy: Selected Essays*, ed. David S. Evans, pp. 361–419.

Evans, David S. (2003), "Some Empirical Aspects of Multi-Sided Platform Industries," *Review of Network Economics*, vol. 2, pp. 191–209.

Evans, David S. (2003b), "The Antitrust Economics of Multi-Sided Platform Markets," *Yale Journal on Regulation*, vol. 20, pp. 325–381.

Evans, David S., and Michael Salinger (2004), "The Role of Cost in Determining When Firms Offer Bundles and Ties," http://papers.ssrn.com/sol3/papers.cfm?abstract_id=555818.

Evans, David S., and Michael A. Salinger (2005), "Why Do Firms Bundle and Tie? Evidence from Competitive Markets and Implications for Tying Law," *Yale Journal on Regulation*, vol. 22, pp. 37–89.

Evans, David S., and Richard Schmalensee (2001), "Some Economic Aspects of Antitrust Analysis in Dynamically Competitive Industries," in *Innovation Policy and the Economy*, vol. 2, eds. A. Jaffe, J. Lerner and S. Stern, pp. 1–50.

Freiberger, Paul, and Michael Swaine (2000), "Fire in the Valley", (McGraw-Hill: New York, NY), pp. 11–17.

Gawer, Annabelle, and Michael A. Cusumano (2002), "Platform Leadership: How Intel, Microsoft, and Cisco Drive Industry Innovation," (Harvard Business School: Boston, MA).

Hagiu, Andrei (2004), "Platforms, Pricing, Commitment and Variety in Two-Sided Markets," Princeton University Doctoral Dissertation.

Hennessy, John L., and David Patterson (1996), "Computer Architecture: A Quantitative Approach," (Morgan Kaufmann Publishers: San Mateo, CA).

IDC (1988), "Macintosh Peripherals Markets: High-Resolution Monitor and Printers Review and Forecast, 1987–1992," Report #3713.

IDC (1993), "Desktop Operating System Review and Forecast: The Second Phase of the Industry Begins," Report #7445.

IDC (2000), "Worldwide Software Market Forecast Summary, 2000–2004," Report #22766.

Katz, Michael L., and Carl Shapiro (1994), "Systems Competition and Network Effects," *Journal of Economic Perspectives*, vol. 8, pp. 93–115.

Kent, Steven L. (2001), "The Ultimate History of Video Games," (Prima: Roseville, CA).

Kunkel, Paul (1997), "AppleDesign: The Work of the Apple Industrial Design Group," (Watson-Guptill Publications: New York, NY).

Liebowitz, Stan J., and Margolis, Stephen E. (2001), "Winners, Losers & Microsoft," (The Independent Institute: Oakland, CA).

Linzmayer, Owen W. (1999), "Apple Confidential," (No Starch Press: San Francisco, CA), pp. 193–206.

Mace, Jeff (1995), "Printers (The Drivers Manual)," *PC Magazine*, vol. 14.

Malone, Michael S. (1998), "Infinite Loop," (Currency Doubleday: New York, NY).

Manes, Stephen, and Paul Andrews (1994), *Gates*, (Touchstone: New York, NY).

McConnel, Ben, and Jackie Huba (2003), "Creating Customer Evangelists," (Dearborn Trade Publishing: Chicago, IL), p. 13.

Microsoft (1995), "Microsoft Developer Relations: Proving Microsoft's Commitment to Third Parties," Microsoft Corporation White Paper.

Microsoft (1998), "Microsoft Developer Relations: Microsoft's Commitment to Third-Party Developer Success," Microsoft Corporation White Paper.

Rochet, Jean-Charles, and Jean Tirole (2003), "Platform Competition in Two-Sided Markets," *Journal of the European Economic Association*, vol. 1, pp. 990–1029.

Rochet, Jean-Charles, and Jean Tirole (2004), "Two-sided Markets: An Overview," IDEI Working Paper, http://www.frbatlanta.org/filelegacydocs/ep_rochetover.pdf.

Salus, Peter H. (1995), "A Quarter Century of UNIX," (Addison-Wesley Publishing Company: Reading, MA), pp. 209–212.

Stross, Randall E. (1996), "The Microsoft Wag," Addison-Wesley Publishing Co., Reading, MA.

4

Digital Music

Martin Peitz and Patrick
Waelbroeck

4.1 Introduction

With the diffusion of fast Internet connections in home computing, the
music industry is facing one of its biggest challenges.[1] Record companies even claim that unabated Internet piracy could mean the end of
the industry as a whole. Contrary to traditional formats, digital music
files that can be found on file-sharing networks can be separated from
their physical support. They can be compressed and exchanged on the
Internet in a relatively short time, that is, substantially faster than by
renting a CD in a media library or borrowing it from a friend. Facing
such a threat, record companies have started to sue Internet users who
share copyrighted files on peer-to-peer (P2P) networks freely and
anonymously without the authorization of copyright owners. At the
same time technology companies are developing technological measures of protection, known as *digital rights management* (DRM), to control the uses of music in digital format. We are thus witnessing the
birth of a paradox. On one hand, new technologies of information and
communication increase the value of information goods for consumers
who can download songs anywhere at anytime. On the other hand,
new rights management technologies can restrict and even lock the
use of digital music licensed to consumers. The goal of this chapter is
to understand the roots of the paradox and to analyze the economic
consequences of digital music for the record industry. To do so, we
rely heavily on international industry data and data from U.S. surveys.

Recent debates about file sharing, legal and technological protection,
as well as associated business models relate to other chapters in this
book. Part of the debate is how much protection for original work provides sufficient incentives to innovate. This relates to the literature on
patents. Clearly, it is well to evaluate the importance of an innovation

(for an attempt in the context of patents see chapter 2 by Fershtman and Gandal). However, this is much more problematic in the context of music and other artistic creation, for which the horizontal (or taste) dimension is important. Even though there often is a shared understanding of which piece of art is important and which is not, it is difficult to measure this. Why would it be necessary to distinguish between a work that is truly innovative and another that is not? Because one of the debates is whether innovative art would have an increased chance at being produced and consumed via file sharing over P2P and other forms of decentralized information exchange. If this were the case, the music industry's claims of revenue losses due to file sharing would be much less relevant for society; chapter 5 by Liebowitz addresses whether the music industry has indeed suffered from file sharing—this chapter provides some short remarks on the empirical evidence. For the related aspect of potential conflict of interest between creators and intermediaries, see chapter 8 in this volume by Gayer and Shy. A broader part of the debate is the possibility of changing consumer behavior in general, and the attitude toward digital products in particular. This is relevant for the music industry, but also for electronic commerce as a whole—for a collection of facts around electronic commerce see chapter 9 in this book by Dinlersoz and Perreira. The interplay between new technologies (P2P and DRM) and consumer preferences will determine which business models are viable. With respect to pricing, DRM may provide a profitable opportunity for product versioning; see chapter 6 by Belleflamme for a theoretical investigation. With respect to distribution, music sites may simply take the role of a marketplace where artists and consumers meet and the site charges for access and/or usage. To analyze such business models, the emerging literature on two-sided markets seems to be a useful tool; see in particular the analysis of Apple's iTunes in chapter 3 by Evans, Hagiu, and Schmalensee. (In chapter 3, software and related platforms are analyzed from the two-sided market perspective; Jullien's chapter 10 presents a theoretical analysis of two-sided markets that focuses on matching markets.)

This chapter is an attempt to provide a broad perspective on the market for digital music—music that is digitalized and can be distributed easily on P2P networks or other music sites (currently this requires the use of compression formats; however, this is due to the present speed of Internet connections and storage possibilities—in particular, a transfer of uncompressed formats is still too time-consuming). We start our guide by a review of the traditional business of selling music.[2] We then present the causes and the consequences of the digital challenge to the music industry. In section 4.3, we describe the legal and technological measures taken by record companies to protect their digital content. We conclude by describing different ways of selling digital music.

4.2   Challenges to the Music Industry: Facts and Explanations

4.2.1   Traditional Business of Selling Music

The industry for recorded music is worth $35 billion (with around $13 billion in Europe and North America; see IFPI 2004a). Music plays an important role in the life of most people; they often spend several hours per day listening to recorded music. A change in the way music is listened to is likely to affect many people.

In this first section, we describe the players in the industry and present figures related to producing a CD, which at the moment is the dominant format for prerecorded music. This section is voluntarily short, as there are many books that analyze the traditional music industry. (See Vogel 2004 for a recent bibliography).

4.2.1.1   The Cost of a CD   There is little information on the costs of making a CD. In general, a CD can be seen as an example of a good with large fixed costs and low variable costs. According to an article in *Knack* quoting the IFPI, the average price of a CD was around €17 in the EU in 2002 (table 4.1). For a CD sold at €17, record companies make around €11; this is the net price of the retailer's margin and taxes (which varies across countries in the EU). Costs incur at various stages

Table 4.1
Average "cost" of a CD in the EU (in euro)

Recording	2.25
Production	0.25 to 5
Marketing and promotion	0.25 to 5
CD press	1
Margin of retailers	2 to 2.5
Margin of record companies	2.5 to 4
Copyright payment to artist	1.25
Taxes	3.5

Source: IFPI quoted by *Knack* June 11, 2003, p. 59.

of making a CD. Manufacturing costs run below €3.50 (including the costs for recording and pressing the CD). Two other important types of costs are royalties paid to the artist (€1.25), and costs for production, marketing, and promotions (€1–10). Hence costs easily can run up to €15 per CD if the marketing and promotion activities do not generate sufficient sales. Record companies keep an important part of the revenues for themselves (€2.50–4 per CD).

Production, marketing, and promotions are important cost components of a CD. These costs reflect the nature of music as an experience good, which is a good that needs to be "tasted" before consumers can assess its value. Chuck Philips confirmed this when he interviewed music industry executives on the condition that they would not be identified. He states that "it costs about $2 to manufacture and distribute a CD, but marketing costs can run from $3 per hit CD to more than $10 for failed projects" (see Philips 2001). This is due to the cost structure of large fixed costs and relatively small marginal costs.

The Record Industry Association of America (RIAA) elaborates on these costs:

Then come marketing and promotion costs—perhaps the most expensive part of the music business today. They include increasingly expensive video clips, public relations, tour support, marketing campaigns, and promotion to get the songs played on the radio.... Labels make investments in artists by paying for both the production and the promotion of the album, and promotion is very expensive. (RIAA 2005)

An important question in this article is to ask how these costs are likely to be modified by online music distribution.

There are many new releases each year. Consumers need information on the existence and the genre of these new releases. Listening to the radio is the main way consumers obtain information about new songs and artists, discussion with friends and family members being a distant second (see table 4.2).

While most new CDs are sold at similar prices, some become hits, others flops. Indeed record companies lose money on many new releases. Therefore, since few albums become profitable, much of the profits from hits compensate for losses made on other albums. Chuck Philips states that only one out of ten acts ever turns a profit (Philips 2001).

The risky nature of the current music business model was confirmed in Hilary Rosen's statement in the Napster case (Hilary Rosen was president and CEO of the RIAA in 2000. She is quoted from "Rosen's

Table 4.2
Type of media that influenced U.S. consumers to purchase their last CD

Radio	75%
Friends/relatives	46%
Music video channel	45%
Saw in store	42%
Movie soundtrack	37%
Live performance	29%
TV advertisement	24%
Featured in TV show	23%
TV show appearance	22%
Downloaded MP3	19%
Internet site	17%
Magazine/newspaper	17%
Internet radio	15%
Record club	15%
Video game	5%

Source: Edison Media Research, June 2003; in percentage of consumers who have purchased a music CD in the past 12 months.

Statement at Work for Hire Hearing," May 25, 2000, available on the RIAA website[3]):

Record companies search out artists and help to develop their talent and their image. Much goes into developing artists, maximizing their creativity and helping them reach an audience. In addition to providing advance payments to artists for use by them in the recording process, a record company invests time, energy and money into advertising costs, retail store positioning fees, listening posts in record stores, radio promotions, press and public relations for the artist, television appearances and travel, publicity, and Internet marketing, promotions and contests. These costs are investments that companies make to promote the success of the artist so that both can profit from the sale of the artist's recording. In addition, the record company typically pays one half of independent radio promotions, music videos, and tour support. If a recording is not successful, the company loses its entire investment, including the advance. If a recording is successful, the advance is taken out of royalties, but the other costs I mentioned are the responsibility of the record company....

Statistically, this is a very risky business. Typically, less than 15% of all sound recordings released by major record companies will even make back their costs. Far fewer return profit. Here are some revealing facts to demonstrate what I'm talking about. There were 38,857 albums released last year; 7,000 from the majors and 31,857 from independents. Out of the total releases, only 233 sold over 250,000 units. Only 437 sold over 100,000 units. That's 1% of the time for the total recording industry that an album even returns any significant sales, much less profit. Fortunately, when it hits, it can hit big. That's what goes to fund the next round of investments to develop and nurture new artists.

This small success rate is due to the nature of a mass-media market in which exposure to the public is scarce and firms maximize audience by selecting a few number of potential one-size-fits-all superstar artists. Our investigation with respect to cost is summarized by our first observation.

Observation 4.1   Production, marketing, and promotion often are the main cost of making a CD and selling it to consumers.

4.2.1.2   Players in the Market   Record companies or labels sell music and complementary products to consumers.[4] These are the two players we focus on in this chapter. Clearly, music is written by artists, who, if they become well known, play an important role in the industry. Other players are disseminating information about new releases. Figure 4.1 describes the players in the music industry.[5] The dotted ellipse indicates that some economic functions are vertically integrated. It is important to stress that record companies typically carry out most of the marketing and advertising activities.

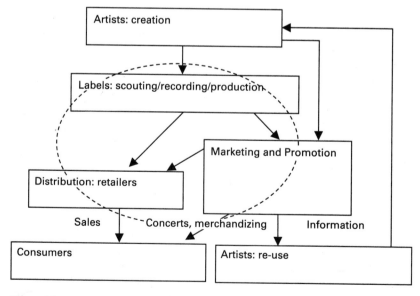

Figure 4.1
The traditional music industry

Artists Contracts between artists and labels are of a complex nature. While many small-audience artists complain that big labels tie them into long-term contracts with unfavorable conditions, record labels complain about successful artists in a similar way. In particular, Philips reports that "successful acts thwart the existing contract system by refusing to deliver follow-up albums until they extract additional advances" (Philips 2001). However, the majority of musicians make only a small part of their income from recorded music; they have other jobs and make money from live performances (see 4.2.1.3).

Record Companies Record companies function as intermediaries between the artists and the consumers. The big record companies own different labels; each label is active in certain segments of the market. For simplicity, we do not distinguish here between a "record company" and a "label." The label's role is to select artists and offer services to artists to make "matches" between the music that is recorded and the consumers. The music industry is highly concentrated—five record companies dominate the market, and the business press often talks of further mergers. Annual data on label market shares are published by the IFPI. The five largest distribution companies, namely EMI, Sony, BMG, AOL Time Warner, and Vivendi Universal, shared 84 percent of the revenues in the North American market and 79 percent of the European market in 2002.[6] Aggregated over all regions, market shares of those five companies total around 75 percent (see IFPI 2003a). Worldwide market share of the top five (now after the Sony BMG merger top four) have been relatively stable over the past five years. The music industry can therefore be seen as a tight oligopoly on all major music markets. Record companies thus have multimarket contact and repeated interaction. Perhaps unsurprisingly, the record companies have a history of alleged price fixing. The most recent case in the United States was settled in October 2002 (see box 4.1).

Retailers Retailers make the final sales to the consumers. They also may have contractual arrangements to promote new releases. However, promotion is mainly done by radio and television playtime.

4.2.1.3 Complementary Products Although a CD is a medium mainly for distributing prerecorded music, it is often packaged with complementary products such as artwork, liner notes, lyrics, or, more recently, videos. Music DVDs include videos and additional audio tracks as well as bonus tracks with interviews, etc. Moreover, some record companies sell or license additional products bearing the artist's

Box 4.1
Alleged price fixing

The top five record labels and three large music retailers (Trans World Entertainment, Towers Records, and Musicland Stores, a division of Best Buy and Co.) agreed to pay $143 million in cash and CDs to settle charges that they cheated consumers by fixing high prices (see for instance CBS News, October 1, 2002). The alleged price fixing goes back to 1995. Over the next several years, the price of a CD rose from $12 to $15. In 2000, twenty-eight states filed a suit against the five major record labels, maintaining that the record labels colluded to fix the prices for music CDs. An out-of-court settlement was then reached in 2002.[1]

1. The FTC condemned the underlying practice of a minimum advertised price. In particular, it condemned this practice because "the arrangements constitute practices that facilitate horizontal collusion among the distributors, in violation of Section 5 of the Federal Trade Commission Act" (see FTC, press release on May 10, 2000, "Record Companies Settle FTC Charges of Restraining Competition in CD Music Market").

name or album title (such as posters), although the revenues from these are likely to be small. Indeed most of the revenues from merchandising go to the artists themselves.

Merchandising differs from concert tours, which typically are not controlled by the record companies at all. According to *Forbes* magazine, the tour business has climbed four years in a row, from $1.3 billion in 1998 to $2.1 billion in 2002 (*Forbes* 2002). For best-selling artists, tours represent a way to promote their new albums. For other artists, net revenues from concert tours are a main source of income. Or, as *Forbes* puts it, "the top 10 percent artists make money selling records. The rest goes on tour" (*Forbes* 2002). Connolly and Krueger (2004) report that ticket prices and revenues from live concerts have increased much more than the consumer price inflation (CPI) over the last two decades.

Because of complementary products such as live concerts, the objectives of artists and the record companies are not necessarily aligned. Gayer and Shy (chapter 8) argue that this tension is exacerbated in a world of file-sharing networks. Record companies are aware of this tension. Possibly as a response to changes in the market environment, contracts have been signed recently that realign the objectives of the two groups. For instance, *BBC News* and *The Economist* have reported that artist Robbie Williams signed a contract giving the record company a large cut of revenues derived from complementary products.

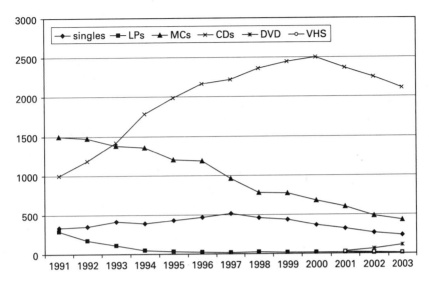

Figure 4.2
World sales by format (units); figures in millions. Source: IFPI, The Recording Industry in Numbers, 2001–2003.

4.2.2   The Challenge: Digital Music

4.2.2.1   Music Sales Over Time   To understand the changes in the music industry during the past five years, we look at worldwide sales of prerecorded music in different formats between 1991 and 2003. The aggregate market was relatively flat between 1991 and 1999 (growth in CDs compensating declines in other formats), but sharply declined starting in 2000 (figure 4.2), both in units as well as dollar amounts. This period coincides with the creation of Napster in the second half of 1999 and new file-sharing technologies in the second half of 2001. It is of course very tempting to attribute the decline in CD sales to the availability of free music files on the Internet. We analyze the possible causes of the decline later in this section.

Sales appear to have stabilized during the second half of 2003, after decreasing by as much as 12 percent, and started to increase in the last quarter to reach an annual drop of 6 percent. The introduction of new formats such as DVD audio and Super Audio CD seems to be helping the music industry.

This negative trend over the past three or four years is observed in many, but not all, developed countries. While the trend is contrasted for CD sales, most markets have experienced a drop in other formats, especially singles, as illustrated by sales in units in the top five markets for prerecorded music (figure 4.3). Interestingly, CD sales increased in France and the UK over the 1999 to 2003 period, although clearly those countries have also faced Internet piracy. Figure 4.3 also documents that the older cassettes and vinyl LP formats are no longer relevant.

Our analysis of CD sales gives rise to observation 4.2.

Observation 4.2   There has been a substantial downturn in CD sales since 2000, with a lot of heterogeneity across countries.

4.2.2.2   Digitalization and New Technologies of Information Distribution   In this section, we describe factors that made digital music available on the Internet. To download and share music online, a computer and a fast Internet connection are required. In most developed countries, a large percentage of the population has access to a computer. In addition, a significant share of households has access to fast Internet connections. A broadband connection is an important prerequisite for sharing files on a peer-to-peer network since the software needs to run continuously and album files take time to download.

Broadband Penetration   Starting in 1999, the number of broadband users has steadily increased in the top markets for prerecorded music. In early 2003, the number of broadband subscribers reached 20 million in the United States. By February 2004, almost 40 percent of United States consumers accessed the Internet using a broadband connection (see table 4.3). This means that a large part of the population has access to music services that can be delivered only through broadband. Suppose that consumers with a strong taste for music are also more inclined to download music. Then for those consumers, a broadband connection is even more important than for the average consumer. This means that the Internet can become a significant channel for music fans to listen to new releases.

4.2.2.3   Peer-to-Peer (P2P) and File-Sharing

Basics of File-Sharing Technologies   The principle of file-sharing technologies is very simple. Users run the search engine of the software, looking for specific files. Typically, a user types the name of an artist or even the title of a particular album or song. In the second step, the software returns "file results" found on computers connected to the file-swapping network at the time of the search. In the last step, the user proceeds to download files directly from other users sharing the relevant files. Most file-sharing software have backup technology that enables downloaded portions of digital files to be recovered in case of software crashes or involuntary disconnections of the user.

File sharing consists not only in downloading but also in uploading files. The uploading function of the software is also simple. Downloaded files are by default on the sharing list and thus can be automatically uploaded (unless otherwise specified by the user). In addition, users can transfer songs from a CD into compressed digital format (such as MP3) and upload them in a similar way. Most P2P technologies have a built-in priority rating system that provides information about the material shared by users. For instance, Kazaa priority rating is a measure of how many megabytes have been uploaded compared to how many megabytes have been downloaded over a period of time. Such a system benefits users who share large popular files such as recent movies compressed in DIVX format, or pornographic files. (Measuring in megabytes rather than by number of files can lead to surprising results; for example, a Palisade study of 2002 found that the majority of requested files were pornographic files.)

Private Costs and Benefits of File-Sharing Sharing and downloading files on P2P networks involve several costs including the opportunity cost of using computers and the Internet to download and burn files. The main benefit of music downloaded from file-sharing networks is the acquisition of compressed music files that have a technical quality close enough to the original CD. A digital copy also can be stored on hard drive for later listening, recorded on a CD-R to share with others, or transferred to a portable MP3 player. Moreover, digital files are less cumbersome to carry than a CD, mainly because more songs can be carried using the same (CD-R) or smaller (MP3) device. Finally, MP3 files offer new opportunities for consumers to listen to music. An Ipsos survey in 2002 found that Internet users download music to listen to single tracks instead of looking for complete albums that are sometimes difficult to find in record stores (see table 4.4). They also use the Internet to sample music, that is, to try new music before making a purchase decision (see section 4.3). There are several costs of downloading:

• Waste of time searching, downloading, and testing files; it is only possible to assess the technical quality as well as the content of a file

USA

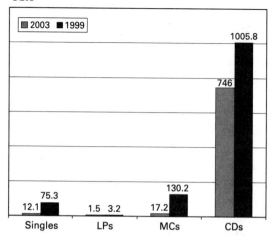

France

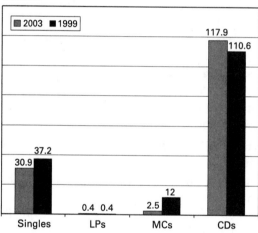

UK

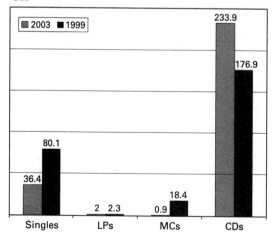

Japan

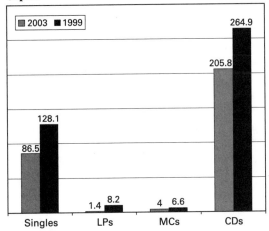

Germany

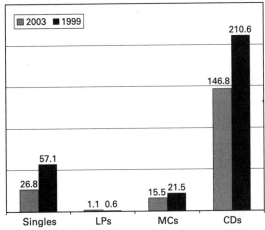

Figure 4.3
Top five markets for prerecorded music. Source: IFPI, The Recording Industry in Numbers, 2003.

Table 4.3
Broadband penetration in top music markets (percent of households)

Country	Internet	Broadband
USA	61	23
Belgium	47	29
Denmark	65	28
France	43	13
Germany	50	14
Italy	37	9
Netherlands	71	21
Spain	32	11
Sweden	70	26
UK	52	11
Japan	52	28
South Korea	76	75
Taiwan	13	1

Source: IFPI, The Recording Industry in Numbers, 2003.

Table 4.4
Digital music attitude (U.S.)

I download music that is not easily available in stores.	65%
I download songs that I want, without having to buy an entire album.	69%
I like being able to sample music online before making a purchase decision.	73%

Source: TEMPO, Keeping pace with digital music behavior, 2002 (n = 740).

after downloading it, thus wasting time for downloaders; moreover it is difficult to find nonmainstream files (due to the nature of the sharing technology, popular artists and songs are easy to find, while marginal artists are more difficult to find).

• Erroneous, incomplete, poorly compressed files; downloaded files could not correspond to what the user expected, mainly because the file name has been changed or was badly encrypted or needed special software.

• Download limitation by providers; many Internet Service Providers (ISP) limit the number of gigabytes that can be downloaded.

• Worm viruses; there are specific types of viruses that proliferate on P2P networks; they either use P2P networks to propagate viruses and infect victims or they use P2P to construct worms to communicate with one another; worms do not infect other programs but copy them-

Box 4.2
Most prevalent viruses on the Internet, January 2004

1. Worm/MyDoom.A
2. Worm/Sober.C
3. Worm/Bagle.A
4. Worm/MiMail.I
5. Worm/Gibe.C
6. Worm/Klez.E (including G)
7. Worm/MiMail.J
8. Worm/BugBear.B
9. Worm/MiMail.A
10. Worm/Dumaru.A

Source: Central Command, Inc., 2004.

selves and look for specific files that they try to destroy; worms also can replicate in memory and slow down the computer; worm viruses were the biggest threat in January 2004 (for the most prevalent ones see box 4.2).

• Adware/spyware; consumers must internalize the cost of viewing ads and installing spying software that can violate their privacy.

• Storage and transfer; storing files on the hard disk requires space and transporting files to portable media or burning CDRs is time consuming (if this is the intended use).

Because of the built-in priority rating that determines how fast a user can download the requested files, the main benefit of uploading is to improve this rating. Uploading files has cost mainly because sharing files drains computer resources and increases the risk of being sued. There may also be "moral" cost for those who believe that file sharing amounts to theft and that theft is immoral. Finally, uploading files opens the computer to intruders who can hack system files or install spyware; the computer is more vulnerable to viruses.

To sum up, using file-sharing networks is time-consuming and involves different types of risks. Therefore, we expect P2P networks to be used mainly by consumers with a low opportunity cost of spending time online, especially teenagers and college students. Teenagers and college students have substantial discretionary income and can benefit from more flexible pricing schemes. In the long term, file sharing may have a positive effect on CD sales due to an income effect. Indeed, by

Table 4.5
Frequency of use of P2P (U.S.)

Never	60%
Less than once a month	17%
1–3 times a month	11%
1–3 times a week	9%
Daily	3%

Source: Parks and Associates, Broadband Access @ Home II, 2003; n = 297.

downloading free music, teenagers and college students can acquire information on the songs and albums that they like. As they become older and increase their purchasing power, these Internet users may "legalize" their music archives. In this case, teenagers and college students only temporarily reduce their spending on prerecorded music.

Frequency and Number of Downloads Although Napster, Kazaa, and the likes have made headline news, survey data suggest that the majority of consumers do not use these services and that only a small fraction of broadband users share files on a regular basis. This is documented in table 4.5. While all survey responses could be biased as they are self-reported, the perception of legal risk was low before the summer of 2003 when the RIAA announced plans to sue P2P users. All survey data that we present in this section cover the period prior to June 2003.

An analysis of the distribution of downloaders according to the number of music files downloaded and stored on computer (figure 4.4 from a survey in 2000 and table 4.6 from a survey in 2003) suggests that there is heterogeneity among downloaders: many download very few files, but others download a substantial number of songs. This pattern is confirmed by an NPD survey in 2003. In this survey, participants who had digital music files on their hard drives were asked how many files they had. Fifty-six percent answered that they had between 1 and 100 files, 28 percent between 101 and 500 files, 8 percent between 501 and 1000 files, and 8 percent more than 1000 files. Note that some of the files reported in table 4.6 have been ripped from CDs and were not downloaded. However, NPD says that two thirds of all digital music files can be attributed to file sharing.

Age Structure of Downloaders File sharing is popular among Internet users age twenty-four or under. In particular, a large proportion of

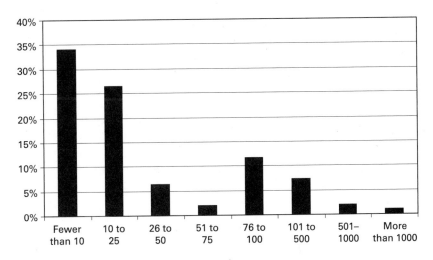

Figure 4.4
Number of files downloaded (percentage of population who ever downloaded music, U.S.) Source: PEW Internet Report, July–August 2000 (based on 238 respondents).

Table 4.6
Number of music files stored on PC (U.S.)

<50	47%
50–99	9%
100–199	14%
200–299	9%
300–399	4%
400–499	1%
>500	16%

Source: Parks and Associates, Electronics Living @ Home, 2003; n = 297.

P2P users are teenagers and do not represent a significant percentage of the population with large purchasing power, although they have discretionary income from their parents. The relationship between age and downloading behavior is documented in a number of surveys. A study by Parks and Associates finds that the number of downloads is much lower for households with the household head older than forty-five (table 4.7). Note that the average number of files in this survey is 297 per computer, which is comparable to numbers presented in figure 4.4.

Respondents to a December 2002 Ipsos survey were asked whether they have downloaded digital music files (or MP3 files) from an online file-sharing service (such as Morpheus, Napster, or Kazaa). Table 4.8

Table 4.7
Average number of MP3 files on home computers by age of user (U.S.)

Age	Average number of files
65+	72
55–64	124
45–54	177
35–44	340
25–34	721
18–24	348

Source: Parks and Associates, April 2002; n = 711.

Table 4.8
Downloading using P2P according to gender and age (U.S.)

Gender or age (number observed)	Ever	In the past 30 days
Total (1112)	19%	9%
Male (566)	26%	13%
Female (546)	12%	6%
12–17 (111)	52%	32%
18–24 (138)	44%	24%
25–34 (181)	23%	8%
35–54 (394)	12%	5%
55+ (282)	3%	1%

Source: Ipsos-Insight, TEMPO: Keeping Pace with Online Music Distribution, December 2002.

suggests that teenagers and adults between 18 and 24 are the most likely to have used file-sharing networks and that they tend to do so on a regular basis (last column). Only 8 percent of adults between 25 and 34 admitted to using file-sharing services during the previous month in December 2002. This percentage becomes almost insignificant for adults over 55. The profile of music downloaders reported by Pew Internet Report (table 4.9) confirms that young adults (18–24) are more likely to have downloaded music from the Internet than older adults. The respondents, all Internet users, were asked whether they ever downloaded music files over the Internet so that they can play them at any time. The probability of having downloaded music decreases with the income of the household.

How many Internet users upload music? Table 4.10 shows that, while the whole population has embraced the Internet revolution, the

Table 4.9
Downloading behavior according to demographic characteristics (U.S.)

	July 2000	February 2001	March 2003
All adults	22	29	29
Men	24	36	32
Women	20	23	26
Whites	21	26	28
Blacks	29	30	37
Hispanics	35	46	35
Age cohorts			
18–29 years	37	51	52
30–49 years	19	23	27
50+ years	9	15	12
Household income			
Under $30,000	28	36	38
$30,000–$50,000	24	31	30
$50,000–$75,000	20	29	28
$75,000+	15	24	26
Education			
Less than high school	38	55	39
High school	25	31	31
Some college	25	32	33
College degree or more	15	21	23
Internet experience			
Less than 6 months	20	27	26*
6 months to 1 year	20	25	
2 to 3 years	24	28	29
3 or more years	22	33	59

Source: Pew Internet Tracking Report, April 2001 and July 2003; n = 2515, *less than a year.

Table 4.10
Sharing on P2P networks (U.S.)

Internet users who download music files onto their computers so that they can play them anytime they want	Internet users who allow others to download music or video files from their computers	
	yes	no
yes	12%	17%
no	9%	62%

Source: Pew Internet Report July 2003; n = 1555.

number of persons who upload music files on P2P networks represents less than 21% of Internet users in the United States in July 2003. The number of downloaders is somewhat larger, namely 29 percent, because there are more people who download than upload. Our analysis of downloaders, based on survey data, provides us with observation 4.3.

Observation 4.3   A large number of people download copyrighted music without permission from copyright owners. Fewer upload music on file-sharing networks.

4.2.2.4   Audio-Streaming   The Internet also gave birth to audio streaming. On one hand, Internet radio stations are owned by sites independent of major technological distribution companies. On the other hand, specific streaming technologies owned by large software producers and content providers (such as Microsoft, Apple, AOL, and RealNetworks) have obtained licenses to broadcast music from copyright owners. Indeed the Digital Millenium Copyright Act requires webcasters and commercial broadcasters to pay licensee fees (see section 4.3.2.1). Many small websites had to shut down because they were not able to pay these royalties.

On the Cost and Benefits of Audio-Streaming   Contrary to sharing music files on the Internet, audio-streaming is legal. Most of the time it is easy to purchase the original music provided that a link to merchant sites can be directly accessed from the software. However, just as for radio, there is no digital copy of the music played on the audio-stream.[7] Moreover, many audio-streaming sites are ad-based, which can annoy some Internet users. More generally, sampling is more difficult since playlists are preprogrammed. More than 35 percent of Americans age 12 and older were "streamies" in July 2002, according to an Arbitron/Edison Media Research. The active audio-streamer is more likely to be older (between 35 and 54) than the active music downloader (see table 4.11).

4.2.3   Potential Causes of Current Decline in CD Sales
Several explanations for the downturn in music sales have been proposed, among them the negative economic environment, substitution of music formats, substitution with other forms of entertainment, and Internet piracy. We analyze these factors from an international perspective. Liebowitz (2003a) discusses the impact of these factors on the

Table 4.11
Profile of audio-streamers (percent of respondents, U.S.)

	Broadband	Dial-up
Men	59	47
Women	41	53
12–17	17	13
18–24	13	11
25–34	15	18
35–44	20	23
45–54	22	20
55–64	9	11
65+	4	6
$50K+ household income	59	48
Online listening habits		
Listened to radio stations online last month	18	12
Listened to radio stations online last week	7	5
Listened to music online	62	49
Number of MP3 files downloaded	48	30
Downloaded music that is not available from local radio	37	26

Source: Arbitron/Edison Media Research, July 2002; n = 2511.

U.S. market. These factors are presented as potential causes because of a lack of data at the individual or album level.

4.2.3.1 Prices Trivially, the demand for recorded music depends on its price. We first focus on the price of a CD over time. The decline of CD unit sales in recent years (see section 4.2.2.2) would be hardly surprising if it were accompanied by a drastic rise in CD prices. Price is very difficult to measure because we have information only on list prices. Prices paid by consumers display more volatility due to temporary promotions, record clubs, etc.

Using implicit prices of music, we find that over the past five years, real prices of music exhibit different patterns in the top five countries with no significant trends. In figure 4.5, price changes have been computed by dividing total retail value in local currency by the total number of units sold (singles, LPs, cassettes, and CDs; except for 2003 where music DVDs were added). We then subtracted inflation to obtain figure 4.6. It should be emphasized that CDs represent more than 85 percent of the available formats during the period; therefore

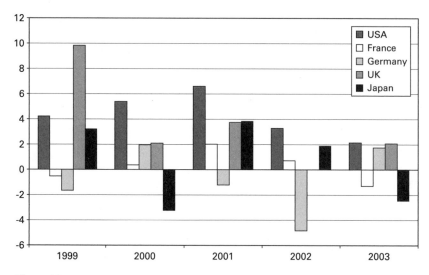

Figure 4.5
Nominal price changes (in percentage)

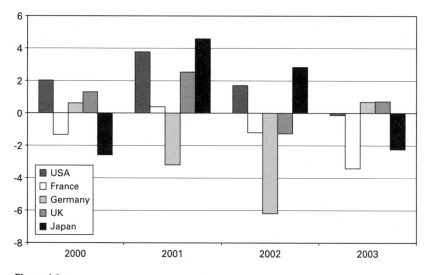

Figure 4.6
Real price changes (in percentage) Source: IFPI, The Recording Industry in Numbers, 2001–2003, and own computations. Data for 2003 computed by including music, VHS, and DVD sales.

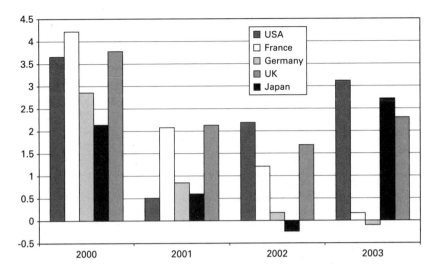

Figure 4.7
GDP in top music markets (in percentage changes) Source: *The Economist.*

changes in nominal and real prices can be attributed mainly to changes in CD prices.

4.2.3.2 Economic Environment The demand for CDs depends on the economic environment, measured by GDP growth (figure 4.7). In fact we find that it is one of the main reasons CD sales have declined during the period from 2000 to 2001 in the econometric study that we discuss in section 4.2.3.6. Moreover, economic conditions after the burst of the Internet bubble in 2000 to 2001 probably impacted consumer CD purchase decisions, especially because people who suffered the most from the crash were 25- 35-year-old people starting day trading. Historically, this share of the population has a strong desire for music.

4.2.3.3 Quality and Variety in New Releases The number of new releases is not available for 2000 and after. Some analysts of the music industry have argued that consolidation in the radio broadcasting industry due to mergers have favored the superstar system and reduced variety on radio time. Provided that consumers depend on the radio to motivate purchase (as documented for the United States in table 4.2), reduced variety offered from radio playlists could influence music

Table 4.12
European Platinum Awards

Year	Total albums receiving awards	New releases receiving awards	Number of artists receiving awards
2003	70	21	57
2002	92	32	77
2001	87	30	69
2000	80	35	73
1999	81	39	68

Source: IFPI, The Record Industry in Numbers, 2003.
Note: In an article in *Business Week* ("Big Music's Broken Record," February 13, 2003), Jane Black discusses a study of Soundscan that found that the number of new releases decreased by as much as 20 percent in 2001.

Table 4.13
New album releases

	1999	2001	2002
Number of new releases	38,900	31,734	33,443

Source: Nielsen Soundscan quoted in *Business Week*, February 13, 2003.

sales. The net effect is ambiguous because increased radio playtime favors sales of music superstars.

To document the trend in the number of new releases over the past five years, we report in table 4.12 the number of European Platinum Awards and in table 4.13 the number of new releases in 1999, 2001, and 2002. European Platinum Awards are awarded to albums selling more than 1 million units. There seems to be a negative trend in the number of new releases receiving the award. More research is needed to confirm this finding, since this award is only a simple measure of the total number of new releases in a given year.

Consumer purchases are also influenced by CDs seen and listened to in record stores (see table 4.2). Therefore, a shift in distribution channels could reduce the exposure of consumers to the potential variety of releases. Again the net effect on sales is ambiguous because each superstar should see their sales increase due to more exposure of their music to the public. Figure 4.8 reports the shift from record stores to other stores in music distribution for the United States.

Changes in distribution channels have been overlooked, but more recently, articles in the specialized press have noted that the strategies

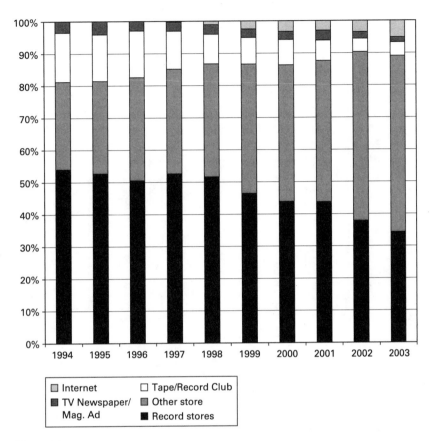

Figure 4.8
Channels of music distribution (U.S.) Source: RIAA, Consumer Profile, December 2003.

of marketing and promotion of large retail stores (low inventories, high turnover in shelves, decreasing shelf space due to the popularity of DVDs, and focus on top-selling artists together with large price volatility due to temporary price discounts that confuse the consumers about the value of the CD) are not suited to increase the value of music to consumers and are detrimental to new artists.

4.2.3.4 Demographics It appears that the younger consumer has purchased less music over the past decade. However, the older population seems to be replacing its LP collection with the CD format, as illustrated in figure 4.9.

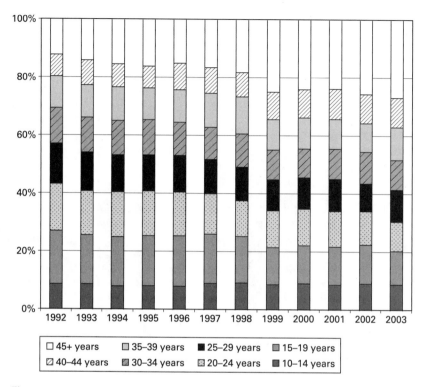

Figure 4.9
Music consumption by age (U.S.) Source: RIAA, Consumer Profile, December 2003.

4.2.3.5 Substitution with Other Media and Devices Substitution among different types of media potentially can explain the downturn in CD sales. Figure 4.10 indicates that the year 2000 coincides with the end of a strong substitution and replacement effect between cassettes and CDs.[8] When such a replacement no longer continues, revenues are lost.

With the replacement of music cassettes by CDs more or less completed in the United States and Western Europe, the music industry is introducing new formats.

Music on DVD As of 2001 a new type of medium has become more and more popular: music on DVD. Apart from the improved copy protection (see section 4.3), record companies hope that the replacement of CDs by DVDs will increase revenues. As for any new format, the industry is gambling on its acceptance by consumers. However, different

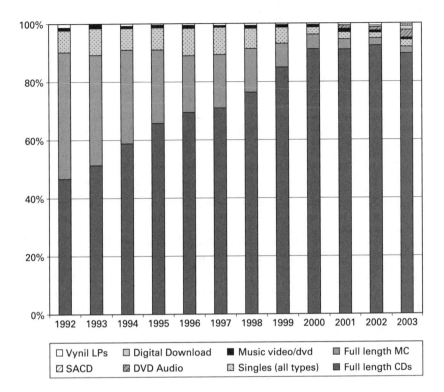

Figure 4.10
Substitution between different types of media in the United States. Source: RIAA and own calculations.

from other formats, DVDs already have a market in film. DVD player penetration in U.S. households was 41 percent in 2001. It climbed to 70 percent in 2003. In Western Europe and Japan the respective numbers were 19 percent and 28 percent in 2001, and 47 percent and 42 percent in 2003 (IFPI 2004a). Table 4.14 shows that the sale of music DVDs is picking up in the major markets. For the moment, it cannot fully compensate for the decrease in CD sales. The music industry also has high hopes for the Super Audio CD (SACD), which provides better sound quality than a regular CD and offers surround sound.

MP3 Players and Portable Devices Ipsos-Insight (TEMPO, Dec. 2003) found that 19 percent of U.S. downloaders own a portable MP3 player, up from 12 percent in September 2003. This is confirmed by Parks Associates (Sept. 2003) who found that 20 percent of digital music users own an MP3 player. However, according to their survey data,

Table 4.14
Music on DVD and CD in units of millions

	DVD			CD			
	2001	2002	2003	2000	2001	2002	2003
North America	8.8	12.3	21.5	1,008.2	942.7	860.7	799.1
Europe	7.3	14.3	35.2	861.8	857.5	854.2	807.6
Asia	16.0	30.2	38.9	363.3	332.3	308.3	286.7
Latin America	1.7	3.1	4.4	198.3	162.4	156	198.3
Australasia	0.9	2.6	5.7	53.3	59.7	56.8	53.3
World	34.7	62.8	105.7	2,504.9	2,372.2	2,253.4	2,111.6

Source: IFPI, The Recording Industry in Numbers, 2003.

only 8 percent plan on purchasing an MP3 player in the next twelve months. Similar figures are available from a Jupiter Research survey, (Dec. 2003) which found that 6 percent of online adults said they would be buying a portable device in the next twelve months, and the likely buyer is male (79 percent) and under age thirty-five (more than 65 percent). Jupiter Research also expects U.S. shipment of MP3 players to double in 2003 to more than 3.5 million and to continue to grow almost 50 percent per year for the next several years. IDC forecasts the worldwide MP3 player market to grow to $44 billion in revenues by 2007, with an annual growth rate of 30 percent. New media are likely to play an important role in the market for recorded music in the near future.

Observation 4.4 There is a strong (potential) demand for new media, such as DVD audios, Super Audio CD, and MP3 portable devices.

There are, however, three other types of substitution that have taken place, but from which the music industry does not benefit. First, due to the penetration of CD burners, consumers can more easily make copies of CDs they do not own by making a copy of a friend's CD or by burning songs downloaded from the Internet. Second, watching movie DVDs and playing computer games is taking time away from listening to prerecorded CDs. Finally, broadband connections at home allow Internet users to start new forms of activities.

Penetration of CD Burners In many countries, the penetration of CD burners is such that the majority of the population can easily record CDs. In a September 2003 survey, Parks and Associates found that 80 percent of PC users in the United States owned a CD burner. This sta-

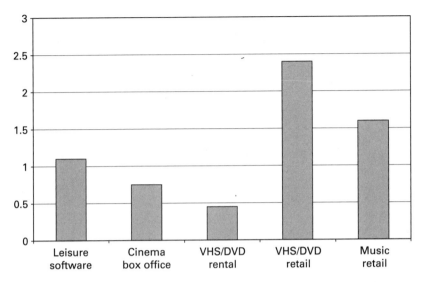

Figure 4.11
UK entertainment spending. Source: Screen digest from industry sources, 2004.

tistic combined with the fact that more than 90 percent of U.S. households have computers at home and that sales of CD-Rs have also increased indicates that many consumers could use their burners to make copies from existing CDs. Similarly, the shipments of DVD burners increased 416 percent in one year to 22.92 million units worldwide, and 362 percent to 5.93 million units in the Japanese market. Jeita, the association that conducted the survey, expects global sales of DVD recorders to hit 88 million units by 2006, and the market share of DVD recorders to exceed that of CD-R/RW devices by that time. The 2003 shipments of optical disk devices rose by 114 percent from a year earlier to 222 million units in the global market, and by 113 percent to 20.06 million units in the Japanese market.

DVDs and Computer Games   There is some evidence that consumers have substituted listening to prerecorded CDs with playing computer and video games and watching prerecorded DVDs. Figure 4.11 indicates that UK consumers now purchase more DVDs than they purchase music.

Internet Activities   A high-speed Internet connection at home offers new ways to spend leisure time. Among these digital activities, looking for information on hobbies, products, travel, and news are prominent, as illustrated by a survey from Pew Internet Report (see table 4.15).

Table 4.15
Internet activities in 2000 and 2001 (in percentage of Internet users, U.S.)

Activity	March 2001	March 2000
Communication activities		
Email	100	75
Instant messages	48	36
Fun activities		
Hobby information	83	64
Online just for fun	66	53
Video/audio clips	56	40
Download music	40	30
Play game	40	30
Sports scores	38	28
Information activities		
Product information	82	63
Travel information	72	55
Movie, book, and music information	69	53
News	64	52
Health information	64	47
Government website	60	42
Job-related research	52	41
Financial information	45	38
Look for job	44	31
Look for place to live	32	20
Religious/spiritual information	27	18
Transactions		
Buy a product	58	40
Buy a travel service	46	29
Online banking	25	14
Online auction	22	12
Buy/sell stocks	13	10

Source: Pew Internet Report, Getting Serious Online, March 2002; n = 862 (March 2001), n = 723 (March 2000).

Table 4.16
Daily Internet activity by connection (in percentage of respective category, U.S.)

	All home broadband	Broadband elite (25%)	Other broadband (75%)	Dial-up
Communications				
Email	67	58	80	52
Instant messaging	21	48	14	14
Chat rooms	10	23	7	5
Information seeking				
News	46	56	49	24
Product information	32	68	24	18
Information producing				
Share computer files with others	17	50	8	4
Create content (e.g., web pages)	16	38	10	3
Downloading				
Download games, videos, pictures	22	61	12	4
Download music	17	43	10	6
Download movies	5	17	2	n/a
Media/streaming				
Watch video clip	21	55	12	6
Listen to music/radio station	19	48	11	4
Transactions				
Buy a product	21	59	11	3

Source: Pew Internet tracking survey February 2002 (broadband) and August–September 2001 (dial-up); elite broadband users are doing on average 10 or more activities on a daily basis and represent 25% of the broadband population; n = 507 (broadband users), n = 1391 (dial-up users).

Analyzing daily music-related activities, we find that broadband users are more likely to have experimented with music downloads and file-sharing networks (table 4.16). Overall, there are slightly more broadband users who use audio-streaming technologies (19 percent) than broadband users who download music files (17 percent). An Arbitron Media Research 2002 survey reports that many people have substituted time spent using traditional media (newspapers, radio, prerecorded music) with online activities (see table 4.17). Substitution is stronger for activities that require full attention, such as watching

Table 4.17
Internet and other forms of entertainment (U.S.): "Are you spending less time with each activity due to the time you spend online?"

Activity	Percent spending less time
Watching TV	37
Reading newspapers	31
Reading magazines	27
Listening to the radio	20
Listening to music CDs	19

Source: Arbitron/Edison Media Research, July 2002; n = 2511.

television, than for music (one can listen to music while reading newspapers or surfing the Internet). The use of broadband Internet connections is likely to generate broader changes.

Observation 4.5   There is evidence that the increasing availability of broadband is changing the spare time activities of consumers in favor of online activities.

4.2.3.6   Effect of Internet Piracy and Music Downloads on CD Sales   In this section, we investigate what the main effects of Internet piracy on CD sales are. We start with a review of the economics of Internet piracy to understand what economic mechanisms increase or decrease sales. Next, we discuss recent survey data and summarize econometric studies.

The economic rationale of intellectual property protection is to give incentives for creative activities that involve large sunk costs. With the traditional distribution technology, the cost of creation includes costs of recording, marketing, and promotion. Since this activity is risky, it seems efficient to share revenues of intellectual property between artists and distribution companies. We argue that the situation has changed and that online distribution services have a different cost structure.

By giving exclusive rights to authors of original artistic work, the copyright law tends to increase market power in the music industry (even if ignoring collective efforts such as price fixing). Ex post facto, this situation is inefficient: it is optimal to price a "public good" at its marginal cost, which is very small. Ex ante, this situation is necessary. The tradeoff between "investment" incentives and ex post efficiency is at the core of the optimal copyright and patent policy debate.

Despite the technological breakthrough of file sharing, the debate on the implications of piracy goes far back in the economic literature on unauthorized copies of copyrighted material—this literature is reviewed in Peitz and Waelbroeck (2003a). Instead of duplicating the review here, we discuss the arguments of the literature that can be applied to the music industry.

When copyright owners can monitor the amount of copies likely to result from the purchase of original material, they can indirectly appropriate revenues by charging a higher price for the original (see Liebowitz 1985, Besen and Kirby 1989, and Bakos et al. 1999). The first argument is related to the pricing of a club membership and the nature of the cost to copy. The second argument is related to the literature on bundling and how club formations can reduce the variance of the demand of the club as a whole compared to individual demands. Potentially, indirect appropriation could arise if users of file-sharing technologies were ready to pay a premium to purchase the original version of a hit song to improve their priority rating on a P2P network (see Liebowitz 2002). However, both arguments are unlikely to play a key role in P2P technologies since it is extremely difficult to monitor file exchanges.

Most of the time, the copy is of lower quality than the original; widespread use implies that the increase in consumer surplus more than compensates for the static losses of producers. This argument is easily understood since the ex post total surplus-maximizing price is equal to the marginal cost (which can be assumed to be zero). However, in a long-term perspective, such profit loss results in less incentive to provide quality on the market (an important contribution to this idea should be credited to Novos and Waldman [1985]). Because of reasons given in section 4.2.2.3, it can be argued that digital music files have a lower expected value than an original CD; therefore, some elements of product differentiation should be part of the debate on Internet music piracy.

In some cases, positive network externalties generated by copies can benefit copyright owners, as shown by Conner and Rumelt (1991), Takeyama (1994), and Shy and Thisse (1999). There is a case for network effects in music consumption if users place a value on the number of people listening to the same music. These *social network effects* can result from the fact that consumers want to belong to a community or be able to talk about music in social gatherings. In principle, network effects could depend on both the number of originals and copies.[9]

Finally, digital copies can provide information on the genre and style of CDs that consumers want. For instance, Takeyama (2003) shows how copies that give information on the characteristics of a durable good can solve adverse selection problems. Arguments based on sampling are developed by Duchêne and Waelbroeck (2003) and Peitz and Waelbroeck (2004a). In particular, Peitz and Waelbroeck show how a multi-product firm can benefit from better *matching* consumers to their ideal products through better sampling on P2P networks, despite the negative *competition effect* from the availability of digital copies. We believe arguments based on the informational role of copies are important for music consumption. Liebowitz provides in his chapter a somewhat conflicting view arguing that sampling is likely to reduce purchases of recorded music.

After a fast increase, the number of people using P2P applications started to decline in the second half of 2003, following the legal actions taken by the RIAA. Numbers on the popularity of P2P networks can be obtained by monitoring the use of file-sharing software applications running at a given time. Following the summer 2003 announcement of the RIAA to sue P2P users, most file-sharing networks saw their number of users drop by 10 to 30 percent (figure 4.12).

The IFPI tracks the number of infringing music files on the Internet and also reports a significant decline after summer 2003 when the RIAA announced it would sue music uploaders (table 4.18).

A 2002 survey commissioned by the RIAA found that only 15 percent of music downloaders who burn music onto CD-Rs spent more money on music purchases, while 27 percent spent less. An Ipsos 2002 survey found the opposite, as reported in table 4.19. Therefore, survey data do not give a clear-cut effect of music downloads on CD purchases. We document empirical studies on the effect of Internet piracy on music sales in the Econometric Studies section.

Finally, a recent Pew Internet Report interviewed 2,755 musicians in the United States and asked them their opinions of file sharing on the Internet. Results are reported in tables 4.20a and 4.20b. Only 5 percent of the musicians answered that free music downloads had a negative impact on their career. However, these survey data are constructed from a nonrepresentative sample and should therefore be interpreted with caution.

As a first attempt, in Peitz and Waelbroeck (2004b), we try to estimate the effect of music downloads on music sales (mainly CDs, music cassettes, and singles), controlling for other factors during the period

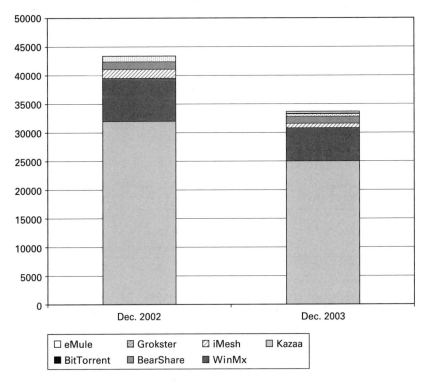

Figure 4.12
Unique users of file-sharing (worldwide, 2002–2003) Source: comScore, 2004; data in millions.

Table 4.18
Number of infringing music files on P2P networks (world); figures in units of millions

June 2004	700
January 2004	800
June 2003	1000
April 2003	1100
November 2002	900
June 2002	500
April 2002	600

Source: IFPI, Online Music Report, 2004.

Table 4.19
Probability of purchase after downloading (U.S.): "Since you initially began downloading music or MP3 files off the Internet," would you say that your compact disc purchases have now changed?

Decreased	19%
Increased	24%
Stayed the same	57%

Source: IPSOS TEMPO 2002; n = 834.

Table 4.20a
What are musicians saying about free downloads? (U.S.): "How has free downloading on the Internet affected you?"

	Increased	Decreased	No effect	Does not apply to me	Don't know/ refused
Sales of your CDs or other merchandise?	21%	5%	34%	25%	14%
Radio play of your music?	19%	1%	39%	28%	13%
Attendance at your concerts or live performances?	30%	0%	29%	27%	13%

Source: Pew Internet Report, June 2004.

Table 4.20b
What are the musicians saying about free downloads? (U.S.): "In general, how would you say that free downloading on the Internet has affected you?"

Helped my career	35%
Hurt my career	5%
Not made any difference in my career	37%
Has both helped and hurt my career	8%
Don't know	15%

from 1998 to 2002 for which we have cross-country survey data on music downloads. We find that there are three main factors that significantly influence cross-country variation in sales over that period: GDP growth, MP3 downloads, and broadband penetration. The overall impact of Internet piracy on *music* sales is estimated at 20 percent for the period. In Peitz and Waelbroeck (2004c), we show that MP3 downloads led to a 7 percent reduction of *CD* sales worldwide and to a 12 percent reduction in the United States during the period from 2001 to 2002. Subsequent drops hardly can be explained by music downloads only. These two studies should be taken with caution since we consider a small number of countries in the econometric analysis.

Zentner (2003) uses individual survey data from large European countries in October 2001. Preliminary estimation results suggest that music downloads do not significantly reduce the probability of purchasing music. However, after controlling for unobserved heterogeneity in music taste, Zentner finds that music downloads reduce the probability of purchasing music by 30 percent. Assuming that people who download music purchase as much as people who do not, Zentner finds that Internet piracy could have decreased CD sales in units by 7 percent in the countries considered. This study gives roughly the same aggregate effect as in Peitz and Waelbroeck (2004c) for the same period.

These analyses use download data based on surveys. This can be questioned for a number of reasons. We mention only two. First, survey data on downloads may be biased because some respondents might be aware of the illegality of their actions (although in the period considered, legal concerns were not as high as in the second half of 2003). Second, the survey data used are not sufficiently rich because they do not distinguish between frequent and occasional downloaders.

Oberholzer and Strumpf (2004) use actual download and sales data. They determine which albums were downloaded most on file-sharing networks during the last quarter of 2002. Controlling for possible endogeneity issues, they show, contrary to the previous studies, that the number of times an album has been downloaded does not have a statistically significant effect on sales. They also conclude that "estimates are of moderate economic significance." This study has been criticized by some academics and representatives of the music industry. Liebowitz (2005) argues that the effect of file sharing on sales of individual albums is hard to extrapolate at the industry level and questions the validity of the instruments chosen by the authors. IFPI market research director Keith Jopling, quoted by *BBC News* (April 1, 2004), criticizes the choice of the last quarter of the year to carry an empirical study because of the changing nature of music sales due to Christmas. He adds that "they [Oberholzer and Strumpf] establish no causality between file-sharers and music sales. The link they make is tenuous at best."[10]

Rob and Waldfogel (2004) use a survey of college students to determine which albums have been downloaded most at the individual level. Using a list of hit albums (hit list) and a list of albums acquired by the respondents during the past year (current list), Rob and Waldfogel explain variation in individual CD consumption by the number of albums downloaded from the corresponding list. They find a statistically negative effect of downloaded albums on CD purchases for the current list and a much weaker effect for the hit list. Next they use answers to valuation questions to determine if students download high- or low-value albums. Data suggest that depreciation and the nature of music as an experience good can explain the difference and the correlation between ex ante and ex post valuations and that students download low-valuation albums.

Overall, the empirical results so far do not give a clear indication whether music downloads have a significant effect on current CD sales. However, the available evidence suggests that the qualitative claim by the music industry should be taken seriously—for a complementary analysis with much stronger conclusions, see chapter 5 in this volume by Liebowitz). He provides a more detailed discussion of the paper by Oberholzer and Strumpf and describes some additional empirical contributions.

Different factors, which are not captured in the regressions, may at least partly explain the recent downward trend in CD sales. One such factor may be the effect of the diffusion of fast Internet connections on leisure activities. People are listening to audio clips and Internet radio more than they are downloading music files. While it is not clear how audio streaming will affect record companies in the future, streaming is only one of the many activities that broadband users are doing on any given day instead of listening to CDs. Other forms of digital activities include instant messaging, looking for news, job and hobby information, creating online content (pictures and web pages), watching video clips and movies, playing online games, purchasing products online and undirected browsing. These new forms of entertainment that have been embraced by broadband users are clearly a substitute to traditional forms of entertainment. Indeed, as documented in section 4.2.3.5, survey data provide evidence that heavy Internet users already have reduced the amount of time watching television and listening to music.

There has also been self-selection. Teenagers and college students with low purchasing power have the highest propensity to use file-sharing technologies and for this reason adopted the technology first. Older Internet users are late adopters with higher purchasing power and a high opportunity cost of using file-sharing networks to download music. Using the terms defined previously, the *matching effect* may dominate the *competition effect* for older Internet users, while the converse may be true for teenagers and college students. This would imply that the reaction by older Internet users to music downloads may actually be to increase spending. There may also exist heterogeneity within groups such as college students; in particular, student music enthusiasts may show different patterns than those students who are less enthusiastic about music.[11]

The interpretation that early adopters behave differently from late adopters is compatible with our empirical study that indicates that music downloads have had a large impact on CD sales in the early period of file-sharing networks and a much smaller impact from 2002 onward. It is also compatible with the study of Boorstin (2004) who finds that the number of teenagers and adults younger than twenty-four who have Internet access significantly decreases total CD sales in a given area, but that the number of older adults with Internet access significantly increases total CD purchases. However, with respect to Boorstin's study, it is problematic to equate Internet access to Internet piracy, as we have argued that Internet access can serve a number of purposes, only one of them being downloading music from file-sharing networks. Moreover, analyzing the effect of Internet access of a subpopulation on *total* sales does not provide the correct partial effect of that subpopulation.

Finally, the music industry has experienced several technological cycles related to the introduction of a new format. Cassettes partially replaced LPs. In the main markets for prerecorded music, CDs have replaced cassettes and LPs. In particular, consumers have over time replaced their LP collection by purchasing the same albums on CDs. This substitution pattern seems to be approaching an end. New formats

have been introduced also such as the Super Audio CD and music
DVDs, as documented in this section. However, it remains to be seen
whether these new formats can trigger a new replacement cycle of the
same magnitude. As suggested by Oberholzer and Strumpf, consumers may be busy building up a DVD collection of movies and cut-
ting down on CD purchases; see also the discussion in chapter 5 by
Liebowitz who dismisses this explanation.

4.3 (Re)actions and Opportunities

High-speed Internet has created new technological opportunities to
distribute music to consumers. On one hand, the technology of selling
digital music is built on a new cost structure. On the other hand, technological protection of digital music files raises new economic and legal challenges for players in the market and for policy-makers. From a
legal perspective, new amendments to the U.S. Copyright Act make it
a crime to circumvent technological measures of protection of digital
content. This has opened the market to firms producing so-called *digital rights management* (DRM) solutions that can monitor and control
access to digital music. As a matter of fact, all business models that
we describe in this section rely on DRM to distribute digital music to
consumers.

4.3.1 What Has Changed?

4.3.1.1 Cost of Digital Music Distribution   In most of the business
models that we describe in this section one music download costs one
dollar. Box 4.3 provides a breakdown of this price according to ClNet,
an Internet company specializing in technology news.

The large fixed cost of setting up a CD press and reproducing CDs
has vanished, which means that potentially it can become profitable
for artists with a smaller audience to distribute. However, fixed marketing costs are still necessary to provide consumers with information
on new releases, but probably to a lesser extent, as we argue at the end
of this section. Although costs related to financial intermediation
existed already, their proportion is larger for digital music. It remains
to be seen if new payment methods can bring that cost down. Overall,
one can say that variable costs relative to fixed costs are more important for music downloads than for CDs. This suggests that acts with a
smaller audience can succeed in the digital music market. As a conse-

Box 4.3
Digital music distribution: A dollar divided

Labels   Receive 60–70 cents. This includes publishing rights of about 10–12 cents per song, which are bundled with the labels' cut in the kind of wholesale arrangement reportedly brokered by Apple.

Financial transaction   Costs 10–15 cents. Credit card companies stipulate transaction minimums of up to 30 cents, making this one of the biggest line items for download retailers. Experienced music executives said micro-payments are prohibitively expensive at fewer than three downloads per purchase. "Credit card fees can eat you alive," asserts Yahoo Launch CEO Dave Goldberg.

Marketing   5–10 cents. Assumes marketing budget of $5–10 million a year.

Staff   3–5 cents. Assumes 30–50 employees at $3–5 million a year in salary and benefits.

Bandwidth and hosting   2–5 cents. This includes the cost of delivering the bits to the customer and is highly sensitive to volume. Large numbers of downloads can mean big savings, assuming rates have been locked in advance.

Start-up costs   2–3 cents. Assumes a $20–30 million investment—about what Sony and Universal put into the Pressplay service being sold to Roxio—amortized over 10 years.

Total $0.82–1.03.

Profits $17 million gain to a $4 million loss.

Source: C|Net News.com, "Microsoft, Again: Apple's Old Nemesis," May 29, 2003.

quence, we might observe more music diversity and a less skewed distribution of sales among artists.

4.3.1.2 New Players   Since digital music does not require a physical product, new players can sell digital music to consumers: traditional and hybrid stores (Fnac, Amazon, Walmart, and BuyMusic), technology companies (Apple's iTunes and iPod, Microsoft Media Player, and RealNetworks), online content providers (Yahoo! Launch), online music sites (MP3.com and OD2), electronics companies (Sony Connect Store), and Internet Service Providers.

Moreover, copyright owners need to choose the digital format of the music they intend to sell to consumers. They also have to determine their restriction policy, that is, how much freedom consumers have with respect to streaming, transferring, and burning music files (see section 4.3.3.5 on DRM in this chapter).

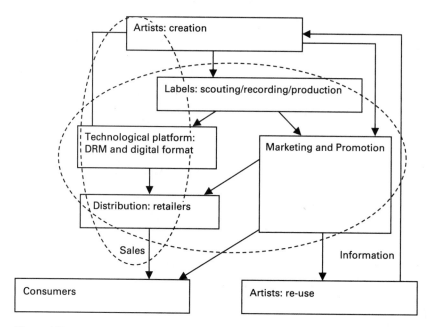

Figure 4.13
Players in the digital music industry

The organization of the digital music industry is represented in figure 4.13. Dotted ellipses indicate potential sources of vertical and horizontal integrations.

4.3.1.3 Consumers' Behavior and Digital Music In this section we present facts on digital music available in compressed format on the Internet. Clearly, downloading music files is only one way to get access to music with the computer. A 2001 survey carried out by Ipsos-Reid in the United States (with a representative sample of 1,112 respondents) provides an early picture: approximately a quarter of the respondents said they had downloaded music from the Internet. A similar number of all respondents said they listened to Internet radio, streamed music clips, or audio files. At that point, more than one third had listened to a prerecorded CD on the computer.

In this subsection, we focus on consumers' attitudes with respect to music downloads and audio streaming. Music downloads can be used to

• sample new songs,

• add songs to a playlist on the computer (and transfer them to other computers),

• burn songs on CD, and

• transfer music to a portable device (MP3 player).

For the first two purposes no additional devices are needed. To burn a CD, a CD burner obviously is needed, and for portable use an MP3 player is required. Hence, to assess the importance of burning music files onto CDs or transferring files on portable players, it is relevant to analyze the penetration of CD burners and MP3 players in households. Although consumers purchase CD burners for a variety of reasons, burning music and video files onto CDs is likely to be the main use for most consumers. However, while a CD burner is a prerequisite for burning downloads onto a CD, the possession of a CD burner does not indicate the intent to use it for an infringing purpose.[12] MP3 players are used almost exclusively to listen to recorded music (see section 4.2.3.5).

Sampling   When sampling occurs, consumers purchase music on CDs after downloading or streaming the songs from the Internet. This means they do not fully substitute CDs with digital music. To assess the interaction between downloading and purchasing behavior, we document in table 4.21 answers to surveys on sampling. In a Pew Internet Report survey only 26 percent of downloaders are freeloaders, while 50 percent of music downloaders say they actually purchase the original on a regular basis.

When they sample, downloaders can discover new artists. According to table 4.22, 31 percent of music downloaders have listened to new artists. This percentage can be seen as a lower bound of the size of the sampling effect because currently P2P networks are not good at providing cross-recommendations, customized playlists, etc.

An indication that sampling can affect music consumption is provided by a 2002 survey of Ipsos. Thirty percent of participants acknowledged that they have changed their listening or purchasing habits since they started downloading music. Twenty-seven percent of those who answered the survey reported that their listening or purchasing habit has changed because they are able to experiment with new music (see table 4.23).

Burning   There is little data on the behavior of P2P users with respect to burning downloaded files. One survey with a small sample size

Table 4.21
Downloads and music purchases (U.S.): Did you buy the music you downloaded, or did you get it for free?

Bought it	15%
Got it for free	79%
Don't know/refused	9%

Did you download music that you already own on a CD or tape, or did you download new music?

Music already owned	28%
New Music	63%
Don't know/refused	9%

After you downloaded music to your computer and listened to it, how often—if ever—have you bought that same music on a CD or cassette?

Most of the time	21%
Some of the time	29%
A little of the time	19%
Never	26%
Don't know/refused	5%

Source: Pew Internet Tracking, July–August 2000; n = 218.

Table 4.22
Downloading new music (U.S.)

What type of music have you downloaded?	Yes	No	Don't know/ refused
Music you'd heard before by artists you were familiar with	86	9	5
New music by artists you were already familiar with	69	27	4
Music by artists you had never heard before	31	65	4

Source: Pew Internet Tracking, July–August 2000; n = 218.

finds that the majority of Internet users who download music burn a small number of files (see table 4.24). This pattern is compatible with the distribution of files stored by music downloaders presented in section 4.2.2.3. We summarize our findings by the following observation.

Observation 4.6 Digital music downloads have a number of purposes, the most prominent being sampling, burning, adding to computer playlists, and transferring to portable MP3 players.

Table 4.23
Downloading and changes in music taste (U.S.): Has the genre of music that you typically listen to or purchase changed since you began downloading music or MP3 files off the Internet?

No	71%
Yes	30%
In what ways? (n = 242)	
Was able to experiment with different forms of music	27%
Like a range of music	23%
Introduced to new age, techno, or electronica	10%
More aware of new bands, groups, artists, or songs	10%
Listening to more country or introduced to it	6%
Listening to more classical or introduced to it	5%
Listening to more pop or introduced to pop	4%
Listening to more hip-hop and rap or introduced to it	4%
Listening to more jazz or introduced to it	4%
Other	19%

Source: Ipsos-Insight, TEMPO: Keeping Pace with Online Music Distribution, 2002; n = 834.

Table 4.24
Number of music tracks burned to CDs (U.S.)

<50	54%
50–99	5%
100–199	10%
>200	11%
Don't know	20%

Source: Parks and Associates, Electronic Living @ Home, 2003; n = 285.

4.3.2 Legal Protection of Digital Music

Technological protection, which is at the core of all business models proposed by the major players in the music industry, has its foundation in the Digital Millennium Copyright Act. To understand the new economic challenges posed by technological protection of digital content and the legal actions undertaken by the record companies, it is necessary to review some key elements of U.S. copyright law.

4.3.2.1 Basic Facts about Copyright The U.S. copyright law serves the purpose of protecting authors of "original works of authorship," including literary, dramatic, musical, and artistic works. The protection is available for published and unpublished work. In addition to protection, copyright gives an exclusivity right on the revenues generated by the copyrighted work. Two U.S. acts are of particular importance for the music industry: the Audio Home Recording Act and the Digital Millennium Copyright Act.

Audio Home Recording Act   The U.S. Congress enacted the Audio Home Recording Act (AHRA) in 1992 in response to the appearance of home digital audio recording devices. The law imposes monetary duties on equipment and supplies, but noncommercial users are protected from copyright infringement. According to the Alliance of Artists and Recording Companies (AARC), a nonprofit organization representing featured performing artists and record companies, at a first approximation 40 percent of the Sound Recordings Fund (two thirds of total royalty payments; the other third goes to the Musical Works Fund) is distributed to artists and 60 percent to copyright owners (that is, music distribution companies) in proportion of their sales. The royalty payment is under AHRA section 1004—2 percent of the transfer price of the device and 3 percent for the media. A digital audio recording device is, according to the law, "the digital recording function of which is designed or marketed for the primary purpose of, and that is capable of, making a digital audio copied recording for private use." Congress also used the AHRA to introduce a DRM known as the Serial Copy Management System (SCMS), which authorizes unlimited first copies of copyrighted material but prevents additional copies of the first copies. Devices that do not include such technological protection can not be sold in the United States. There is much debate on the definition of "digital audio recording device" and the increasing obsolescence of the AHRA itself in the fast evolving technological environment around digital music.

Digital Millennium Copyright Act   Following the 1998 World Intellectual Property Organization (WIPO) convention in Geneva, Congress enacted the Digital Millennium Copyright Act (DMCA), which extends the Copyright Act. The DMCA

• makes it a crime to circumvent antipiracy measures built into most commercial software (except for research and nonprofit libraries, etc.),

• limits liability of copyright infringement of Internet Service Providers (ISP) and institutions of higher education,

• requires webcasters and commercial broadcaster to pay licensee fees (these fees are set to 0.07 cents per performance (i.e. unicast stream) with a minimum of $500 per year), collected by the Copyright Arbitration Royalty Panel (CARP),

• does not affect exemptions of copyright infringements, including fair use.

DMCA lays the legal foundation of pay-per-use, even for material that is no longer protected by copyright law.

4.3.2.2 Exemptions to Copyright Infringement In most countries, the copyright law includes several exemptions to copyright infringement. In the United States, the most ambiguous exemption, especially in the digital era, is fair use. Four elements must be balanced to determine whether an activity is within fair use: the purpose of the use, the nature in which the work is being used, the amount of the work used, and the effect of the use on the market for—or value of—the original work. We return to these elements in the context of the Napster case. In Europe an legislation, the exemptions are listed; however, more music-related products and services are taxed. The proceedings are redistributed to copyright owners.

In 2002, collections for broadcasting, public performance, and other sound recording royalties topped $605 million at the forty-nine collecting societies reporting to IFPI's income survey. This is an increase from $566 million in 2001 and $505 million in 2000. Of the collected revenues, $59.5 million were distributed to companies in the UK, $59 million in Japan, $47 million in France, $43 million in Germany, $17 million in the Netherlands, and $9 million in North America (IFPI 2003b).

4.3.2.3 Napster: The Court Decision A year after its creation in 1999, the pioneer file-sharing company Napster was sued by the RIAA. The Ninth Circuit Court, in some cases using simplistic arguments, found that the four elements weighted against fair use in the Napster case. The court found that the use of Napster harmed the music industry on two economic grounds: the loss of CD sales and a heightened barrier to entry of the music industry in the online distribution market.

The empirical study for the RIAA used to show that music downloading harmed the music industry provided only weak evidence of a decline in CD sales in record stores near college campuses and ignored the effect of online sales of CDs. At the same time, the argument of sampling that Napster used, according to which higher CD purchases are generated, was supported by an empirical study that the court ruled out as flawed and nonobjective.

The court also ruled out computers, MP3 players, and hard drives that can be used for purposes other than listening and copying music as "digital audio recording devices," which made the AHRA exemption difficult to apply. In other words, music downloaders are not exempted from copyright infringement when they use computers and the Internet to acquire MP3 files without authorization. The court did not resolve the question of whether Napster was an ISP, and the question never went to trial. However, this issue was raised in the series of legal actions taken against file-sharing network developers and users.

4.3.2.4 Kazaa, the RIAA, and File-Swappers Two series of legal actions were taken by the RIAA against file-sharing networks: the first against developers of P2P networks, and the second against uploaders of MP3 files on P2P networks such as Kazaa.

In early 2003, the RIAA sued campus file-swappers who created P2P or indexing services at Rensselaer Polytechnic Institute, Princeton University, and Michigan Technological University. The software ranged from indexing technologies to local and generic search engines. Four campus file-swappers agreed to pay between $12,000 and $17,000 each to the RIAA to settle piracy charges.

Kazaa became the most popular P2P network after the departure of Napster. Contrary to its predecessor, Kazaa files are exchanged in a decentralized way. Kazaa therefore claims that it is not responsible for copyright infringement and that it should be treated like an ISP.[13] Services like Kazaa and their users were the next RIAA target.

After monitoring file-sharing activities on P2P networks in the summer of 2003, the RIAA launched a massive series of lawsuits targeting individual file-swappers. While many observers of the music industry view the strategy of suing one's own customers as extremely risky, and only leading to the development of better anonymous file-sharing technologies, the RIAA has totaled an impressive 2,454 cases as of May 2004. Many charges were settled out of court for $3,000 each. According to Jason Schults, a staff attorney at Electronic Frontier Foundation defending music uploaders, "many of the people who have called us

who have been sued have been single parents whose children were using the computer while the parent was at work" (Wired News 2003).
At the same time, the number of unique users of P2P networks has
decreased 15 to 50 percent during the second half of 2003. However,
while many people stopped using the popular Kazaa software, some
switched to less well-known file-sharing software such as Bittorent
and Emule.[14]

On the legal front, the lawsuits against Kazaa and its users have
brought key interpretations of the Copyright Act. First, a federal judge
from Los Angeles, Judge Stephen Wilson, ruled that Streamcast (a parent of Morpheus) and Grokster were not liable for copyright infringement from users of their software. This ruling does not directly affect
Kazaa. The decision was partly based on a comparison with companies
selling home video recorders or copy machines. The difference between Napster and new P2P technologies is that the latter do not
control content that circulates through their applications. The ruling
follows a court decision in the Netherlands in March 2002 that ruled
that Kazaa could not be liable for copyright infringements done by
people using their software application. A reference was made to the
Betamax Case of 1984, which made the sales of VCRs legal.

Second, the RIAA initially won a court order forcing Verizon Communications to divulge the identity of Kazaa users suspected of copyright infringements (putting ISPs into the middle of a huge copyright
mess threatening the privacy of individuals). However, reversing the
previous decision in favor of the RIAA, a Washington DC appeals
court decided that the law does not allow the RIAA to send subpoenas
asking ISPs the identity of P2P users without a judge's consent. In
other words, record companies must file a lawsuit to obtain a sub-
poena to uncover the identity of P2P users, which substantially
increases the cost of tracking P2P users. Finally, Judge Konrad von Fin-
kelstein in Canada ruled that uploading music files is not in itself a
breach of copyright and that "before it constitutes distribution, there
must be a positive act by the owner of the shared directory, such as
sending out the copies or advertising that they are available for copying." We thus make the following observation.[15]

Observation 4.7 Active uploading is considered to be illegal distribution of copyrighted material, but developers of P2P networks are
not held responsible for the files that are being exchanged on their
networks.

4.3.2.5 Concluding Remarks on Legal Protection Copyright law is alive and has been tailored to the digital era. U.S. copyright law includes complex definitions that are subject to interpretation for digital products. Computers are not exempted by the AHRA. Fair use has been interpreted as follows: transformative uses are strongly favored but digital copies are not transformations of CDs; music is considered a creative work and fair use is narrow in this domain; effects on current and future markets are taken into account.

The rest of the world is enacting legal protection of digital content. For instance, the EU Intellectual Property Rights Enforcement Directive was passed in March 2004 and seems comparable to the controversial DMCA. However, it has one amendment that says action should not be taken against consumers who download music "in good faith" for their own use.

4.3.3 Technological Protection of Digital Music

The DMCA legally enabled DRM, a small piece of software that can detect, monitor, and block unauthorized use of copyrighted material.

New DRM solutions for digitally compressed music files open the door for new ways of distributing digital content, as well as for second-degree price discrimination.[16] From a legal perspective, DRM requires a rethinking of the notion of fair use.

DRM for music generally includes copy control, watermarking (digital identification inserted in digital files, that is, ex ante constraints), fingerprinting (converts the files content into a unique identification number, that is, ex post control), authentication, and access control.

DRM protection on original CDs has proved to be quite unpopular. For instance, EMI is fighting a lawsuit against European organizations for the protection of consumers who claimed that some of the legitimately purchased CDs would not play in old stereos or in cars. New DRM protection of digital files has similar problems. For instance, it is difficult to stream legally purchased files onto wireless audio receivers or to transfer music files to video-editing software.

4.3.3.1 Uses and Misuses of DRM The fact that digital music can be compressed, exchanged, and monitored over a network has implications for both users and producers of music.[17] Where users are concerned, DRM can protect any digital content even if it is not protected by the copyright law, such as documents in the public domain. It reduces the value of fair use and can force consumers to listen to undesirable content (such as ads). Because of these restrictions, DRM is sometimes called by its critics "Digital Restrictions Management" (Samuelson 2003). Moreover, it can protect potentially for an infinite amount of time, which is contrary to the spirit of the Copyright Act. In a sense, DRM creates the basis for a perpetual payment system.

Fair Use and Indirect Appropriation   Fair use is an exemption to copyright infringement and is economically justified when the cost of writing a formal contract to authorize use is less than the benefit to the user (Gordon 1982). DRM can reduce the value of fair use if digital music cannot be used as before. Indeed nothing in copyright law prevents legitimate owners of digital music to include songs in video-editing software, for instance—an action that is sometimes difficult with current technological protection. However, DRM is not necessarily hostile to fair use. It could be designed with symmetric rights (see section 4.3.3.3). There is currently a debate on whether fair use is still necessary when copyright owners can monitor and appropriate all uses of digital music. Indeed one could imagine in a not-so-distant future an environment in which all music is streamed from a centralized server (which is called *digital locker*).

Does Contract Law Override Copyright Law?   Digital rights management is linked to a contractual agreement (clickware) that can conflict with copyright law if it reduces the set of actions permitted by copyright. Moreover, DRM can protect work in the public domain, over an infinite period of time, which is contrary to the spirit of the copyright law. It is not clear whether contract law overrides copyright law, but if it does, potential conflicts need to be resolved.

First Sale Doctrine (Exhaustion Principle)   There is currently a debate on whether the first sale doctrine could be applied to digital music files. The first sale doctrine states that a legitimate purchaser and owner of a copyrighted work can resell or rent it on a secondary market. Although this doctrine could be applied in principle to digital media files, it is difficult to realize for the following reason: copying and transmitting digital files require making a temporary copy in the memory of the receiving computer, which could be considered an infringement to copyright.

Privacy   Privacy can be defined economically as the ability to control information (in and out) about one's actions in a private intellectual space. Privacy is protected in general in places where one can consume intellectual goods (libraries, video-rental stores, cable subscription). DRM can invade privacy by monitoring and constraining unauthorized uses. DRM also can invade privacy by forcing consumers to view or listen to undesirable content (for example, spam). However, firms could use DRM to collect information to sell products better suited to the tastes of consumers. There is currently a debate on who should protect privacy: should it be protected by the law or should consumers protect themselves with personal firewalls? The latter scenario raises the possibility of a technological protection war between users and producers of digital music.

Price Discrimination, Versioning, and Targeted Offers Because DRM allows producers to price discriminate, Liebowitz (2002) argues that DRM is unlikely to significantly reduce use compared to the social optimum. In the extreme case of first-degree or perfect-price discrimination, use is not reduced at all. However, price discrimination tends to reduce the surplus to consumers and raises distributional concerns. DRM can also be used to target different segments with different types of restrictions and pricing schemes. Since DRM can transmit information on consumers' behavior, firms can use DRM to version their products to consumers' needs.

Promoting New Acts As discussed, there is a strong heterogeneity of tastes in music consumption. It is therefore difficult for a consumer to evaluate a cultural good from a catalog. For this reason, music can be classified as an experience good that consumers need to "taste" before they can make an informed purchase decision. Transmitting this information is the first challenge. A second and related challenge is to predict the success of a new act. DRM could solve both challenges if properly designed. Limited free sampling gives useful information to both consumers and record companies. Different from free downloads on Kazaa, DRM-protected files make it so artists and record companies do not forego future earnings since free use is restricted in time (see the discussion of the DRM-protected files available at Kazaa in section 4.3.3.5).

Some record labels' executives have discreetly looked at music download data to assess how well an act is doing. Maverick Records used download data to promote Story of the Year's "Until the Day I Die" that was a top-twenty-downloaded song, selling half a million copies. Similar strategies have been said to be used by Warner Bros. to promote the song "Headstrong" from the band Trapt (see Chmielewski

2004). However, the popularity of an artist's songs on P2P networks does not necessarily translate into commercial success. For instance, Ben Jelen and Atreyu, are bands that are often exchanged on P2P networks. Atreyu has half of Ben Jelen's P2P audience but nevertheless manages to generate stronger album sales (see BigChampagne.com, which tracks the success of these two bands). This phenomenon can be explained by the variety offered on music download charts targets different consumers than those who purchase singles. As an illustration, we report in box 4.4 the top twenty UK singles and downloads charts for September 2004. The two most downloaded songs are not even in the top twenty singles chart. However, in a world in which most people buy their songs online, the difference is expected to fade away. Changes in popularity on chart rankings in the file-sharing era have been recently studied by Gopal et al. (2004).

4.3.3.2 Designing DRM DRM could increase substantially the cost of creation if artists must check and clear melodic lines belonging to other artists. There is no market mechanism for processing information contracts efficiently, although many new genres rely on sampling (electronica and rap, for instance).

However, there is nothing in the nature of DRM that prevents subsequent use or diminishes consumers' rights. In principle, one could design a value-centered DRM that respects interests of various parties. Indeed the "R" in DRM stands for rights—but not only producers' rights.

Some authors have advocated the use of "rights expression language" to enhance creativity and deal with multiple rights owners (Bechtold 2003). Others are proponents of a "Copyright Commons," where DRM is used to control copyrighted works that are registered in a metadata system (Lessig 2001; DRM is used to enforce openness and enrich the commons). Several artists have released content under Copyright Commons licenses: Chuck D., Beastie Boys, David Byrne, Gilberto Gil, and Cornelius (see *BBC News* Oct. 5, 2004).

Finally, other observers of the music industry have strongly argued that the current levy system on digital audio material in Europe is not compatible with the current restrictions imposed by DRM solutions. In most European countries, there are taxes on blank media, MP3 players, and CD burners that are redistributed to the copyright owners (see Bechtold [2003] for the numbers in Germany). These taxes give copyright owners remuneration without control of the way music is

Box 4.4

UK top 20 songs (September 2004)

Downloads	
1. Flying Without Wings	Westlife
2. Blazin Day	Blazin Squad
3. She Will Be Loved	Maroon 5
4. Lola's Theme	Shapeshifters
5. American Idiot	Green Day
6. This Love	Maroon 5
7. Dry Your Eyes	Streets
8. Bedshaped	Keane
9. Laura	Scissor Sisters
10. Apocalypse Please	Muse
11. Sick and Tired	Anastacia
12. Dumb	411
13. Everybody's Changing	Keane
14. Left Outside Alone	Anastacia
15. My Happy Ending	Avril Lavigne
16. Guns Dont Kill People Rappers Do	Goldie Lookin' Chain
17. Single	Natasha Bedingfield
18. Harder To Breathe	Maroon 5
19. Hey Ya	Outkast
20. Sunshine	Twista
Singles	
1. My Place/Flap Your Wings	Nelly
2. Leave (Get Out)	Jojo
3. Sunshine	Twista
4. These Words	Natasha Bedingfield
5. Baby Cakes	3 Of A Kind
6. Dumb	411
7. Gravity	Embrace
8. You Should Really Know	The Pirates feat. Enya/ Ama/Boss/Ishani
9. She Will Be Loved	Maroon 5
10. Guns Don't Kill People Rappers Do	Goldie Lookin' Chain
11. Wishing on a Star	Paul Weller
12. Popular	Darren Hayes
13. Is It Cos I'm Cool	Mousse T feat. Emma Lanford
14. Thunderbirds	Busted
15. My My My	Armand Van Helden

Box 4.4
(continued)

16. Jesus Walks	Kanye West
17. Caught In A Moment	Sugababes
18. All These Things That I've Done	Killers
19. Girls	Prodigy
20. Stand Up Tall	Dizzee Rascal

Source: The Official UK Charts, September 2004.

consumed. However, DRM currently allows both remuneration and control of copyrighted work and represents an additional financial source that is at odds with the existence of a levy system.

4.3.3.3 Alternative DRM-based Remuneration Systems
Sobel (2003) distinguishes two extreme forms of copyright arrangements. These forms are the following:

• Anticopyright models: they would eliminate copyright entirely; DRM is only used to tip some artists.

• Beyond copyright models: DRM could be used to control all form of access to digital work, even noncopyrighted work.

Note that all DRM-based models authorize some form of price discrimination according to use. Among copyright-based models, Sobel (2003) distinguishes between the following:

• Statutory license models: authorize noncommercial use against a levy on providers.

• Tax and royalty system: tax ISP access and technologies to play digital files; the tax is redistributed to copyright owners.

Both models use DRM to determine the amount of copyrighted work that has been flowing over the ISP network and have been advocated, for instance, by Lessig (2001). The basic idea of this tax and royalty scheme is to tax ancillary products such as blank CDs, CD writers, ISPs, etc. A compulsory license requires that the copyright owners make their work available to users at a given price, usually fixed. The compulsory license is based on the blanket license for which broadcasters pay a group of copyright owners a fee that is redistributed among copyright owners. Broadcasters are thereby cleared from copyright infringement. The advantages of a compulsory license are that it would eliminate wasteful resources spent on filing lawsuits and monitoring P2P networks and users, which could violate users' privacy. Moreover, consumers could download as many MP3 files as they want without fear of being sued. Finally, a compulsory license could simplify contractual disputes over which albums can be released online: there is usually a conflict of interest between copyright owners who benefit from putting an album online and artists who fear they might not be fairly compensated.

As Liebowitz (2003b) discusses, compulsory license models suffer from several shortcomings. First, making MP3 downloads legal could reduce CD sales further. Second, a tax would introduce inefficiencies to the market. Third, the right price (tax) would be difficult to compute, especially in a distant future, since it is arduous to get accurate statistics now on MP3 downloads in a given country in an internetwork environment. Fourth, it would be difficult to assess how much money should be raised by the tax, especially over a long period of time. Finally, how would the money be distributed? It should depend on the relative importance of music downloads by artists. But this statistic is hard to find and manipulatable and does not translate into the number of lost purchases (the harm).

4.3.3.4   DRM and the Music Industry

DRM = Down-Right Messy? Because DRM can be implemented in the hardware, operating system, and player, which are provided by different firms, the issue of setting standards and ensuring that all platforms are compatible cannot be neglected. For these reasons, some observers of the computer industry consider DRM as "Down-Right Messy."

DRM and Competition between Platforms Clearly, a music site needs to offer a large variety of music, at least for the music segment in which it is active. Among the record companies, it is useful to distinguish between those who are backing a particular music site and those who are not. For instance, Napster 2.0 and Sony Connect are owned by Bertelsmann and Sony, respectively. This means that the music sites have access to the available repertoire of the labels owned by the respective companies. For the time being, however, to become a major music site other labels have to be on board as well. Other labels must be assured of not being discriminated against, or must have the right to cross-license their distribution technologies. Thus, it may turn out to be a disadvantage for a music site to be owned by a major label. (Note that the incentives for Sony to start a music site are different from those of a record company, because Sony is primarily a consumer electronics firm.)

At the moment, labels multihome, that is, they offer their repertoire on different sites. This implies that the same track is available in a number of different proprietary formats. One of the open questions is whether the market will tip at some point so that eventually only one or two music sites will attract most of the traffic.

DRM to Control Ancillary Markets   Proprietary DRM can be used to control ancillary markets: the DMCA prohibits reverse engineering, and, as a consequence, Apple's DRM could use its first-mover advantage to control the portable market with its iPod player. Effectively, it creates an entry barrier to the market for portable players ("The iPod makes money. The iTunes Music Store doesn't"—Apple Senior Vice President Phil Schiller).

DRM to Control the Evolution of Technology and Business Models
Proprietary DRM can be used to control technological development: content providers can ask technology companies to comply with their business strategy if they want to distribute digital content. For instance, record companies have asked Apple to reduce the number of times a playlist can be burned to seven times, down from ten.

4.3.3.5   Examples of DRM

iTunes.com   Apple iTunes service uses the Advanced Audio Coding (AAC) format in combination with FairPlay DRM. Users can burn a playlist seven times and transfer music files to five computers. Users need to de-authorize old computers when they purchase a new one or when they sell them. This procedure is relatively straightforward. iTunes users can offer their playlists for preview to other members of the community, and offer musical gifts to other subscribers. The iPod player is compatible with music files in MP3 format.

Microsoft   Microsoft has developed its own series of DRM solutions. Their first type of DRM protection is implemented in its Windows Media Audio (WMA) music format that is used by many e-tailers and works like Apple's DRM, restricting the number of CD burns and transfers to desktop computers. The most recent DRM solution, named

Janus, can also limit the use of a music file, thus enabling business models based on subscription services to not limit the number of computers or portable players the music file can be loaded on. In terms of business strategy, it is rent versus buy.

Music.walmart.com   Walmart also offers songs in the Microsoft WMA format. Products must be downloaded within 90 days of purchase and played within 120 days. Music files can be burned ten times to a CD and transferred an unlimited number of times to a portable device. Files are downloaded to a computer and can be backed up on two additional computers. However, this procedure is not straightforward (see box 4.5). It is not possible to sell the songs, share them with friends nor offer them as gifts. This set of restrictions is common to all songs offered on the site.

BuyMusic.com   BuyMusic.com uses the Microsoft WMA format with a DRM that authorizes transfers to three to five computers and limits the number of burns to seven to ten. Different from Music.walmart .com, songs and albums are priced individually with different usage rules.

Sony   In May 2004, Sony launched its Connect store, which offers music for downloads of released and unreleased songs and remixes. Sony uses the ATRAC3 format and developed its own OpenMG and MagicGate DRM technology that is used in most of its portable CD and digital music players. The existing restrictions limit the transfer of music files to only one computer. Restrictions on the use of music files depend on the artist and the album. Music downloads are only compatible with the Sony SonicStage software and portable players that use the OpenMG and MagicGate DRM. Moreover, many Sony portable players do not accept the MP3 standard. Sony announced that it will change its compatibility policy in future portable players. Some industry analysts see the Connect store as an attempt to improve sales of Sony's portable players versus Apple's iPod and other MP3 players.

Kazaa, Altnet, and Cornerband   Kazaa tries to provide a platform for information sharing. It licenses its software free of charges. The business model is built on a two-sided marketplace in which advertisers pay for advertising and users do not receive payments for receiving advertisements. Kazaa also offers "premium content" for which users are charged. This is a pay-per-download service. Users can sample songs a limited number of times. After the sampling period, the user

Box 4.5

Backing up files with Microsoft Windows Media is not straightforward

---

1. Copy and transfer song files

Copy song file(s) and transfer (via email, on CD, or through a shared network) to a designated music folder on another computer.

2. Back up license files

Go to the Tools menu on Windows Media Player and click on License Management.

Choose the location to store the license backup files.

Click on Back Up Now to save all your license files to this location.

3. View license files

License files are hidden by default until you change your folder viewing options.

You must show hidden license files in order to transfer them to another computer.

Open the file where you placed your license backup files.

Go to the Tools menu and click Folder Options.

Select the View tab and click Show Hidden Files and Folders.

Click OK.

4. Transfer licenses to a different computer

Copy your license backup files. (Look for filenames drmv1key.bak, drmv1lic.bak, drmv2key.bak, drmv2lic.bak.)

Transfer all license files (via email, on CD, or through a shared network) to a designated music folder on the new computer.

5. Restore licenses

You must restore the licenses on the new computer before you can play the songs.

Go to the Tools menu on Windows Media Player and click on License Management.

Point to the location where you saved the license files on the new computer.

Click on Restore Now to allow Windows Media Player to access the licenses on the new computer.

Open the song to play it.

Source: Walmart.com.

sees a window with a link to a merchant site. Artemis Records has used Kazaa and other file-sharing networks to distribute music files by artists such as Lisa Loeb, Ricky Lee Jones, and Steve Earl.[18] They use a DRM technology developed by a partner of Kazaa that allows the first use for free and after that the downloaders usually must pay 99 cents to purchase the song (see Chmielewski March 31, 2004). This probably comes closest to a fee-based business model in which consumers pay per download and in which there is limited sampling.

Observation 4.8   Labels and intermediaries have undertaken a series of uncoordinated efforts to use DRM as a part of their distribution strategies.

4.3.4 Legal Downloads and New Business Models

4.3.4.1   The Demand for Legal Downloads   A 2002 survey from Ipsos-Reid (documented in Ipsos, TEMPO 2002) shows that the average respondent in the population as a whole is not eager to use online subscription services and fee-based downloads. When asked how likely the respondent would be to pay to download or stream music from the Internet if there were no free material available, only 1 percent answered that this was likely, 11 percent answered that this was somewhat likely, and an overwhelming 84 percent answered that this was not likely. While a 2003 Jupiter Research survey confirmed a strong reticence to pay for downloads in consumers who do not sample much using the Internet (last two rows of table 4.25), there is evidence that Internet users who do sample a lot are ready to pay for music—even more so if there is a charge per download rather than a subscription fee.

Table 4.25
Demand for music subscriptions and downloads in 2003 (U.S.)

Type of consumer (number sampled)	Subscriptions	Downloads	Will not pay for music
Music aficionados (357)	21%	25%	46%
Free-music fans (514)	13%	19%	60%
CD purists (280)	10%	16%	71%
Passive populace (746)	7%	10%	79%

Source: Jupiter Research 2003.

4.3.4.2 Demand from College Students It is worthwhile to take a closer look at college students because they represent an important share of music buyers. They are also typically leaders in technology adoption; future trends for the whole population can be anticipated by analyzing students' behavior. There were 14.5 million students, or 5 percent of the population, enrolled in U.S. colleges and universities in 2002. According to comScore Media Matrix, 7.7 percent of U.S. Internet users connected from college- and university-based PCs in 2001. The Harris Interactive/360 Youth fall 2002 study finds that 93 percent of college students access the Internet in a given month, 88 percent own a computer, and 56 percent have a broadband connection.

According to the Pew Internet Project (1,021 college students in March–June 2002), the percentage of college Internet users who have downloaded music is larger than the percentage of the total Internet population who have done so (60 percent compared to 28 percent overall). The college user is also three times as likely to download music on any given day (14 percent compared to 4 percent overall, a percentage similar to the respective percentage for broadband users). College students also lead other Internet users in file sharing of all kinds (44 percent against 26 percent overall). Moreover, they share files other than music in a greater proportion: 52 percent downloaded files other than music compared to 41 percent for the overall Internet population.

There is serious money to be made from college students. According to the Harris Interactive/360 Youth fall 2002 study, students spent more than $210 billion in 2002. Around two thirds of college students have paying jobs, which represents $53.9 billion in discretionary spending annually. Most of the spending goes to entertainment and leisure related expenses. College students were spending $5 billion on travel, $790 ongoing to the movies, $390 million on music concerts, $318 million on amusement parks, and $272 million on professional sporting events.

College students are high-volume music consumers and are likely to be influenced by new technological opportunities, such as P2P networks. This is documented by the fact that several websites among the top twenty sites where the total and relative amount of traffic from colleges is particularly high are related to music. All sites in tables 4.26 and 4.27 had more than one million total U.S. home, work, and college visitors in August 2002.

Table 4.26
Selected websites visited by college students (U.S.)

Website	Primary activity	Proportion of traffic that comes from college PCs
audiogalaxy.com	P2P file-sharing service	18.1%
billboard.com	Online music magazine	17.7%
imesh.com	P2P file-sharing service	17.1%
azlyrics.com	Resources for song lyrics	16.4%
winamp.com	Entertainment site for winamp downloads	15.7%
astraweb.com	Portal for MP3 and song lyrics search engines	15.5%
lyrics.com	Song lyrics search engine	14.6%

Source: comScore, 2002.

Table 4.27
Selected online purchases by college students (U.S.)

Website	Primary activity	Proportion of traffic that comes from college PCs
cdnow.com	Music retail	13.3%
allposters.com	Online poster and print store	11.8%
bestbuy.com	Electronics and media retail	11.2%
ticketmaster.com	Entertainment ticketing site	10.2%
emusic.com	Subscription MP3 music service	10.2%

Source: comScore, 2002.

4.3.4.3 Digital Music Initiatives from Established Agents Backed by Major Labels

Online distribution companies offer different listening options that we review in box 4.6. Digital music distribution is not the exclusive business of dedicated music services anymore. With the appearance of iTunes in the United States and OD2 in Europe, technology companies, as well as traditional retailers, have started to distribute music online.[19]

Dedicated Music Sites Pressplay, acquired by Roxio and distributed by Yahoo and Microsoft, offers downloads, streaming, 99-cent-per-song CD burns, and a catalog that includes more than 300,000 songs. Pressplay is a subscription service with limited portable downloading, available for U.S. residents (as of March 2003). For $9.95 per month, it allows unlimited streaming and downloading; for $17.95 per month, it

Box 4.6
Listening options for digital music

À-la-carte download   Most services allow users to pay a single fee for one song, which they download to their PC hard drive or to a portable music player.

Tethered download   These allow consumers to "rent" tracks for a given period of time. These tracks are nontransferable to portable music players, but sit on the consumer's PC hard drive until they "time-out" or the subscription ends. These have been popular on European services and are a good way for consumers to preview songs before they decide to buy.

Download an album   A popular option that enables consumers to pay a single fee for one album.

Download a bundle   Some services enable consumers to download a "playlist" that has been suggested by other consumers, or perhaps the artist. Such "bundles" may also include video content or artwork and photography.

Streaming   Allows the consumer to listen to a song once and is very low cost. Streaming is ideal for listening to exactly what you want without having to pay to own a copy of the song. It is the preferred option for consumers who want to explore a broad range of songs, artists, or genres.

Customized streaming   These services offer subscribers the ability to compile their own program of tracks based on their favorite genre or artist, or choose an already-compiled program.

Source: IFPI Online Music Report 2004, p. 9.

allows an additional ten monthly portable downloads (as of March 2003). Pressplay offers content from the five big labels, namely EMI, Sony, Universal, Warner, and BMG, and is pushed by MSN and Yahoo!, as well as MP3.com. Pressplay offers songs in the WMA format. Downloaded files, which are not portable, can be listened to only on the computer where the file was downloaded and can be backed up to one additional computer. Such files can be listened to only as long as a subscription is active. Recently, Roxio also bought the Napster brand and now combines both services under the name Napster 2.0.

Similar offers are available from real.com with its Harmony DRM that favors compatibility between formats and portable players, and listen.com, which distributes Rhapsody, an online subscription service. Harmony, distributed by RealNetworks, is a subscription service that allows downloads, streams, and access to a limited number of CD burns per month; it's catalog includes more than 250,000 songs. Rhapsody has a $9.95 monthly subscription fee that allows access to unlimited streams and 99-cent-per-song burns; the catalog includes more than 250,000 songs. In the past, Sony started a number of initiatives, such as the Sony Connect store. On its website, Sony has offered its U.S. customers CDs on demand (as of March 2003); for example, each customer can select twelve Bob Dylan tracks (in any sequence) and Sony will press the custom CD on demand (charging $15 plus shipping). Sony also offers official bootleg CDs and MP3s for all U.S. concerts for $15 plus shipping (as of March 2003); This can be seen as an attempt to appropriate revenues that would otherwise be lost to illegal bootlegs. Consumers sign up before the concert and then they have access to MP3 downloads one day after the concert; they receive the CD about two weeks after the concert.

Technology Companies Apple's iTunes Music Store offers downloads of 200,000 tracks at 99 cents per single and $9.99 per album using Apple's AAC format, and some music videos. A year after its creation, 70 million music files had been sold; this increased to 150 million by November 2004. Buyers can store their music on five computers (up from three) and burn a playlist seven times (down from ten). No subscription service is planned. iTunes also offers the ability for consumers to offer their playlist for preview and purchase to other consumers. Microsoft aggregates at windowsmedia.com promotional music videos, Internet radio stations, and downloads from a variety of sites using its Windows Media technology; Microsoft's MSN Web portal also offers various music selections, from ad-supported and premium radio stations to music videos and free downloads. Microsoft is also pushing its Media Center PC, which will be a convergence of different technologies from the computer and electronics industries. Microsoft Janus DRM allows users to stream content from online and to play on portable players for a limited time. It is implemented in all songs that are sold on the recently introduced MSN Music site. The music service is fully integrated in the Web portal msn.com and the Windows Media player. Standard features are available such as thirty-second preview, fan recommendations, and artist and video pages. Note that Microsoft and Apple follow two very different business strategies, that is, rent versus sell.

RealNetworks offers free access to Internet radio and some music videos on its website, recently including an exclusive live concert clip of The Vines, as well as paid content through its music store Internet service. The basic service is free, and the premium subscription service costs $9.95 per month. Similar streaming models have been proposed by Napster 2.0 and Musicmatch. In addition, RealNetworks develops an interoperability policy that ensures that songs purchased from different stores can be played with the RealPlayer. Sony's Connect store is also welcoming the distribution of international and independent labels. Some industry analysts see the Connect store as an attempt to improve sales of Sony's MiniDisc Player as an alternative to Apple's iPod and other MP3 players. The price of individual songs and albums can vary from one artist to the other and over time, and consumers can offer gift coupons to other subscribers of the store.

Retailers   Amazon.com offers free downloads in MP3 and Liquid Audio formats from major artists and newcomers, with customer ratings. Tower Records offers free and retail downloads in MP3, Microsoft Windows Media, and Liquid Audio formats. Singles cost between 99 cents and $1.49, while albums typically sell for $9.99. Meanwhile, Walmart sells individual songs at 88 cents and has a DRM policy that does not vary across artists and albums. Buymusic.com, however, sells individual songs and albums at different prices and has a DRM policy adapted to each product. Table 4.28 presents the differences between the major services' business models.

To sum up, new business models propose music experience from à-la-carte downloads to customized streaming and transfer to portable players. Most services offer a technology that allows users to exchange audio and video samples, playlists, and recommendations.

Observation 4.9   Most new business models combine information-push and information-pull technologies. Both streaming and downloading services are available.

4.3.4.4   Other Initiatives   In this section, we list a number of recent initiatives by artists and P2P network developers.

Artists Initiatives   Matador Records offered free MP3 singles from its most active bands, such as Wilco, posted on the label's website. The company also allowed downloads of the album "Yankee Foxtrot Hotel" for much of the year before its release, most likely to create word-of-mouth. The follow-up EP "More Like the Moon" was released free on WilcoWorld.net. Madonna sold her "American Life" single on Madonna.com, and Kristin Hersh allows fans to subscribe to a series

Table 4.28
Major services' business models

Service	Core offer	Payment method	Unique offering
iTunes	À-la-carte downloads	Pay per song, music allowance accounts, gift certificates sold at iTunes and Apple stores	Audiobooks, exclusive tracks and on-demand videos, customized playlists, transfer to portable player (iPod)
Napster 2.0	Track streaming, customized streaming, à-la-carte downloads	Monthly subscription for Napster Premium, Napster Card sold at more than 14,000 retailers	Playlist recommendations and sharing, exclusive material, transfer to portable player
Rhapsody	Track streaming, customized streaming	Monthly subscription with additional charge for CD burning	Access music from any PC
Musicmatch	Track streaming, customized streaming, à-la-carte downloads	One-time fee for Musicmatch Jukebox Plus, pay per song thereafter	Transfer to portable players, personalized CD package, new music recommendation based on customer playlist
OD2 (branded by HMV, Fnac, MSN, etc.)	Track streaming, à-la-carte downloads	Prepayment credits, pay per song, subscription	Discounts for products paid with credits, transfer to portable player, news and special features with artists

Source: IFPI Online Music Report 2004, p. 7.

of MP3 demos before albums are released through ThrowingMusic .com.

P2P Networks—Legal Downloads Kazaa also signed a deal with Cornerband.com to distribute work by signed artists and to promote so-called emerging artists on its network. Cornerband.com explains: "Thirty new subscribing bands will be selected on a quarterly basis through a combination of an online rating system and a panel of expert judges from the music industry enabling every band and musician a chance to receive mass exposure to the millions of KMD users." (Cornerband.com website 2003). The rating is done by users of Kazaa and Cornerband.com. Cornerband.com writes of itself: "Cornerband .com is an online music community dedicated to the promotion and distribution of secure, downloadable music from emerging artists. The online music service is available on the Kazaa Media Desktop ("KMD"), the most widely distributed peer-to-peer application in the world for finding, downloading, and playing musical content, or directly at www.cornerband.com. This service enables the musicians in the Cornerband.com community to gain exposure to the millions of KMD users worldwide. All Cornerband.com artists will have control over the secure distribution of their music, including the way in which songs are downloaded, sampled and priced to the consumer."

The business model of Cornerband.com can be seen as a partial substitute to traditional labels. It offers online DRM-protected distribution, online sales of CDs, and merchandising (via CD Street). It also selects and promotes emerging artists. However, the company describes itself as an entry ticket into the music industry: the service allows "bands and musicians to securely reach consumers in efforts to secure a major record label contract." (Cornerband.com website 2003). Altnet uses this business model to distribute legal content on Kazaa. Most of the files can be previewed for a set length of time. At the end of the trial period, the user is prompted with information about purchasing the file. Each file has an individual pricing and license agreement.

At MP3.com, free MP3 files are available for downloading (as part of the Vivendi music empire). It promotes artists and lets them sell their CDs through the portal. To do so, artists can select between different service levels of an artist program—the lowest being provided for free, the highest at $99.99 per year (as of March 2003). When artists sell CDs through MP3.com, they upload music in the MP3 format and order material for their cover and booklet. MP3.com then presses the CDs and distributes them through its portal. The artists control the pricing of the CDs and receive 50 percent (or 60 percent if they signed up to the highest level of the program) of all revenues exceeding $3.99 per CD. MP3.com can also be seen as a partial substitute to the traditional distribution channel through a label.

Observation 4.10 There have been several attempts to bypass the major labels or use P2P networks in the selection and the distribution of acts.

4.3.4.5 A New Landscape for the Music Industry To get consumers on a music site, price and nonprice strategies are important additions to music services. The most common pricing strategy is to charge ninety-nine cents for a download—this is, for instance, the pricing strategy chosen by iTunes and OD2. Survey data suggest that subscription-based models are less popular among Internet users, but this is a snapshot depending on time and space (see section 4.3.1).

An important part of the nonprice strategy is the choice of DRM, which defines the potential use of a download. Ceteris paribus, flexibility is appreciated by users. However, labels are likely to reject uses that could reduce CD sales.

It is important to stress that many popular songs and albums have not been cleared to be distributed in digital format online. For instance, the songs of the Beatles can not be purchased in compressed format. Other artists' songs are not for download either: Led Zeppelin, AC/DC, Grateful Dead, and Garth Brooks, to name a few. Other songs can be downloaded only with the full album, including albums by Madonna, Red Hot Chili Peppers, Radiohead (see Ahrens January 19, 2004). Microsoft's MSN Music store plans to offer album-only downloads, which should attract artists such as Metallica who are reluctant to license individual songs.

In addition to DRM, which defines the use of digital music, music sites can enhance the value of a download by providing additional information, additional songs, discussion forums, cross-recommendations, and communication capabilities, which can create virtual music communities like that which made Napster so popular. A music site backed by companies that can provide some of these services (such as Amazon, for instance) is in a stronger position.

The final question is where the money will be made. Companies selling complementary products, such as Apple's iPod, Sony's portable players, and Microsoft's software, may be well placed. This certainly explains Nokia's interest in entering the digital music distribution market. Since devices from Apple and Sony cannot be declared the winners of the battle yet, it is not clear whether a particular complementary product will turn out to be an advantage or a disadvantage. The success of the music site is simply tied to the success of the device and of the DRM standard. Although the practice of tying products is frowned upon by competition authorities, it remains to be seen how their traditional arguments apply to an emerging industry.

Well-known online or hybrid retailers and information sites also have some comparative advantages. They start with a users' base and enjoy brand recognition. Retailers such as Amazon or Fnac can sell products such as DVDs and concert tickets related to the download.

They should be able to offer attractive bundles. Moreover, some retailers have developed already the practice of acquiring information on how well a product is doing. For instance, Amazon has a system of recommendations and a lot of information on its users, which is also valuable to companies selling music downloads. This means that OD2 together with Internet retailers could become successful even though it lacks complementary products such as software or portable devices.

4.4 Conclusion

We have argued that file sharing and other forms of online music distribution can be used as

- a device for consumers to test new music;
- an advertising tool;
- an instrument to open the market to small artists; and
- a source of information on downloads, which is valuable to producers in order to select products and resolve situations of asymmetric information.

We infer from the success of Apple's iTunes that digital music downloaded from the Internet will partly replace music sales on traditional format. In this sense, it would become just another channel through which music is distributed: instead of selling records through record stores, the labels sell downloads through music sites.

However, new online distribution technologies offer new ways to acquire information on consumers and products and are likely to decrease the role of labels. Music sites can collect detailed user information, which allows them to make targeted offers to users. They could become efficient at spotting new trends and potential stars. Also, the promotion of acts could be done partly by the music sites themselves. This means that music sites would take over some of the functions that in the past have belonged to the labels.

This does not mean the death of the big labels, but it is an open question whether Internet music sites will at least reduce the role of labels in selecting music. Moreover, because of vanishing economies-of-scale, the rationale among record companies for staying big has weakened and a larger number of artists could bypass labels. For this to happen, revenues from downloads and complementary products must become an important part of industry revenues.

Notes

1. We would like to thank Marc Bourreau for helpful comments on earlier drafts of this guide.

2. All survey data reported in this article were conducted in the United States unless specified otherwise.

3. www.riaa.com/news/newsletter/press2000/052500.asp.

4. Some complementary products typically are offered by the artists themselves. We discuss the most important one, namely live concerts.

5. Some details are missing to simplify the diagram. For instance, a music band typically has a contract with a manager.

6. Sony Music and BMG merged their music units to form Sony BMG Music Entertainment in August 2004.

7. In principle, it is always possible to record music from an Internet radio on analog devices and convert it to a digital file. This is referred to as the "analog hole." However, doing so is time-consuming and results in a degraded technical quality of the song.

8. From year 2000 onward cassette sales contribute little to overall music sales. However, the replacement effect may continue to work for a while beyond 2000 because consumers need time to build up their CD collections.

9. There is a another rationale for the existence of network effects among copiers using file-sharing technologies. Namely, the fact that the speed of downloading music files grows along with the size of the network. However, if there is only a small number of users sharing a large number of files, the extent of network effects will be limited (see Peitz and Waelbroeck 2003a).

10. For an elaborate and critical discussion of the current empirical evidence see chapter 5 in this volume by Liebowitz.

11. Bounie, Bourreau, and Waelbroeck (2005) administered an anonymous online survey in two French graduate schools from May 26 to June 3, 2004. This allowed them to analyze the factors that influence the probability of increasing CD purchases after acquiring MP3 files and those that influence the probability of decreasing CD consumption. Their estimation results suggest that there are two populations of music consumers: people who sample a lot (the explorers) and those who do not sample (the pirates). They argue that MP3 consumption leads to an amplification of consumption patterns: music fans use MP3 files to discover new genres, artists, and albums, which tends to increase their purchases of CDs, while people with little interest in music use MP3 files as a direct substitute for CDs.

12. If consumers own the original CDs and copy them for their own use, for example, for playing in the car or at work, this does not constitute a copyright infringement.

13. Before installing the Kazaa Media Desktop software users have to accept the end-user license agreement (as of March 2003). It contains the following paragraphs:

5 Things you need to do when using the Kazaa Media Desktop. 5.1 It is your responsibility to ensure that you obtain all consents, authorizations and clearances in any data owned or controlled by third parties that you transmit, access or communicate to others

using the Kazaa Media Desktop. 5.2 Sharman will not be liable in any way:...5.2.3 for any allegations or findings of infringement of copyright or other proprietary rights as a result of your use of the Software. 6 Copyright Infringement 6.1 Sharman respects copyright and other laws. Sharman requires all Kazaa Media Desktop users to comply with copyright and other laws. Sharman does not by the supply of the Software authorize you to infringe the copyright or other rights of third parties. 6.2 As a condition to use the Software, you agree that you must not use the Software to infringe the intellectual property or other rights of others, in any way. The unauthorized reproduction, distribution, modification, public display, communication to the public or public performance of copyrighted works is an infringement of copyright. 6.3 Users are entirely responsible for their conduct and for ensuring that it complies with all applicable copyright and data-protection laws. In the event a user fails to comply with laws regarding copyrights or other intellectual property rights and data-protection and privacy, such a user may be exposed to civil and criminal liability, including possible fines and jail time....15 Termination 15.1 It is your responsibility to comply with the terms of this License and to obey the laws of your jurisdiction. Your rights under this License will terminate immediately and without prior notice if: you violate any term of this License, including violating any applicable laws or rights of any third party including the intellectual property rights of any such third party. You may be subject to legal action if you continue to use the Kazaa Media Desktop in violation of this License.

(Other file-sharing software contain similar provisions.) In its written statements the Kazaa website discourages the sharing of those files that infringe copyright or other proprietary rights (as of March 2003), quite in contrast to some other websites offering file-sharing software.

14. The latter creates serious legal issues as it belongs to an open-source movement and is not backed up by a commercial company.

15. We may have to modify our observation in the future if other courts (and in particular the U.S. Supreme Court) find differently. When this chapter was written decisions were still outstanding.

16. Offering different transfer possibilities allows the targeting of different consumer segments. To the extent that one of the offerings is more restricted than the other, the arguments found in the literature on damaged goods initiated by Deneckere and McAfee (1996) are applicable. More generally, versioning allows for second-degree price discrimination. For an overview see chapter 6 by Belleflamme in this volume.

17. This section builds on Gasser (2004) and Bechtold (2003).

18. As a side remark, this discredits the major labels' claim that the file-sharing systems such as Kazaa do not have a significant legitimate use. Also, the fact that some labels use download data to promote acts shows that labels derive some benefits from file-sharing systems such as Kazaa.

19. Part of this information on business models is taken from ClNet News.com, "State of the Art: A Medium Reborn," May 28, 2003.

References

Ahrens, F. (2004), "Music Fans Find Online Music Box Half-Empty," Washington Post, January 19.

Bakos, J. Y., E. Brynjolfsson, and G. Lichtman (1999), "Shared Information Goods," *Journal of Law and Economics* 48, 117–156.

Bechtold, S. (2003), "The Present and Future of Digital Rights Management: Musing on Emerging Legal Problems," in Becker et al. (eds.), "Digital Rights Management—Technological, Economic, Legal and Political Aspects," Springer, 597–654.

Besen, S. M., and S. N. Kirby (1989), "Private Copying, Appropriability, and Optimal Copying Royalties," *Journal of Law and Economics* 32, 255–280.

Boorstin, E. (2004), "Music Sales in the Age of File Sharing," Senior thesis, Princeton University.

Bounie, D., M. Bourreau, and P. Waelbroeck (2005), "Pirates or Explorers? Analysis of Music Consumption in French Graduate Schools," mimeo.

Chmielewski, D. (2004), "Music Labels Use File-Sharing Data to Boost Sales," Mercury News, March 31, 2004.

Conner, K. R., and R. P. Rumelt (1991), "Software Piracy—An Analysis of Protection Strategies," *Management Science* 37, 125–139.

Connolly, M., and A. Krueger (2004), "Rockonomics: the Economics of Popular Music," forthcoming in: *Handbook of Cultural Economics*, Elsevier, Amsterdam.

Deneckere, R., and P. McAfee (1996), "Damaged Goods," *Journal of Economics and Management Strategy* 5, 149–174.

Duchêne, A., and P. Waelbroeck (2003), "Legal and Technological Battle in Music Industry: Information Pull vs. Information Push Technologies," mimeo, CERAS-ENPC, Paris.

Gasser, U. (2004), "iTunes: How Copyright, Contract, and Technology Shape the Business of Digital Media—A Case Study," Berkman Center for Internet & Society at Harvard Law School Research Publication, no. 2004–2007.

Gopal, R. D., S. Bhattacharjee, and G. L. Sanders (2004), "Do Artists Benefit From Online Music Sharing?" mimeo.

Gordon, W. J. (1982), "Fair Use as Market Failure: A Structural and Economic Analysis of the Betamax Case and its Predecessors," *Columbia Law Review* 82, 1600.

IFPI (2003a), The Recording Industry in Numbers, 2002.

IFPI (2003b), IFPI Network, December 2003.

IFPI (2004a), The Recording Industry in Numbers, 2003.

IFPI (2004b), Online Music Report.

Landes, W., and R. Posner (1989), "An Economic Analysis of Copyright Law," *Journal of Legal Studies* 18, 325.

Lessig, L. (2001), "The Future of Ideas: The Fate of the Commons in a Connected World," Random House.

Liebowitz, S. (1985), "Copying and Indirect Appropriability: Photocopying of Journals," *Journal of Political Economy* 93, 945–957.

Liebowitz, S. (2002), "Re-thinking the Networked Economy: The Real Forces that Drive the Digital Marketplace," Amacom Press, New York.

Liebowitz, S. (2003a), "Will MP3 Downloads Annihilate the Record Industry? The Evidence So Far," in G. Libecap (ed.), "Advances in the Study of Entrepreneurship, Innovation, and Economic Growth," JAI Press.

Liebowitz, S. (2003b), "Alternative Copyright Systems: The Problem with a Compulsory License," mimeo.

Liebowitz, S. (2005), "Pitfalls in Measuring the Impact of File-sharing," CESifo Economic Studies 51, 435–473.

Novos, I. E., and M. Waldman (1984), "The Effects of Increased Copyright Protection: An Analytic Approach," *Journal of Political Economy* 92, 236–246.

Oberholzer, F., and K. Strumpf (2004), "The Effect of File Sharing on Record Sales: An Empirical Analysis," mimeo.

Peitz, M., and P. Waelbroeck (2003), "Piracy of Digital Products: A Critical Review of the Economics Literature," CESifo Working Paper 1071, electronic document available at www.ssrn.com/sol3/papers.cfm?abstract_id=466063.

Peitz, M., and P. Waelbroeck (2004a), "File-sharing, Sampling and Music Distribution," International University in Germany Working Paper 26/2004, electronic document available at www.ssrn.com/sol3/papers.cfm?abstract_id=652743.

Peitz, M., and P. Waelbroeck (2004b), "The Effect of Internet Piracy on Music Sales: Cross-Section Evidence," *Review of Economic Research on Copyright Issues* 1, 71–79.

Peitz, M., and P. Waelbroeck (2004c), "The Effect of Internet Piracy on CD Sales: Cross-Section Evidence," CESIfo Working Paper 1122, electronic document available at www.ssrn.com/sol3/papers.cfm?abstract_id=511763.

Philips, C. (2001), "Record Label Chorus: High Risk, Low Margin," *Los Angeles Times*, May 31, 2001.

RIAA (2005), "Cost of a CD," electronic document available at www.riaa.com/news/marketingdata/cost.asp.

Rob, R., and J. Waldfogel (2004), "Piracy in the High C's: Music Downloading, Sales Displacement, and Social Welfare in a Sample of College Students," NBER Working Paper 10874.

Samuelson, P. (2003), "DRM, {And, Or, Vs.} the Law," Communications of the AACM 46, 41–45.

Shy, O., and J. Thisse (1999), "A Strategic Approach to Software Protection," *Journal of Economics and Management Strategy* 8, 163–190.

Sobel, L. S. (2003), "DRM as an Enabler of Business Models: ISPs as Digital Retailers," Berkeley Technology Law Journal 18, 667–695.

Takeyama, L. N. (1994), "The Welfare Implications of Unauthorized Reproduction of Intellectual Property in the Presence of Network Externalities," *Journal of Industrial Economics* 42, 155–166.

Takeyama, L. N. (2003), "Piracy, Asymmetric Information and Product Quality," in Wendy J. Gordon and Richard Watt (eds.), "The Economics of Copyright: Developments in Research and Analysis," Edward Elgar, Cheltenham.

Vogel, H. (2004), "Entertainment Industry Economics: A Guide for Financial Analysis," 6th edition, Cambridge University Press, Cambridge, UK.

Zentner, A. (2003), "Measuring the Effect of Online Piracy on Music Sales," mimeo, University of Chicago.

5 Economists Examine File Sharing and Music Sales

Stan J. Liebowitz

5.1 Introduction

The decline in sales of music CDs and the recording industry's attempts to reverse the decline have been much in the news over the past few years. Since this decline began at the same time that file sharing became popular, and since file sharing would be expected to lead to a decline in sales, file sharing is the leading candidate among possible causes of this decline.

The recording industry has tried to stem this decline in the United States and several other countries by suing, or threatening to sue, individuals heavily engaged in file sharing. The motion picture industry has expressed concern that its sales are likely to suffer a similar fate to that of the sound recording industry if nothing is done to stem the unrestricted use of file-sharing software, and it too has engaged in lawsuits against file sharers. These lawsuits have attracted a good deal of publicity, discussion, and criticism. A rather influential school of thought has formed in opposition to the corporate players in these industries, and these lawsuits have provided fodder for their critiques of traditional copyright.[1]

At the center of the file-sharing debate is the empirical issue of whether or not file sharing decreases sales. I should note, particularly given the prominence given to this point in chapter 8 by Gayer and Shy, that file sharing can have a strong negative impact on sales even when a majority of downloads do not replace a sale. There are several estimates that the number of music files exchanged on file-sharing networks is larger than the number purchased through legitimate channels. If so, file sharing could cause a major loss of sales even if only a relatively small percentage of unauthorized downloads translated into a lost sale. Nevertheless, estimates of the number of music files downloaded in file-sharing networks varies widely (see Liebowitz 2004b).

In this chapter I examine the different empirical methodologies that have been chosen by economists in an attempt to shed some light on this issue. The studies use different methodologies but nevertheless find, almost unanimously, that file sharing has led to a serious decline in record sales, except for one highly publicized study that reaches very different, and in my opinion, highly implausible conclusions.

5.2 Background

Sound recordings, movies, and television occupy the large bulk of our time spent on leisure activities, with the average American watching four and a half hours of television and listening to more than three hours of music each day.[2] The advertising industry is primarily based around these industries, as is the consumer electronics industry, which includes all forms of stereo equipment, televisions, DVD players, VCRs, and so forth. Sometimes it appears that the youth of advanced economies are interested in little else besides music, movies, and video games. Chapter 4 in this book by Peitz and Waelbroeck provides a useful description of much of this activity.

The products of these entertainment industries have proven amenable to digitization, allowing them to be transferred over peer-to-peer file-sharing networks.[3] Napster was the first well-known peer-to-peer file-sharing system, but others have followed in the wake of the preliminary injunction that effectively shut Napster down. Current replacements have surpassed Napster in popularity. As examples, from single websites, Kazaa has been downloaded 350,000,000 times, Morpheus 131,000,000 times, and iMesh 90,000,000 times.[4] It has been claimed that file sharing represents over one third of all material transferred over the Internet and that music files are downloaded to the tune of billions of files per month, although Liebowitz (2004b) suggests that these claims may be wildly exaggerated.

In what follows I focus on the sound recording industry because that is the market that has attracted the most attention. Since most computer users have enough bandwidth to download MP3 files and also have in place the requisite CD burners that allow the listening of this music in locations not tied to a computer, this is the arena where most file sharing is taking place.

It is always useful to examine the predictions of economic theory. To that we now turn.

5.3   Economic Theory of File Sharing's Impact

One topic that has received too little attention in the recent literature is the theory underlying predicted impacts of file sharing on the marketplace.[5]

On one hand, a downloaded file can substitute for the purchase of an original CD or single song. Substitution of a free alternative is easily understood to have a negative impact on sales and does not need any more elaboration.

On the other hand, the claim has been made that users might merely use downloaded songs to become more familiar with potential music. Although this was referred to originally as the *exposure effect*,[6] it is currently called the *sampling effect*. Under this scenario users sample from available music and then purchase those songs and albums that are found to be most suitable to the tastes of the users. This sampling hypothesis is usually associated with a claim that sales will increase if consumers are allowed to become more familiar with the product before they purchase it, although, there has not been much analysis of this claim.

There is also a claim of potential network effects. As more downloaders listen to music, this theory goes, other consumers derive greater value from their legitimate purchases. It is suggested that this might lead to an increase in the sales of CDs. Gayer and Shy present such a model in their paper in chapter 8.

Finally, there is a possibility that sellers of original files can capture the value from later copies indirectly by charging a higher price of originals, a concept known as indirect appropriability.

I examine each of these last three claims in turn.

5.3.1   Sampling
Although sampling is often put forward as having a positive impact on sales, the impacts of sampling are far more subtle. Indeed a more complete analysis leads one to expect that sampling would lead to a decrease in sales in this market.

The sampling story basically argues that file sharing allows consumers to experience music in a more complete manor prior to purchase than they would have been able to do were they to use the more traditional methods of learning about music—hearing it on the radio or at a friend's house. With file sharing, listeners can become as familiar with a song as they wish, listening to it over and over again until they are certain they like it.

At that point, according to the sampling theory, the listeners go out and purchase the music. A natural question is to ask why they would purchase it when they already have the item for free. There are several possible answers. First, they might be uncomfortable listening to music they have not purchased. This discomfort might arise from a sense of honesty or a sense of wishing to support their favorite musicians. Alternatively, listeners might get to know three or four songs on an album, which then allows them to feel comfortable buying the entire album and avoid the efforts involved with downloading the rest of the album.

Assuming that sampling occurs in this manner, what would be the likely economic impacts of sampling?

Assume that those engaged in sampling have no intention of listening to MP3 files after the sample period. Instead they either purchase the music or throw it away. This is a pure analysis of sampling independent of any pirating motive.

There are few explications of the impacts of sampling.[7] Presumably, after sampling, consumers have more information about which CDs to purchase, allowing them to purchase CDs that provide greater utility than CDs purchased without sampling. Although it is natural to think that consumers would be led to purchase more CDs if CDs can provide greater utility than they did without sampling, this is not necessarily the case.

To see this it helps to analogize the CD to a candy bar, following a line of reasoning developed by Jack Hirshleifer (1971).[8] Each individual consumer has particular tastes in music, and some CDs are better than others at satisfying these tastes. Consumers, after all, do not derive utility from the CDs per se but derive enjoyment from listening to the music contained within the CD. The underlying demand can be thought of as the demand for music-listening services, which is met to differing degrees of success by various CDs. Those CDs that better satisfy the consumer can be thought of as providing more music-listening services within the fifty or so minutes of music contained within the CD. Since those CDs contain more of what the consumer wants, they can be analogized to providing consumers larger candy bars containing more of the candy that the consumer ultimately desires. Sampling has the impact of increasing the amount of music listening services on the CDs purchased.

In the candy bar case, it is natural, but wrong, to think that if candy bars remain constant in price while increasing in size, that the quantity of candy bars sold will increase. After all, each large candy bar provides more utility than a small candy bar. This is apparently the thinking of those claiming that sampling MP3s increases the sales of CDs.

The story, however, is not so simple.

First note that the price of candy (music services) is effectively lowered when the bar (CD) becomes bigger, holding the price of the candy bar (CD) constant. If the demand for candy (music services) is elastic, then revenue in the market will increase when candy (music services) goes down in price, as it does when constant-price bars (CDs) become larger. If revenues increase in this way, and the price of bars is unchanged, then more candy bars are purchased. The inverse of this story will hold when the demand for candy is inelastic. Making candy bars larger rotates the demand curve so that the price is higher at small quantities but lower at large quantities—in other words, the demand curve rotates and becomes steeper. Satiation occurs at a smaller number of bars since each bar is bigger.

Support for this style of analysis can be found in other markets, such as the introduction of cable television. Cable allowed television viewers who were previously accustomed to having a very constrained choice of broadcast signals to be able to choose from dozens of channels. This should have increased the probability that viewers would find, in any half hour period, a program more to their liking than they were likely to have found with only the limited original choices. The analogy to the sampling hypothesis is very strong since allowing viewers to find a better program in a thirty-minute television time slot is similar to allowing listeners the ability to find better selections in their choices of CD, as sampling is claimed to do.

Yet providing more choice to consumers did *not* increase the time they spent viewing television.[9] Thus the claim that providing consumers the ability to fine-tune their product selections does not necessarily increase their consumption is seen to have real-world explanatory power.

Observation 5.1 Sampling might lead to either an increase or a decrease in revenues.

There is, however, some additional information in this market that helps to resolve this imprecision. CDs are thought to have low variable costs of production and high fixed costs. It is common in theoretical models of markets like software or music to assume a zero marginal cost of production. Although this is merely a theoretical convenience, since the variable costs are clearly not zero, variable costs do appear to be quite low in the case of sound recordings.

What are some of these variable costs? The cost of a blank CD is only a few cents and putting music on CDs appears to cost less than a dollar. Although the artists normally receive a royalty that is expressed as a function of sales, those payments are usually paid up-front as a nonrefundable advance against future royalties, so for most units sold, marginal royalties paid by the producers are effectively zero. Promotional costs for CDs are usually also taken out of up-front advances, removing another potential variable cost from the variable cost column. There is a variable payment made to the composers of songs that are included in the CD, however, with a statutory maximum payment (in the United States) of approximately seventy cents per CD.[10]

It seems reasonable to conclude, therefore, that variable costs are quite low relative to the wholesale price of CDs, which is in the vicinity of twelve dollars.[11]

This datum of variable costs being a relatively unimportant component of costs provides some important additional information about elasticity of demand facing each CD. Profit maximization, when marginal costs are zero, is equivalent to revenue maximization, and the elasticity of demand is one at the profit-maximizing price.

The elasticity of demand for CDs maps directly into the elasticity of demand for music-listening services. If the price elasticity of demand for CDs equals one, so too must the price elasticity of demand for music-listening services. After all, if the marginal revenue of another unit of music service is negative, so too must be the marginal revenue of the CD containing that unit.

Because there is competition between record titles, we should expect that the elasticity of demand for music-listening services (whether defined by musical genre or the entire industry) will be less than the elasticity of demand for individual firms or individual record titles for the same reasons that price elasticities of demand for industries have lower elasticities than their constituent firms. This implies that the elasticity for the industry will be less than one.

It matters little, however, whether the price elasticity is less than one or equal to one. In either case, revenues (and profits) fall when the price is lowered.[12] The effect of sampling (more music-listening services at a constant CD price) is to lower the price of music-listening services. The net effect should be to lower the revenues generated by music-listening services. *With a price per CD that is independent of the sampling effect, this implies that the quantity of CDs will fall due to sampling.* This analysis assumes, as does the candy bar problem, that the price of CDs is exogenous to the change in music-listening services created by CDs.

5.3.2 Network Effects

Some products have network effects. These occur when consumers' values of a product change depending on the number of other users of the product. Telephones and fax machine are two examples of products where the value of those products depends on the number of individuals using those products.

It sometimes has been claimed that network effects might be important to understanding the impact of copying. Conner and Rumelt (1991), Takeyama (1994), and Shy and Thisse (1999) each examine models where the existence of unauthorized users creates additional value to the purchasers of legitimate copies and thus might increase the profits of the seller. These models are put forward usually in the context of software, where it appears to be a more natural fit, although elsewhere in this volume Gayer and Shy apply such a model to file sharing.[13]

The network effects story applied to file sharing goes like this: File sharing is likely to increase the number of individuals who listen to prerecorded music (although it is far from clear that it increases either the number of people listening to music or the amount of time spent listening to music). If there is more "consumption" of music on the part of file sharers, the value of music for non-file-sharing individuals might increase and the non-file-sharers would then be expected to purchase more music.

There are several issues to be addressed in the context of possible network effects for sound recordings. The first is whether there even are network effects at work in music listening and what the nature of those effects might be. The second is whether file sharing strengthens network effects from a regime without file sharing.

5.3.2.1   Are There Network Effects? If So, What Kind?   As normally modeled, network effects depend on the number of other users of the product. The more telephones, the more valuable it is to have a telephone. It really doesn't matter whether the other telephones are used five minutes or five hours per day; the fact that more people have them increases the value to any potential telephone owner. In these models the utility of a user is a function of the number of other users. It is easy to show, in this type of model, that having additional unauthorized users of the product might increase demand for legitimate units.

Unlike telephones, where network effects are obvious, or software, where the ability to transfer files might be important, the linkage of values between different music listeners is far less clear.

What might be the nature of network effects in music? Although it is a common event that one person hears music at a friend's house and decides to buy it, this is not sufficient for a network effect to exist. Just hearing new music is merely a form of sampling. For it to be a network effect, the value of the music once it has been heard must be higher because others also like to listen to this music. Alternatively, consumers may enjoy being part of a crowd and value particular songs more highly when they understand that others also listen to those songs.

Which brings us to the question of whether network effects, if they exist for musical works, have the impact mainly of shifting output from one musical composition to another or whether they have the impact of changing the overall size of the market. The question that almost never is addressed, but crucially needs to be, is do consumers need to be listening to the same exact music for the network effect to operate? We can refer to these as *specific network effects*. Specific network effects could easily imply that any particular song might benefit from unauthorized copying since that song might become more valuable to purchasers of legitimate copies as the number of listeners of illegitimate versions increases. But specific network effects work to rearrange the sales of individuals songs and do not necessarily have any impact on the overall sales of songs or CDs. Specific network effects work mainly to allocate a consumer's utility from one CD to another depending on shifts in popularity, and they can have a neutral or negative impact on overall sales.

Yet it is possible that the act of listening to music, any music, increases the value of that music to others when they listen to it.

This type of *general network effect* implies that purchasers of CDs have greater value for CDs the more other people listen to music in general. Since just about everyone listens to music, the factor that would affect the utility of users could not be the number of listeners but would need to be something like the total man-hours of music listening. Note that it is not only the number of man-hours listening to prerecorded music. Radio equally should be able to impact this network effect. Note that, under these assumptions, any type of increase in overall music listening would increase the demand for CDs from those who do not engage in file sharing.

Is there any reason to believe that such general network effects are at work? I am not aware of any direct evidence on this point, but it does not seem terribly likely that music listeners care very much about how much music everyone else listens to. Why should they? Specific network effects seem far more likely to occur.

Observation 5.2   Network effects based on quantity of music listened to seem unlikely to be important.

5.3.2.2 Would File Sharing Increase Network Effects?   Let us assume that there are such general network effects so that the utility of purchasing any particular CD increases as other individuals listen to more music. This general network effect is most consistent with the theoretical models mentioned at the beginning of this chapter. Nevertheless, those models demonstrate, at most, that there are certain theoretical conditions under which general network effects might benefit music sellers.

A precondition for such a result is that file sharing actually increase the man-hours spent listening to music since that is the mechanism that would lead to increased value for CDs. It seems unlikely that file sharing will actually increase the total time spent listening to music, however.

It usually is assumed that file sharing must increase music listening since songs are made available for free that otherwise would require payment. It is a truism to economists that if the price is lowered the quantity consumed must increase. But in fact the alternative to file sharing might not be the purchase of CDs, but instead might be the activity of listening to radio. Radio is another free method for music listening. Although file sharing is likely to increase the time spent listening to nonbroadcast music, it will not necessarily increase the time spent overall listening to music. It is true that file sharing is likely to give consumers a better choice of music to listen to since consumers cannot control what is on the radio but can control the choice of downloaded music. But just because an hour of listening to downloaded files might provide greater utility to listeners than an hour listening to radio does not mean that file sharing will increase the time spent listening to music. We are back, here, to the candy bar story.

Observation 5.3   It is unlikely that there are new network effects at work for file sharing that were not operating already for broadcast radio.

Thus for file sharing to increase record sales due to network effects, several rather long chains of possibilities all need to go the right way. First, network effects need to be general and not specific, which is questionable. Second, file sharing needs to increase the general consumption of music, which is questionable. And finally, the network effects need to increase the demand by those who purchased CDs prior to file sharing by more than the effect of a free substitute that diminishes demand. These are a set of conditions that seem highly unlikely to occur. This is why network effects seem an unlikely factor to eliminate the negative impact of file sharing on the sales of legitimate purchases.

5.3.3   Indirect Appropriability

The final impact of copying that might apply to file sharing is indirect appropriability. This is a concept coined in Liebowitz (1985) and analyzed for the case of file sharing in Liebowitz (2002), which I summarize later in this section. It has recently been discussed by Boldrin and Levine (2004), whose work was then critiqued by Klein et al. (2002). The basic idea is that originals from which copies are made might undergo an increase in demand as those making copies incorporate the extra value derived by the users of unauthorized copies.

If, for example, everyone who purchased a CD made one cassette to play in their automobile, then the demand for the original CD would increase by the value of being able to make the tape, and the producers of CDs could capture some of this higher value by increasing the CD price, as would happen when demand increased. This value is captured indirectly since there is no direct payment made by the user of the copy. A precondition for this is that the value from the copy needs to be transmitted to the buyer of the original.

For indirect appropriability to work, however, one of two additional conditions must hold. First, the variability in the number of copies made from each original must be small, as in the example above. Or else the seller needs to be able to charge higher prices for those originals from which the most copies are made, as in the real-world example of photocopies. The most heavily photocopied copyright materials are journals, and most photocopying of journals takes place in libraries. Thus publishers of journals were and are able to charge higher prices to libraries than they charge to individual subscribers to take account of photocopying and indirectly appropriate some of the value from copying. Support for this thesis came from empirical work revealing that the now common practice of libraries paying higher prices than individuals was practically unheard of prior to the advent of the photocopier, and the most heavily copied journals were also those with the greatest price differential.

Indirect appropriability seems highly unlikely to work in the case of file sharing. First, it is unlikely that the value received by downloaders from file-sharing networks is registered with those making the file available. Second, there is great variability in the number of copies made from each original. Third, it is not possible to identify the originals that are going to be copied to file-sharing networks.

Observation 5.4   The mechanisms that allow indirect appropriability to function appear unable to function in the case of file sharing.

5.4   The Basic Case Against File Sharing

Data on the sales of recorded music tend to be available on a yearly basis from organizations of record producers, such as the Recording Industry Association of America (RIAA) and the International Federation of the Phonographic Industry (IFPI). The United States is by far the largest single market.

Figure 5.1 represents the per capita sale of full-length albums sold in the United States since 1972.[14] The recent decline in sales is readily apparent. Clearly, there are yearly fluctuations in this series. I have stripped out the impact of singles because their decline appears to be part of a much longer secular decline quite separate from file sharing. Nevertheless, the current decline stands at 30 percent.

This recent decline is obviously the largest that has occurred in the past thirty years. In absolute terms (units per capita) it is more than

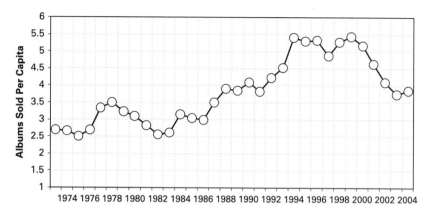

Figure 5.1
Source: RIAA.

twice as large as the next closest decline, and in percentage terms it
is nearly 50 percent larger than the next largest decline, which may
also have been impacted by copying.[15] Another way to gauge the
size of the drop is to count how many years back one would need to
go to equal the new lower sales level. In the case of the current drop,
one needs to go back to 1987—seventeen years—before encounter-
ing a year with lower sales per capita.[16] The second largest decline
ended in 1982 and erased the (much smaller) gains of the prior seven
years.

This recent decline is sufficiently striking that it would appear that
something unusual has occurred in the past few years. Such a large
change would be caused by either an unusually powerful but established factor, an unusual confluence of established factors, or some
completely new factor.

Napster, which was the forerunner of modern file sharing, came into
existence in the second half of 1999, which also happens to be the peak
year in sales. At the time, CD burners were still relatively expensive
and did not yet have a large market penetration. Although Napster
was closed down in 2001, file sharers soon migrated to other file-
sharing services.

The confluence of file sharing's birth and the decline in record sales,
the rapid growth to an immense size of file-sharing activities, and the
unusually large decline in the sound recording market are consistent
with a claim that file sharing is responsible for the decline in sales.
Add to this the predictions of economic theory that file sharing should

lead to a decline in sales and we have what appears to be a very strong case that file sharing is the cause of the decline.

In 2004 the sales slide ended, at least temporarily. This small increase was due to an increase in sales for the first half of 2004. Liebowitz (2004b) documents that this increase in the first half of 2004 occurred at the same time that file sharing decreased (due to record industry lawsuits against individual file sharers). This continued linkage between the size of file sharing and the sales of sound recordings provides additional support for the claim that file sharing harms sales. Further evidence comes from the fact that three genres of music that are less susceptible to file sharing—country, jazz, and classical—each experienced an increase in sales even while sales of other genres fell.

5.5   More Refined Analyses

Various analyses have been undertaken using different data and different approaches, and more are sure to come. Although measuring the impact of file sharing on the sound recording industry provides important information, it is only part of the analysis that would be required to answer the question about file sharing's impact on social welfare or even its impact on the industry's ability to appropriate value. Nonetheless, economists have limited themselves to the more prosaic question of whether or not file sharing has decreased revenues to the sound recording industry.[17] This is a useful first step, but we need to remember that it is only a first step.

5.5.1   Using Countries or Cities as the Unit of Analysis

There are several papers that take this approach. The idea is straightforward enough: compare changes in sales of sound recording in different geographic locations over time using some measure, such as the share of Internet users, to proxy for the impact of file sharing across these regions.

Liebowitz (2004b) examines the sales of CDs in ninety-nine U.S. cities by the number of individuals in various age groups within a city both with and without Internet access. Using Internet access as a proxy for file sharing, he finds that large young populations with Internet access reduce record sales. The coefficients are of sufficient size to support a conclusion that file sharing could explain the entire decline in sales. Peitz and Waelbroeck (2004) use data from sixteen countries for the period from 1998 to 2002. They find a 20 percent decline in the sales of music for the world. Zentner (2004) uses international cross section data from a very large number of countries during the period from 1997–1998 to 2001–2002. He finds a worldwide decline of 15 percent and a U.S. decline of 30 percent.

Difficulties with the approach used by these authors include the fact that there are many factors that differ across geographic areas that cannot be accounted for by these regressions. In some instances these areas have different levels of organized piracy; speak different languages; and have very different levels of per capita income, CD sales, Internet use, and stereo equipment. This potential heterogeneity creates a lot of noise that the statistical technique would need to cut through. For example, CD writers make downloaded music much better substitutes for the purchase of a CD. In countries where there are fewer CD writers per computer, downloading will have a smaller impact on sales. Statistics on the number of CD writers are frequently difficult to come by, thus potentially clouding any analysis. Attitudes toward piracy are also likely to differ by geographic area, which is another variable that we do not have information about. Age distributions are also likely to differ by area. The size of the data sets are usually relatively small because the number of geographic areas with data on file sharing and Internet use is not large, making analyses using these data sets less likely to find statistically significant results.

Therefore, it is either surprising or fortuitous that the results that have been found are as strong as they have been.

5.5.2 Using Records as the Unit of Analysis

There are two papers using this approach: a highly publicized paper by Oberholzer and Strumpf (O&S) and a dissertation by Blackburn.[18] Oberholzer and Strumpf were allowed access to actual download logs on a server that was part of a file-sharing system, whereas Blackburn used data provided by Big Champagne Online Media Measurement. Oberholzer and Strumpf have the advantage of having actual downloads, but the disadvantage of have information from only a single, small part of the file-sharing endeavor. Blackburn's data is based on the entire industry but does not directly measure downloads, instead having the number of files available on hard drives for individuals to download. Both papers assume that their samples are representative of the entire market and provide some evidence to support this view. Both papers then match their estimates of music downloads to the recordings where the songs appeared and then both papers used data from SoundScan to compare the downloads of CDs to the sales of CDs. Nevertheless, these two papers come to diametrically opposed conclusions.

Each paper finds that for the average CD, file sharing has a negligible impact. Of course, it is incorrect to give each CD equal weight if the purpose of the analysis is to determine the overall impact of file sharing on CD sales, since a small number of popular CDs are responsible for the dominant share of industry sales. Blackburn interacts a measure of prior artist popularity with his measure of downloading and finds that file sharing has a positive impact on relatively unknown artists, but more importantly, has a strong negative impact on CDs from more popular artists, leading him to conclude that file sharing has a large negative impact on record sales. Oberholzer and Strumpf used two techniques to determine how their measured impact differed by type of album. In the original version of their paper, they divided their sample into quartiles based on how successful the album was in the market, and found that file sharing had a small, insignificant negative impact on the less successful albums, but a large positive impact that was on the border of statistical significance for the more successful albums. This result is, in my opinion, so contrary to expectations that they most likely indicate a serious problem somewhere in their analysis. The newer version of this paper removes the tables providing details of the regression results by quartiles. Instead the authors use interaction terms (based on prior popularity) similar to those of Blackburn and produce a result strikingly at odds with their prior analysis: now the more popular artists are negatively impacted by file sharing, although, contrary to Blackburn's results, they are not significant. To my mind, current popularity is more important than past popularity, and breaking up the sample by the success of the actual album is the more natural way to test for these impacts, and both papers would benefit from reporting such results.

There are several potential problems with this methodology. First, it is unclear that an analysis using records as the units of observation can provide information about the impacts on the entire industry, as opposed to the impacts on individual recordings. There is a potential fallacy-of-composition problem here. Just as the impact of advertising on a firm's sales may be very different than the impact of advertising on industry sales, so too the impact of downloading on individual CDs may be very different from the impact of downloading on the entire recording industry.

Even ignoring this potential fallacy-of-composition problem, there are other difficulties in these analyses. There is a serious simultaneity problem in the data because popular songs are going to be both heavily purchased and heavily downloaded. Overcoming such a simultaneity problem is no easy task and the major thrust of both of these papers is in trying to overcome that simultaneity.

Oberholzer and Strumpf and Blackburn use very different instruments to try to overcome the simultaneity. Blackburn uses the impact of RIAA lawsuits and O&S use variables such as the number of German schoolchildren on holiday, which appears to me to be a very problematic variable.[19]

The difficulty with choosing proper instruments is illustrated by comparing the O&S estimates for their pooled sample in the first paper and those in their revised paper. In their first version of the paper, they use several instruments and yet the coefficient on downloads (which is biased upward due to the aforementioned simultaneity) actually increases, although the diagnostic tests performed by O&S do not indicate any problems. Perhaps in response to criticisms, O&S add an additional instrument into the latter paper (misspelled song titles) and the coefficient in this version declines to a less outrageous level. Since their diagnostics did not indicate any problems in their original paper, why should we believe that the now seemingly more reasonable results are correct? Perhaps the addition of even more instruments will further change the coefficients?

5.5.3 Using Surveys

There are four papers in this group based upon surveys. Both Hong (2004) and Michel (2004) use data from the Consumer Expenditure survey.[20] Rob and Waldfogel (2004) use data based on a survey of college students, and Zentner (2004) uses data based upon a survey of consumers in several European countries.[21]

All these studies conclude that file sharing is harmful to record sales. Michel finds that file sharing causes a decline larger than the decline that would have occurred naturally, while Hong finds that file sharing causes a decline less than half of the actual decline. Zentner finds a decline in sales of 8 percent from what they would have been as of 2002, but his results are based on seven European countries and it is not clear whether this change is larger or smaller than the actual change that occurred. Rob and Waldfogel find that each downloaded album reduces legitimate sales by half an album, which is a large enough result that it could explain the entire decline in record sales. It is not clear, however, that college students are representative of all file sharers, and thus their results might not generalize to the entire population.

As is true for all studies, there are potential problems. Surveys can be misleading because respondents may not know the answers to questions asking for detailed information about purchases, or because they are unwilling to answer questions honestly.[22] Given the highly politicized nature of file sharing, it would not be surprising if respondents tried to minimize their reported reduction in CD purchases. If so, results based on such surveys would be biased toward understating the true impact on sales.

Zentner and Rob and Waldfogel have direct information about MP3 downloading in their data, whereas Hong uses Internet access as a proxy and Michel uses computer ownership. Data used by Zentner, Michel, and Hong are no more recent than 2001, which precedes much of the CD sales decline and might well understate the impact of file sharing since CD burners were less prevalent then than they are now.

Further, the two studies with direct measures of downloading suffer from a simultaneity problem in that those individuals who are most interested in music tend to be heavy purchasers as well as heavy downloaders. Thus they each resort to instrumental variable techniques in an attempt to overcome the simultaneity. Since the key assumption of instrumental variables—that they are not correlated to the error term—cannot be tested, there always is a risk that the results might be untrustworthy.

5.5.4 Examining Alternative Explanations

Another method to help determine whether the hypothesis above is correct is to examine, at a market level, whether there are other possible explanations for the decline in record sales. There are too few data points to run a regression, but that hardly seems necessary. One can examine the set of variables that might be used in a regression analysis. Given that there is a precipitous drop in sales beginning in 2000, it is merely necessary to know if other variables changed at about the same 7time. If these other variables did not have a fairly large deviation at about that time, a regression analysis using these variables would not have concluded that these variables were responsible for the decline.

Examination of other factors that might impact record sales is the approach taken in Liebowitz (2004c). There are four main alternative factors to examine.

Table 5.1
Dependent variable = change in number of albums sold per capita

	Coefficient/ robust standard error	t	Beta	P > t
Change in disposable income per capita	0.0005341	2.67	0.35035	0.014
Change in portable penetration	1.862218	1.13	0.23302	0.27
Constant	−0.050119	−0.63	.	0.535
R-squared	0.1948	# of obs.	26	
Root MSE	0.32383			

5.5.4.1 Price and Income Changes   Although the claim is made often that price increases are responsible for the decline in CD sales, the evidence does not support this view. Real list prices have been virtually constant for the last decade, and the increasing share of the market generated by discount sellers probably has lowered the average transaction price.[23] Prices, therefore, are ruled out as an explanation of the sales decline.

Regressing first differences in albums per capita on changes in real per capita disposable income and changes in penetration of portable devices over the period from 1973 to 1999 gives the results found in table 5.1.[24] The penetration of portable players has a positive impact on album sales although the results are not statistically significant. The impact of disposable income on sales over the past thirty years is statistically significant, but a change in real per capita disposable income of one thousand dollars would alter per capita sales by only half a unit and the largest sustained decline in real per capita disposable income during the past thirty years was approximately $715 in 1979 to 1980. Although the United States experienced a recession in 2001, it was far too mild, given the historical impact of income on sales, to be able to explain the decline in sales that occurred, because per capita disposable income did not fall.

In fact from 1999 until 2004 real disposable income per capita has increased by $1,156 (in 1983 dollars), which, according to the regression, should have led to an increase in sales of 0.62 units per capita. The year-by-year sales figures after 1999, based on changes in income, are provided in figure 5.2 as the line with diamond markers. Of course,

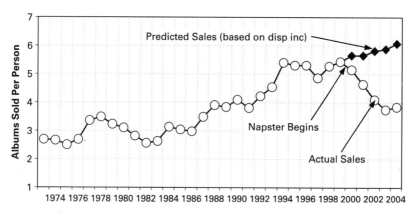

Figure 5.2

Table 5.2
Correlation of change in per capita record sales and change in revenue and unit sales

Movie revenue	0.199	1973–1999
Videogame revenue	0.265	1991–1999
Units of recorded video	0.177	1990–1999

the variables in the regression are not capable of explaining all that much of the prior changes, so there are obviously other factors at work.

5.5.4.2   The Impact of Substitutes, Such as the DVD Market   One frequently encountered claim is that record sales are down because alternatives, such as video games, movie viewership, and DVDs are up.

Table 5.2 lists correlations between yearly changes in the sound recording industry and changes in these other industries. These forms of entertainment seem to be impacted by similar factors since yearly changes in each are positively related to one another. In some instances the number of observations is quite small, however, due to the relatively recent creation of these markets.

More detailed information on whether changes in these markets can possibly explain the changes in record sales is in figure 5.3. Here we compare the changes in these markets since 1990, with 1990 values normalized to equal one. We know that record sales began their steep dive in 2000. None of the markets reported here has any sort of abrupt shift around that time, thus none is a convenient candidate to explain the decline in record sales. Although not shown, there was an abrupt

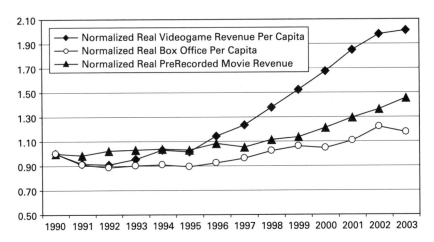

Figure 5.3
Source: Adams Media, MPAA, Ebrain.

increase in *sales* of prerecorded movies beginning in 2000, but the *rental* of movies fell during that period, with the total expenditure for prerecorded movies shown in figure 5.3. Some analysts (Oberholzer and Strumpf) have inadvertently focused on just the sale of DVDs to claim that spending on DVDs is a good candidate to explain the decline in record sales.

Which, naturally, brings us back to the question: why did these other media move generally in tandem with CD sales? One possibility is that interest in electronic gizmos, like other trends in consumer tastes, goes through cycles, and that music and video both tend to benefit from increased interest in home entertainment. Even under such circumstances, where both the video and sound recording markets are impacted by the same outside factor(s), the simple correlation that results between sales in these two markets still provides useful information. As long as that third factor continues to be the dominant impact in both markets, video and sound recordings would be expected to continue to move together. Again, the divergence of the fortunes in the CD markets indicates that something changed in the year 2000. The most viable candidate is file sharing.

5.5.4.3 Has the Music Changed?   When the record industry has a decline, critics of the industry will often claim that sales fell because the music was not interesting. Thus, it is not surprising that this has

Table 5.3
Fall 1998–Fall 2000

Age/group	Decline in listening
12+	9.30%
12–17	11.67%
18–34	13.48%
35–64	4.27%
65+	5.75%

emerged as an answer to the question: "If MP3s are not hurting the industry, what is?"

I looked at two pieces of evidence related to the "quality" of music. One was the financial success of concerts from 1990 to 2001. Although there are defects with this measure, the years 2000 and 2001 had the largest real increases in concert revenues—at the same time the record industry was experiencing unusually large decreases in revenues.

A second potential source of data is time spent listening to radio. If music is losing its luster, then radio listening should decline. Data from the past five years, shown in table 5.3, do reveal a fairly serious decline in listening—9 percent. The decline, however, is across the board, not just for groups that listen to new music. It is implausible that those over the age of sixty-five, for example, would find their attraction to radio diminished because contemporary musical compositions were not to their liking.

Further doubt about any claimed doldrums in current music composition comes from examining the listening shares of radio formats. If current music were inferior to past music, its share of listening should fall relative to old music and nonmusic categories. Yet the category of "News and Information" is up only 1.8 percent over this period. The largest decline in radio listening (51.3 percent) is for the "Adult Standards" category, which consists of music from the prerock era, hardly a repository of new music. The categories of "Contemporary Hits" and "Urban," both of which have a great deal of new music, each increased their shares (5 percent and 23 percent, respectively) and "Alternative" (modern rock) was down only 2 percent.

The evidence on musical quality is far too weak and scant to provide a great deal of confidence. Nevertheless, there is no support in the data for a claim that a decline in music quality can explain the very large decrease in sales that has occurred.

5.5.4.4 Changes in the Supply of Music Some have claimed that
the number of new titles has fallen in recent years and this decline in
new titles is responsible for the decline in sales.[25] Of course, the number of new releases is not exogenous and we would expect the quantity
of releases to fall if demand fell because of file sharing. Unless we are
willing to entertain the possibility that the supply of songwriters and
musicians suddenly dried up at the same time that file sharing started,
we would expect that changes in demand are more likely to influence
the number of new titles than would changes in underlying supply
conditions.

Further, this discussion has suffered from an imprecision in the measured numbers of new releases.[26] One factor that is clear, however, is
that the large majority of new releases, between 65 percent and 80 percent, are from independent record labels that account for merely 10 to
15 percent of industry sales. Looking at industrywide new releases
overweights independent albums at the expense of major labels and is
like having the tail wag the dog. Thus the total number of new releases
is a misleading statistic with regard to the overall sales in the industry,
and really cannot be a useful barometer of supply even if it were exogenous. It would be like comparing the total footage of home movies
shot year-by-year to explain the yearly economic performance of motion pictures. They are not really part of the same market.

5.5.5 Using Genres as the Unit of Analysis

I had high hopes for this methodology, although no one has formally
attempted to use it to my knowledge. With data such as that created
by Strumpf and Oberholzer, one could determine the variation in file-
sharing proclivity by genre, measured as the number of files downloaded as a share of total sales. It is likely that certain groups of users
(perhaps rock or hip hop) would be far more likely to engage in file
sharing than other groups (classical).

If data on yearly sales by genres were reasonably stable, then we
could look to see if those genres with the greatest incidence of file sharing suffered relative to genres with the least incidence of file sharing.
As a control, we could use the share of radio listenership by genre.

My high hopes faded when I purchased data on genre sales from
SoundScan. First, the data had only seven genres plus a catchall genre
called "current." Second, and more important, sales by genre had extremely large changes over very short periods of time. Table 5.4, showing two genres, has a 170 percent increase in sales in the metal genre in

Table 5.4
Comparison of metal and R&B by year

Year	Metal	R&B
1994	38,739	80,819
1995	31,101	80,718
1996	26,409	74,035
1997	28,983	141,613
1998	30,086	166,379
1999	82,698	175,339
2000	89,924	197,141
2001	88,158	195,498
2002	74,677	160,183
2003	74,629	149,972

Table 5.5
Ratio of sales to radio listenership

Year	Classical	Country	Jazz/smooth jazz
1999	8.07416	5.821573	5.456752232
2000	6.979109	6.09621	5.269958006
2001	8.414178	6.361194	5.538243224
2002	8.590823	7.410973	5.495995581
2003	10.55179	6.795402	6.110928962

1999 and a 100 percent increase in the R&B genre in 1997. Without more information that might help explain such sudden jumps, these data seem unlikely to prove reliable enough to use for any important empirical tests.

Nevertheless, Oberholzer and Strumpf have claimed that the data on genres are inconsistent with the thesis that file sharing is harmful to record sales. They state that "musical genres which are not heavily downloaded on file sharing networks experienced the same reduction in sales as other genres."[27] More specifically, they claim that two categories of music (catalogue and country) are not heavily downloaded yet sales have fared poorly.

Table 5.5 presents evidence on three categories of music that are not heavily downloaded. Given the evidence on variability in sales by genre, we should be careful to make any strong statements. But the evidence here is contrary to the claims of Oberholzer and Strumpf. Sales of these three genres are up in absolute terms (not shown) as well as the more relevant comparison to radio listenership. This occurred in spite of the very large overall sales decline.

Observation 5.5   The overwhelming majority of empirical evidence to date supports a claim that file sharing harms copyright owners.

This, of course, is contrary to the assumptions of the Gayer and Shy paper in chapter 8, which create a model suggesting that file sharing might be beneficial to copyright owners. Models, unfortunately, cannot answer empirical questions.

5.6   Conclusions

The analysis of file sharing is a relatively new phenomenon. Economists are just getting started. Nevertheless, progress is being made.

The theory underlying the analysis of file sharing has not received the attention that it deserves. It has always been clear that some possible aspects of file sharing would harm copyright owners, such as the substitution of copies for the purchase of originals. What has not been understood is that the use of file sharing to sample products is also likely to harm copyright owners. Although one can still construct theoretical conditions under which file sharing might benefit copyright holders, these conditions seem quite far-fetched. A broad analysis of the various theoretical factors at work supports a view that file sharing is likely to cause serious damage to the owners of copyright materials that are so shared.

The past few years have provided economists with a laboratory of sorts to analyze the impacts of file sharing. The basic evidence in the United States over the past few years—the birth of file sharing and the subsequent decline in CD sales—makes for an extremely compelling and simple explanation in spite of the protestations to the contrary from a large and vocal group of individuals supportive of file sharing.

Empirical examinations by economists must be undertaken against the backdrop of this simple explanation. That these basic facts fit nicely with the economic theory only adds support to this explanation. With such a strong prior expectation, empirical studies need to meet a higher hurdle than normal before they might be considered to overturn this expectation.

All of the empirical works to date suffer from various imperfections. Nevertheless, all the studies except one find results supportive of the thesis that file sharing is causing harm. As more evidence accumulates, both in the world at large and in the pages of academic publications, we can expect to learn more about the impacts of file sharing. The political arena is calling for an answer now, however, and is impatient to wait for academics to reach unanimity—which academics almost never do anyway. If an answer is needed, the answer that appears to have the greatest likelihood of being correct given our current state of knowledge is that file sharing hurts copyright owners and that it is responsible for most, if not all, of the recent decline in sales.

Notes

1. These copyright critics, who are sometimes associated with the concept of the "creative commons," argue that copyright laws are being used by the sound recording, movie, and software industries to thwart competitive forces that would open the market to new competition. This is the thesis of Lawrence Lessig's recent book *Free Culture*, which views the current controversies as extensions of long-running debates regarding the power of cartels to monopolize access to creative works. In this view of the world, file sharing is a wealth-enhancing innovation, likely to democratize the entertainment industry by allowing artists to broadcast and distribute their works without intermediaries such as record companies. In this view, file-sharing systems should be promoted and, if necessary, copyright law should be altered to allow file sharing to proceed apace.

2. See table no. 909, "Media Usage and Consumer Spending: 1993 to 2003," in the 2000 U.S. Statistical Abstract.

3. For a highly detailed description of file-sharing activities see Peitz and Waelbroeck in chapter 4.

4. On Download.com, as of March 2005, although the Kazaa figure comes from May 2004. Download.com was no longer providing totals for Kazaa in March 2005.

5. For discussions of the economics of copying and copyright see Watt (2004) or Varian (2005).

6. See Liebowitz 1985.

7. The closest might be a paper by Gopal, Bhattacharjee, and Sanders (2005). They attempt to analyze the theoretical impacts of file sharing using a fairly typical model. Sampling plays an important role in their model, but they do not analyze the impacts of sampling by itself. If the full cost of sampling were zero, consumers in their model would sample all music to find the most highly valued music. Whether they would then purchase the preferred music depends on other costs, such as costs of punishment if caught pirating, the sound quality differentials between sampled and purchased music, and the revealed value of music. If sound quality were identical between original and copies and if there were no punishment for copying, consumers would pirate all their music and purchase none.

8. By working with the underlying characteristic of the good, we can avoid problems caused by the fact that CDs are not perfectly homogenous. This is done by assuming that CDs are differentiated by the different quantities of the underlying music-listening service characteristic.

9. See Liebowitz (1982), which compares the link between viewing hours and cable penetration across different Canadian metropolitan areas and finds an insignificant but sometimes negative relationship. Also see Weimann (1996), which examines viewers in Israel after the introduction of a multichannel cable system where previously there had been but a single public channel (a more extreme increase in choice than would be found normally). After a year, there was virtually no difference in changes in viewing between a group with cable and a control group that did not receive cable (the cable group increased its viewing by sixteen minutes over the control group). There are several papers looking at the impact of cable on different European countries and reaching largely the same conclusions that can be found in Becker and Schoenbach (1989).

10. This is a compulsory license that amounts to ninety cents for each CD. In the common case where the performer is the composer, however, it is typical to have a "controlled composition" clause, which pays less than the statutory payment (75 percent appears to be a typical rate).

11. If the composer is not the performer of the song, and if the song has not been recorded, this payment will be negotiated. After a song has been recorded by one performer, however, anyone can record the song if they purchase a "compulsory license," which is the statutory payment described in the text. According to statistics on the RIAA webpage, the average price in 2003 was $11.91.

12. Boldrin and Levine (2004) assume that elasticity is greater than one to generate their results.

13. It is unclear how strong network effects are for different categories of software. For some categories, such as personal finance software, network effects might be expected to be weak or nonexistent. In other cases, such as spreadsheets, network effects are thought to be large. Although there have been attempts to measure the strength of network effects for spreadsheets, these attempts were marred by using Lotus 1-2-3 file compatibility as the measure of network effects when such compatibility was also important for upgrading spreadsheet users wanting to remain compatible with their old work independent of any network effects.

14. Data on quantities were reported beginning in 1973. For prior years only the industry revenues were reported. The data on revenues tend to be estimates based on the list price of recordings. I use full-length albums to avoid measurement problems as, for example, with singles, because they have been in a twenty-year secular decline.

15. The second largest decline occurred in 1978–1982. Long playing vinyl records were in decline at that time, being replaced by prerecorded cassettes. This decline coincided with a fairly deep recession and the possibility that blank cassettes were being used to copy records. As I explain in Liebowitz (2004c), cassettes ultimately allowed, for the first time, portability of prerecorded music, leading to a large increase in sales that overcame any negative impacts of copying.

16. 1991 is almost as low, but this still would be thirteen years.

17. Rob and Waldfogel perform a sort of welfare analysis, but they do not claim to be able to measure any lost value from reduced creative activity, which is the major cost normally associated with weaker copyright.

18. The Blackburn paper is available at http://www.economics.harvard.edu/~dblackbu/papers.html and the Oberholzer and Strumpf paper at http://www.unc.edu/~cigar/papers/FileSharing_March2004.pdf.

19. I discuss some concerns about their instruments in more detail on my Web page http://www.utdallas.edu/~liebowit/intprop/germankids.htm.

20. Hong's paper is part of his dissertation at Stanford and is currently available at http://siepr.stanford.edu/papers/pdf/03-18.html.

21. The Rob and Waldfogel article is available at http://ssrn.com/abstract=612076 and Zentner's (Chicago dissertation) is available at http://home.uchicago.edu/~alezentn/musicindustrynew.pdf.

22. In Rob and Waldfogel's survey, respondents reported that they would pay an average of $20,000 to $50,000 to not give up favorite or popular albums. The median values are in the range of several hundred dollars. The higher average values clearly contain some outlandish responses. Nevertheless, the median values seem quite reasonable to me.

23. There was a very slight increase in real list price between 1999 and 2003 (3 percent) with a decline in price from 2002 to 2003. Transaction prices are likely to have risen less because of the shift to low markup vendors. With any feasible price elasticity of demand, only a trivial portion of the decline in sales that occurred could have been due to price changes.

24. It is obviously inappropriate to use the post-1999 data in these regressions since file sharing started in 1999 and we wish to determine the impact of income and portable penetration on record sales in order to judge whether the post-1999 sales were negatively affected by file sharing. If file sharing had an impact on sales, it could distort regression results ignoring file sharing.

25. See for example George Ziemann "RIAA's Statistics Don't Add Up to Piracy," available at http://www.azoz.com/music/features/0008.html. The analyses contained on these pages are probably best described as "rants," but they have nevertheless been taken seriously by some. Understanding the differences between retail sales volume measured by SoundScan's barcode reading technology and wholesale shipment numbers reported by major labels would be useful, but instead the differences tend to be treated in these analyses as some sort of industry conspiracy.

26. The RIAA at one time provided the number of new releases and then stopped. A general statement about new releases on the RIAA was then taken by Ziemann and used in his analyses, although that was apparently an error. See http://www.theinquirer.net/?article=9048.

27. Page 12 of their Brief *Amici Curiae* of Felix Oberholzer-Gee and Koleman Strumpf in Support of Respondents, MGM v. Grokster, no. 04-480.

References

Becker, Lee, and Klaus Schoenbach (eds.) (1989), *Audience Responses to Media Diversification*, LEA, Hillsdale, New Jersey. Frank Olderaan and Nick Jankowski "The Netherlands: The Cable Replaces the Antenna" and R. Bouillin-Dartevelle "Belgium: Language Division Internationalized."

Blackburn, David (2004), "Does File Sharing Affect Record Sales?" Working paper, Harvard University.

Boldrin, M., and D. K. Levine (2004), "The Case against Intellectual Monopoly," *International Economic Review* 45 (2): 327–350.

Conner, K. R., and R. P. Rumelt (1991), "Software Piracy—An Analysis of Protection Strategies," *Management Science* 37 (2): 125–139.

Gopal, Ram D., Sudip Bhattacharjee, and G. Lawrence Sanders (2005), "Do Artists Benefit From Online Music Sharing?" *Journal of Business*. Forthcoming.

Hirshleifer, Jack (1971), "Suppression of Inventions," *Journal of Political Economy* 79, 382–383.

Hong, Seung-Hyun (2004), "The Effect of Napster on Recorded Music Sales: Evidence from the Consumer Expenditure Survey," SIEPR Policy Paper no. 03-018.

Klein, Benjamin, Andres V. Lerner, and Kevin M. Murphy (2002), "Intellectual Property: Do We Need It? The Economics of Copyright 'Fair Use' in a Networked World," *American Economic Review*, 206–208.

Lessig, Lawrence (2004), "Free Culture," The Penguin Press: New York.

Liebowitz, Stan J. (1982), "The Impacts of Cable Retransmission on Television Broadcasters," *Canadian Journal of Economics* 15, 503–524.

Liebowitz, Stan J. (1985), "Copying and Indirect Appropriability: Photocopying of Journals," *Journal of Political Economy* 93, 945–957.

Liebowitz, Stan J. (2002), "Rethinking the Network Economy," Amacom: New York, 2002.

Liebowitz, Stan J. (2004a), "The Elusive Symbiosis: The Impact of Radio on the Record Industry," *Review of Economic Research on Copyright Issues* vol. 1, 20–45.

Liebowitz, Stan J. (2004b), "File-Sharing: Creative Destruction or Just Plain Destruction?" Center for the Analysis of Property Rights Working Paper no. 04-03. http://ssrn.com/abstract=646943.

Liebowitz, Stan J. (2004c), "Will MP3 Downloads Annihilate the Record Industry? The Evidence So Far," Advances in the Study of Entrepreneurship, Innovation, and Economic Growth v. 15, 229–260.

Michel, Norbert J. (2004), "The Impact of the Digital Age on the Music Industry: A Theoretical and Empirical analysis," Working Paper.

Oberholzer, Felix, and Koleman Strumpf (2004), "The Effect of File Sharing on Record Sales: An Empirical Analysis," Working Paper.

Peitz, Martin, and Patrick Waelbroeck (2004), "The Effect of Internet Piracy on Music Sales," *Review of Economic Research on Copyright Issues* 1(2), 71–79.

Rob, Rafael, and Joel Waldfogel (2004), "Piracy on the High C's: Music Downloading, Sales Displacement, and Social Welfare in a Sample of College Students," see www.law.upenn.edu/polk/dropbox/waldfogel.pdf.

Shy, Oz, and Jacques-François Thisse (1999), "A Strategic Approach to Software Protection," *Journal of Economics and Management Strategy* 8, 163–190.

Takeyama, Lisa N. (1994), "The Welfare Implications of Unauthorized Reproduction of Intellectual Property in the Presence of Demand Network Externalities," *Journal of Industrial Economics* 42, 155–166.

Varian, Hal (2005), "Copying and Copyright," *Journal of Economic Perspectives* 19 (2): 121–138.

Watt, Richard (2004), "The Past and the Future of the Economics of Copyright," *Review of Economic Research on Copyright Issues* vol. 1 (1), 1–11.

Weimann, Gabriel (1996), "Cable Comes to the Holy Land: The Impact of Cable TV on Israeli Viewers," *Journal of Broadcasting & Electronic Media* 40, 243–257.

Zentner, Alejandro (2003), "Measuring the Effect of Online Music Piracy on Music Sales," Working Paper.

Zentner, Alejandro (2004), "Measuring the Effect of Music Downloads on Music Purchases," Working Paper.

6   Versioning Information Goods

Paul Belleflamme

6.1   Introduction

Information can be defined very broadly as anything that can be digitized (that is, encoded as a stream of bits): text, images, voice, data, audio, and video (see Varian 1998). Basic information is transacted under a wide range of formats or packages (which are not necessarily digital). These formats are generically called *information goods*. Books, movies, music, magazines, software, games, databases, telephone conversations, stock quotes, Web pages, news, ringtones, etc. all fall into this category. Information goods have the distinguishing characteristic of involving high fixed costs but low (often zero) marginal costs. In this case, cost-based pricing is not a sensible approach for firms and must give way to *value-based pricing*: an information good must be priced according to the value consumers attach to it, not according to its production cost. Moreover, as different consumers attach very different values to the same information good, the producer should set not a single *but several* value-based prices for its information good. This practice is known as *price discrimination*. More precisely, price discrimination implies that two varieties of a good are sold (by the same seller) to two buyers at different net prices, the net price being the price (paid by the buyer) corrected for the cost associated with the product differentiation.[1]

We begin by addressing the *feasibility of price discrimination*. In a perfectly competitive market, there cannot be two different prices for the same product, for it would otherwise be possible to earn a profit by engaging in *arbitrage*, that is, by buying at the low price and selling at the high price. Implicit behind this "law of one price" are the assumptions that arbitrage is perfect (costless) and that agents are perfectly informed about the different prices. However, in the real world (and especially for information goods), examples abound in which different prices are observed for what is apparently the same product. First, it must be the case that firms enjoy some market power, so that they are in a position to set prices. Second, leaving aside the possibility of imperfect consumer information, it must be that arbitrage costs are so high that consumers do not find it profitable to transfer the good between them.[2]

Let us now distinguish between different *types of price discrimination*. Following Pigou (1920), it is customary to distinguish three types, according to the information that firms have about buyers. The most favorable case for the firm is when it has complete information about individual preferences. The firm is then able to charge an individualized price for each buyer and for each unit purchased by each buyer, thereby extracting all of the consumer surplus. In Pigou's taxonomy, this practice is known as *first-degree price discrimination* (or *perfect discrimination*). Shapiro and Varian (1999) propose the more descriptive term of *personalized pricing*. It is often argued that personalized pricing cannot be applied in practice because of the enormous amount of information it requires. However, firms are now able to use information technologies to improve their knowledge of consumers' preferences and, thereby, to personalize price offers.[3]

When the firm does not know exactly each consumer's willingness to pay, it may still manage to extract a fraction of the consumer surplus by relying on some indicators (such as age, occupation, and location) that are related to the consumers' preferences. If the firm can observe a buyer's characteristics, then it can charge different prices as a function of these characteristics. This type of price discrimination is referred to as *third-degree price discrimination* in Pigou's taxonomy, or as *group pricing* in Shapiro and Varian's. This practice is common in the software industry: for example, office software often are sold at different prices to home users and to professionals, and students enjoy special discounts on Mathematica.[4] As group pricing can be seen as a special case of a multiproduct firm's pricing problem (see Tirole 1988), we shall not discuss it further in this chapter.

When buyers' characteristics are not directly observable, the firm still has the option to use self-selecting devices to extract some consumer surplus. The idea is to discriminate between heterogeneous buyers by targeting a specific package (that is, a selling contract that includes various clauses in addition to price) for each class of buyers. The firm faces then the problem of designing the menu of packages in such a way that consumers indeed choose the packages targeted for them. Pigou describes this practice as *second-degree price discrimination*, whereas Shapiro and Varian refer to it, more descriptively, as *versioning*. Examples of such practice abound for information goods (see section 6.2). As Peitz and Waelbroeck indicate in their analysis of digital music (chapter 4), digital rights management (DRM) solutions facilitate the practice of versioning: using DRM, the producer of a digital music file has the possibility to create different versions by attaching different liberalities of use to the file (in terms of, for example, number of access, number of copies on different devices, number of people one can share the file with, rights to modify or excerpt, or even time of possession).[5]

Versioning is our main focus in this chapter. In section 6.2, we present an integrated model that allows us to study how to implement versioning and when it is optimal to do so. Then in section 6.3, we consider a number of specific strategies for discriminating between consumers in the information economy: bundling or tying different goods together, "functional degradation" (that is, creating a new version by disabling some functions of an existing version), and conditioning prices on purchase history. Section 6.4 gives some concluding remarks.

This chapter bears a number of clear connections with other chapters in this book. First, as mentioned already, Peitz and Waelbroeck consider versioning in the digital music sector. Second, Evans, Hagiu, and Schmalensee's survey of the economic roles of software platforms (chapter 3) complements our analysis of bundling; the authors emphasize that computer systems comprise many components and that the contours of these products—what is included or excluded from the bundle of components—are determined by business and design decisions. Third, the preannouncement of information goods, as addressed by Choi, Kistiansen, and Nahm (chapter 7), could be seen as a particular form of intertemporal price discrimination in situations where (in contrast to what is assumed here) consumers have imperfect information about product qualities. Fourth, to analyze copyright enforcement of information goods, Gayer and Shy (chapter 8) use a vertical differentiation model that is similar to the one we use here to study versioning. Finally, our example of functional degradation (that is, Acrobat Reader and Writer) exhibits some form of two-sidedness and can therefore be related to Jullien's analysis of electronic intermediaries (chapter 10) and, also, to Evans, Hagiu, and Schmalensee's analysis of software platforms (chapter 3).

6.2 Versioning: How and When?

In the nineteenth century, Jules Dupuit (a French engineer and economist, quoted by Ekelund, 1970) analyzes the practice of the three-class
rail system as follows:

It is not because of the few thousand francs which would have to be
spent to put a roof over the third-class carriages or to upholster the third-
class seats that some company or other has open carriages with wooden
benches . . . . What the company is trying to do is prevent the passengers who
can pay the second-class fare from traveling third-class; it hits the poor, not because it wants to hurt them, but to frighten the rich . . . . And it is again for the
same reason that the companies, having proved almost cruel to third-class passengers and mean to second-class ones, become lavish in dealing with first-
class passengers. Having refused the poor what is necessary, they give the rich
what is superfluous.

What Dupuit describes is a classical example of versioning: by offering the same product under a number of "packages" (that is, some
combinations of price and product characteristics), the seller is able to
sort consumers according to their willingness to pay. The key is to
identify some dimensions of the product that are valued differently
across consumers, and to design the product line so as to emphasize
differences along those dimensions. The next step consists in pricing
the different versions in such a way that consumers will sort themselves out by selecting the version that most appeals to them.

Examples of such practice abound in the information economy. The
dimension along which information goods are versioned is usually
their *quality*, which is to be understood in a broad sense (for instance,
the quality of a software might be measured by its convenience, its
flexibility of use, the performance of the user interface). Shapiro and
Varian (1998) give a series of specific examples. For instance, referring
to "nagware" (that is, a form of shareware that is distributed freely but
displays a screen encouraging users to pay a registration fee, or dis-
playing ads), they illustrate how annoyance can be used as a discriminating device: some users will be willing to pay to turn off the
annoying screen. Versioning of information goods can also be based
on *time*, following the tactic of delay. For example, new books often appear first in hardcover and later as less expensive paperbacks. Similarly, movies can be viewed first in theaters; a few months later, they
are released on DVD and are shown on premium cable television;

eventually, they are broadcast on terrestrial television. The price of these choices usually declines with the viewing date. Finally, versioning can be based on *quantity*. Meurer (2001) gives some examples: software site licenses often provide discounted royalties as the number of networked machines or users grow; online databases offer discounts based on number of users or on usage by a particular user (measured by the number of searches performed, the quantity downloaded or printed, etc.); music performance licenses use factors like the number of square meters in a bar or store, or the size of the audience for a radio or television station to set quantity-based royalties; magazine and newspaper subscriptions feature quantity discounts.

We now develop a simple model to understand how monopolists should choose prices to induce self-selection of the consumers between different versions of the product. We also identify conditions under which versioning allows the monopolists to increase profits.

6.2.1   A Simple Model of Versioning

We consider the problem of monopolists choosing packages of quality and price level for an information good when consumers have unit demands.[6] The monopolists have identified one particular dimension of the good for which consumers have different value. In particular, we suppose that there is a continuum of potential consumers who are characterized by their valuation, θ, for this dimension of the information good. We assume that the "taste parameter" θ is uniformly distributed on the interval $[0, 1]$. The monopolists can produce this dimension of the good at two levels of quality, which are given exogenously. We note the two levels s_1 and s_2, with $s_2 > s_1$. As for the other dimensions of the information good, consumers are assumed to share the same valuation. Consumers' preferences are then described as follows: when consuming a unit of the good of quality s_i sold at price p_i, a consumer of type θ enjoys a (net) utility of

$$U(\theta, s_i) = k + \theta s_i - p_i, \tag{6.1}$$

where $k \geq 0$ represents the common valuation for the other dimensions of the information good. We assume that $k < s_1$, meaning that the consumer with the highest taste parameter ($\theta = 1$) values the particular dimension (at its lowest quality level) more than all the other dimensions of the good. Finally, we pose that consumers' utility is zero if they refrain from buying.

Monopolists face the following problem. They know the aggregate distribution of the taste parameters but are unable to identify a particular consumer's type. Two options are available: they can either sell a unique quality at a single price, or price discriminate by offering the two qualities at different prices. Let us examine the two options in turn, assuming that there is a constant marginal cost $c_i \geq 0$ to produce one unit of the good of quality s_i (with $c_i \leq k$ for $i = 1, 2$, meaning that the less eager consumer would buy either version if priced at marginal cost). Assumption 1 summarizes the relationship between the parameters of the model. For reasons that will become clear immediately, we also assume that the cost of producing the high quality (c_2) is not too large with respect to the cost of producing the low quality (c_1). Assumption 2 makes this condition precise.

Assumption 6.1 $0 \leq c_1, c_2 \leq k < s_1 < s_2$.

Assumption 6.2 $c_2 < c_1 + x$, with $x \equiv k + s_2 - c_1 - \sqrt{s_2/s_1}(k + s_1 - c_1) > 0$.

6.2.1.1 Selling a Single Quality

Under Assumption 2, the monopolists will choose to produce quality s_2 if they decide to sell a single quality. For a given price p_2 of quality s_2, the marginal consumer who is indifferent between buying and not buying is identified by $\theta_{20}(p_2)$, which solves $k + \theta_{20}(p_2)s_2 - p_2 = 0 \Leftrightarrow \theta_{20}(p_2) = \frac{p_2 - k}{s_2}$. Since all consumers with a higher valuation than $\theta_{20}(p_2)$ will buy the good, the monopolists' profit-maximization problem writes as

$$\max_{p_2} \pi_{1q} = (p_2 - c_2)[1 - \theta_{20}(p_2)] = (p_2 - c_2)\left(1 - \frac{p_2 - k}{s_2}\right).$$

The optimal price and profit are easily computed as

$$\hat{p}_2 = \frac{k + s_2 + c_2}{2} \quad \text{and} \quad \hat{\pi}_{1q} = \frac{(k + s_2 - c_2)^2}{4s_2}.$$

6.2.1.2 Selling the Two Qualities

We need now to find the profit-maximizing price pair (p_1, p_2) that induces some consumers to select quality s_1 and other consumers to select quality s_2. Given (p_1, p_2), we denote by θ_{12} the marginal consumer who is indifferent between consuming either of the two qualities, and by θ_{10}, the marginal consumer who is indifferent between consuming quality s_1 and not consuming at all. By definition, we have

$$k + \theta_{12}s_1 - p_1 = k + \theta_{12}s_2 - p_2 \Leftrightarrow \theta_{12}(p_1, p_2) = \frac{p_2 - p_1}{s_2 - s_1},$$

$$k + \theta_{10}s_1 - p_1 = 0 \Leftrightarrow \theta_{10}(p_1) = \frac{p_1 - k}{s_1}.$$

To achieve price discrimination, prices must be such that $0 \leq \theta_{10} < \theta_{12} < 1$. In that case, the population of consumers is divided into two (possibly three) groups: consumers with $\theta \geq \theta_{12}$ buy quality s_2, while consumers with $\theta_{10} \leq \theta < \theta_{12}$ buy quality s_1 (and if $\theta_{10} > 0$, consumers with $0 \leq \theta < \theta_{10}$ do not buy any quality). Prices must thus satisfy the following two constraints.

$$\theta_{12}(p_1, p_2) < 1 \Leftrightarrow p_2 < p_1 + (s_2 - s_1), \tag{A}$$

$$\theta_{10}(p_1) < \theta_{12}(p_1, p_2) \Leftrightarrow s_1/(p_1 - k) > s_2/(p_2 - k). \tag{B}$$

These are the so-called *self-selection constraints* (also known as "incentive-compatibility constraints"). If the menu $(s_i, p_i)_{i=1,2}$ is to be feasible in the sense that it will be chosen voluntarily by the consumers, then consumers of each group must prefer consuming the package intended for them as compared to consuming the other group's package or not consuming any package. Constraint (A) states that the price of the high-quality version must be lower than the price of the low-quality version, augmented by the quality gap (as valued by the most eager consumer, that is, $\theta = 1$). This is a necessary condition for positive sales of the high-quality version. Constraint (B) states that the low-quality version must offer a better "quality-price ratio" (computed here as $\frac{s_i}{p_i - k}$ for version i) than the high-quality one. This is a necessary condition for positive sales of the low-quality version.

Expressing p_2 as $p_1 + \Delta$, we can write the monopolists' profit-maximization problem as follows

$$\max_{p_1, \Delta} \pi_{2q} = (p_1 - c_1)[\theta_{12}(\Delta) - \theta_{10}(p_1)] + (p_1 + \Delta - c_2)[1 - \theta_{12}(\Delta)]$$

$$\text{s.t. (A) and (B) are met.}$$

That is, the monopolists set the price of the low-quality version (p_1) and the premium over that price associated with the high-quality version (Δ). The two first-order conditions are given by

$$\frac{\partial \pi_{2q}}{\partial p_1} = [1 - \theta_{10}(p_1)] - (p_1 - c_1)\frac{\partial \theta_{10}(p_1)}{\partial p_1} = 0;$$

$$\frac{\partial \pi_{2q}}{\partial \Delta} = [1 - \theta_{12}(\Delta)] - (\Delta - c_2 + c_1) \frac{\partial \theta_{12}(\Delta)}{\partial \Delta} = 0.$$

The former condition shows that an increase in p_1 has a twofold effect on profits: on one hand, revenues are gained from the consumers of the two versions, but on the other hand, margins are lost from consumers of the low-quality version who leave the market because of the price increase. The latter condition indicates two similar effects: a higher premium Δ gives rise to increased revenue from the consumers of the high-quality version but makes some consumers switch to the low-quality version (which is sold at a margin $p_1 - c_1$ instead of $p_2 - c_2$).

Replacing θ_{12} and θ_{10} by their respective value and solving for each first-order condition, we compute the profit-maximizing prices as

$$p_1^* = \frac{k + s_1 + c_1}{2}, \quad \Delta^* = \frac{c_2 - c_1 + s_2 - s_1}{2} \Rightarrow p_2^* = \frac{k + s_2 + c_2}{2}.$$

Do these prices meet the constraints? We first check that the market is not fully covered at these prices: our assumption that $s_1 > k$ implies that $\theta_{10}(p_1^*) > 0$, so that consumers with very low values of θ do not purchase any version. Next, a few lines of computations establish for which regions of parameters the self-selection constraints are met:

$$p_2^* < p_1^* + (s_2 - s_1) \Leftrightarrow c_2 < c_1 + (s_2 - s_1), \tag{A'}$$

$$s_1/(p_1^* - k) > s_2/(p_2^* - k) \Leftrightarrow s_1/(c_1 - k) > s_2/(c_2 - k). \tag{B'}$$

Conditions (A') and (B') are nothing but the self-selection constraints (A) and (B) expressed in the case of marginal-cost pricing (that is, $p_1 = c_1$ and $p_2 = c_2$). We now discuss the optimality of versioning under different scenarios for the values of the parameters k, c_1, and c_2.

6.2.2   When Is Versioning Optimal?
We have just shown that conditions (A') and (B') are necessary for versioning to be feasible. Using a simple "revealed preference" argument, we can also say that versioning is more profitable than selling a single version when conditions (A') and (B') are met. Indeed if the monopolies decide to set a pair of prices that induces some consumers to purchase the low-quality version, it is because this strategy increases profits (otherwise, they would choose prices such that only the high-quality version is purchased).

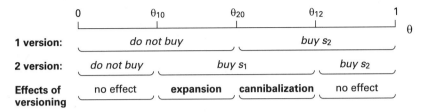

Figure 6.1
Effects of versioning on firm's profits

6.2.2.1   Cannibalization vs. Market Expansion   To understand the importance of the two conditions, let us detail the two conflicting effects versioning induces on the monopolist's profits (see figure 6.1). Under conditions (A′) and (B′), the marginal consumers in the two options are ranked as follows:

$$0 < \theta_{10}(p_1^*) < \theta_{20}(\hat{p}_2) < \theta_{12}(p_1^*, p_2^*) < 1.$$

That is, the effect of versioning on consumers' choices is twofold: first, because $\theta_{20}(\hat{p}_2) < \theta_{12}(p_1^*, p_2^*)$, fewer consumers buy the high-quality good; second, because $\theta_{10}(p_1^*) < \theta_{20}(\hat{p}_2)$, some previous nonconsumers now buy the low-quality good. How does this affect profits? The first thing to note is that nothing changes for the consumers with very high taste parameters $(\theta > \theta_{12}(p_1^*, p_2^*))$: in the two options, they buy quality s_2 at the same price $(p_2^* = \hat{p}_2)$. Going down the distribution of θ, we encounter consumers who would buy quality s_2 if it were the only quality available, but who would buy quality s_1 otherwise. This *cannibalization effect* has the following *negative* impact on the monopolist's profit:

$$d\pi_{ca} = [\theta_{12}(p_1^*, p_2^*) - \theta_{20}(\hat{p}_2)][(p_1^* - c_1) - (\hat{p}_2 - c_2)]$$

$$= -\frac{[s_2 - s_1 - (c_2 - c_1)][s_2(k - c_1) - s_1(k - c_2)]}{4s_2(s_2 - s_1)} < 0.$$

Finally, versioning has a *market expansion effect*: there are consumers who would buy quality s_1 when it is offered but who would not buy quality s_2 were it the only quality available. The *positive* impact on profit is equal to

$$d\pi_{me} = [\theta_{20}(\hat{p}_2) - \theta_{10}(p_1^*)](p_1^* - c_1)$$

$$= \frac{[s_2(k - c_1) - s_1(k - c_2)](k + s_1 - c_1)}{4s_1s_2} > 0.$$

Adding the two effects, we find that under conditions (A') and (B'), price discrimination is indeed the most profitable option:

$$\pi_{2q}(p_1^*, p_2^*) - \pi_{1q}(\hat{p}_2) = d\pi_{ca} + d\pi_{me} = \frac{[s_2(k - c_1) - s_1(k - c_2)]^2}{4s_1 s_2(s_2 - s_1)} > 0.$$

6.2.2.2 Is Versioning Optimal for Information Goods?

Information goods have the distinguishing characteristic of involving high fixed costs but low (often zero) marginal costs. More generally, the marginal cost of production is invariant with product quality. In our setting, this would mean that $c_1 = c_2 \equiv c$. With c being near zero, we observe that assuming $0 < k < s_1$ suffices to guarantee that conditions (A') and (B') are met and that versioning is optimal.[7] Note that for $c_1 = c_2 = 0$, we have that

$$\Delta_{ca} + \Delta_{me} = -\frac{s_2 - s_1}{4s_2}k + \frac{(s_2 - s_1)(k + s_1)}{4s_1 s_2}k = \frac{s_2 - s_1}{4s_1 s_2}k^2 > 0 \Leftrightarrow k > 0.$$

We record our main result below.

Result 6.1 Suppose the consumers' utility for the information good can be separated along two dimensions: a "key dimension" for which consumers have different valuations, and a "secondary dimension" for which all consumers have the same, positive, valuation. Suppose also that some consumers value the key dimension more than the secondary dimension, and that the marginal cost of producing any level of quality for the key dimension is near zero. Then versioning the information good along the key dimension is the most profitable option for the monopolists.

6.2.2.3 Damaged Goods

One extreme form of versioning occurs when firms intentionally damage a portion of their goods in order to price discriminate. Such *"damaged goods strategy"* is widely used in software markets: initially, the producer develops a complete full-featured version and then introduces additional low-quality versions by degrading quality of the original version.[8] Denekere and McAfee (1996) report other instances where firms actually incur an extra cost to produce the low-quality version (for instance, Sony recordable Mini-Discs (MDs) come in two formats—60' and 74' disks—which are sold at different prices. Yet the two formats are physically identical: a code in the table of contents identifies a 60' disc and prevents recording beyond this length, even though there is room on the media). They model this extra cost by assuming that the marginal cost of production is higher for the low-quality version. In the above setting, this would mean that $c_1 > c_2 \geq 0$. Continuing to assume that $0 < k < s_1$, let us examine whether versioning could be optimal under this alternative scenario. Condition (A') is clearly satisfied as $c_2 - c_1 < 0$. As for condition (B'), it can be satisfied if the "damaging cost" $(c_1 - c_2)$ is not too large.

Looking at the examples provided in Denekere and McAfee (1996), one could argue that the damaged good strategy is more likely to require some additional fixed cost rather than an increase in marginal cost. In this case, supposing $c_1 = c_2 = 0$ and letting $F > 0$ denote the fixed cost of creating quality s_1 by damaging quality s_2, we have that the damaged good strategy is optimal if and only if

$$\pi_{2q}(p_1^*, p_2^*) - F > \pi_{1q}(\hat{p}_2) \Leftrightarrow F < \frac{s_2 - s_1}{4 s_1 s_2} k^2.$$

To sum up, the introduction of a different version of the product aims at inducing consumers to reveal their preference for quality, so that the producer is able to extract a larger surplus from them. It is optimal to do so as long as the increase in surplus covers the cost of creating a new version of the product. We record thus the following result:

Result 6.2   Versioning can be feasible, and thus optimal, even if it is more costly to produce the low-quality version of the product.

6.3   Versioning: Applications

We discuss now three specific ways, observed in the information economy, of inducing consumers' self-selection in order to capture a larger share of the consumer surplus: bundling, functional degradation, and conditioning prices on purchase history.

6.3.1   Bundling

Just as inducing self-selection by offering a menu of versions enhances the monopolists' ability to extract surplus, so can selling different products as a combination package. Two such techniques are bundling and tying. The practice of *bundling* consists of selling two or more products in a single package (bundling is said to be "pure" when only the package is available, or "mixed" when the products are also available separately). The distinguishing feature of bundling is that the bundled goods are always combined in fixed proportions. In contrast, the related practice of *tying* (or *tie-in sales*) is less restrictive in that proportions might vary in the mix of goods. It takes only a little reflection to recognize how common practices bundling and tying are in the information economy. Examples abound both on the content side and on the infrastructure side, as illustrated below.

Examples of Bundling in the Information Economy

Content Side   (1) A subscription to cable television is typically a package of channels together, rather than a subscription to each channel separately; similarly for subscriptions to magazines, for CDs (which can be seen as bundles of different songs), or for newspapers (which can be seen as a bundle of news, arts, lifestyle, and sports content). (2) Software companies sell individual products but also offer packages (or "suites") consisting of several applications (for example, Microsoft Office suite). (3) As for software platforms, as indicated by Evans, Hagiu, and Schmalensee (chapter 3), many tasks that were performed by stand-alone applications have become integrated into other applications (for example, spell checkers, which were originally sold separately from word processors) or into the software platform itself. (4) Movie distributors frequently force theaters to acquire "bad" movies if they want to show "good" movies from the same distributor.

Infrastructure Side   (1) Evans, Hagiu, and Schmalensee point out that computer systems comprise many components. Typically, the microprocessor, memory, and other components are combined to create a hardware platform such as a PalmOne Zire PDA, a Nokia mobile phone handset, or an Xbox game console. (2) Audio equipment usually can be bought as separate components or as a complete system. (3) Photocopier manufacturers offer bundles that include the copier itself as well as maintenance; they also offer the alternative of buying the copier and servicing separately. (4) A classic example of tying is the practice adopted by IBM in the era of punch-card computers: IBM sold its machines with the condition that the buyer use only IBM-produced tabulating cards. Current examples involve computer printers (ink cartridges are generally specific to a particular model of a particular manufacturer) or some photographic films (only Polaroid films fit a Polaroid Instamatic).

Economists have given different explanations for bundling and tying. First, some explanations are too transparent to merit formal treatment. In the case of perfectly complementary products, such as

matching right and left shoes, no one questions the rationale of bundling: there is virtually no demand for separate products and bundling
them together presumably conserves on packaging and inventory costs.
In other cases where products are not necessarily complements, various cost efficiencies might provide a basis for profitable bundling.
More interestingly, even in the absence of cost efficiencies, there are
demand-side incentives that make bundling and tying profitable strategies. On one hand, both practices can serve as an effective tool for
sorting consumers and price discriminate between them; it is this rationale we concentrate on in this section.[9] On the other hand, bundling
and tying are also particularly effective entry-deterrent strategies; the
recent case brought against Microsoft by the European Commission
follows this line of argument.[10]

We now present a simple example to illustrate the use of bundling as
an alternative strategy for (second-degree) price discrimination.[11] Consider two monopolized products, which are independent both in terms
of demand (that is, the value a consumer places on one product does
not depend on the consumption of the other product) and in terms of
costs (that is, there are no cost advantages of multiproduct production;
in particular, we assume zero marginal cost for both goods). We still
have a continuum of potential consumers who are characterized by a
taste parameter θ, which is assumed to be uniformly distributed over
the interval $[0, 1]$. Consumers have a unit demand for each of two information goods (indexed by $i = 1, 2$). A typical consumer θ has the
following (gross) utility function:

$$u(\theta) = \begin{cases} u_1(\theta) = \theta & \text{if consuming good 1,} \\ u_2(\theta) = \alpha\theta + (1 - \alpha)(1 - \theta) & \text{if consuming good 2,} \\ u_b(\theta) = u_1(\theta) + u_2(\theta) & \text{if consuming the bundle.} \end{cases}$$

where $\alpha \in [0, 1]$ measures the correlation between the two distributions
of utilities across consumers: for α in $[0, \frac{1}{2})$ there is perfectly *negative*
correlation, for $\alpha = \frac{1}{2}$ there is no correlation, and for α in $(\frac{1}{2}, 1]$ there is
perfectly *positive* correlation. Note that for $\alpha = \frac{1}{2}$ the valuation for product 2 is constant across consumers.

We now compare two options for the monopolists: either selling the
two goods separately (*separate sales*), or selling them together as a bundle (*pure bundling*).

6.3.1.1   Separate Sales   Let p_i denote the price of good i ($i = 1, 2$).
We identify two pivotal consumers:

• Consumer $\theta_1(p_1)$ is such that $u_1(\theta) - p_1 = 0$: this consumer is indifferent between buying good 1 only and not buying any good (or between buying the two goods and buying good 2 only); as $u_1(\theta)$ is an increasing function of θ, consumers with a value of θ larger than $\theta_1(p_1)$ strictly prefer the first option.

• Consumer $\theta_2(p_2)$ is such that $u_2(\theta) - p_2 = 0$: this consumer is indifferent between buying good 2 only and not buying any good (or between buying the two goods and buying good 1 only); if $\alpha \geq \frac{1}{2}$ (positive correlation), $u_2(\theta)$ is an increasing function of θ and consumers with a value of θ larger than $\theta_2(p_2)$ strictly prefer the first option; otherwise (negative correlation), $u_2(\theta)$ is a *decreasing* function of θ and the consumers who strictly prefer the first option are those with a value of θ *smaller* than $\theta_2(p_2)$.

Consider first the case of *negative correlation* $(0 \leq \alpha < \frac{1}{2})$. Using the definition of the pivotal consumers, we see that consumers would prefer to buy nothing if their value of θ was comprised between $\theta_2(p_2)$ and $\theta_1(p_1)$: as $\theta > \theta_2(p_2)$, they are better off buying nothing than buying good 2 only; moreover, as $\theta < \theta_1(p_1)$, they are also better off buying nothing than buying good 1 only. Inverting the argument, we conclude that the monopolists will cover the whole market (that is, sell at least one good to each and every consumer) if they set prices so that

$$\theta_1(p_1) = p_1 \leq \theta_2(p_2) = \frac{1 - \alpha - p_2}{1 - 2\alpha}.$$

Under this condition, consumers are split into three groups: those with $0 \leq \theta < \theta_1(p_1)$ buy good 2 only, those with $\theta_1(p_1) \leq \theta < \theta_2(p_2)$ buy the two goods, and those with $\theta_2(p_2) \leq \theta < 1$ buy good 1 only. The monopolists' maximization program writes thus as

$$\max_{p_1, p_2} \pi_s = p_1(1 - p_1) + p_2 \frac{1 - \alpha - p_2}{1 - 2\alpha}$$

$$\text{s.t. } 0 \leq p_1 \leq \frac{1 - \alpha - p_2}{1 - 2\alpha} \leq 1. \tag{6.2}$$

The unconstrained prices are easily found as $p_1^* = \frac{1}{2} > 0$ and $p_2^* = \frac{1-\alpha}{2}$. One checks that $(1 - 2\alpha)p_1^* < 1 - \alpha - p_2^*$. However, the last constraint is satisfied if and only if $\alpha \leq \frac{1}{3}$. For $\frac{1}{3} < \alpha < \frac{1}{2}$, we have a corner solution: $\bar{p}_2 = \alpha$ and no consumer buys good 1 only. A quick analysis reveals that the latter solution also holds in the special case where $\alpha = \frac{1}{2}$ and all consumers have the same utility for good 2.

Consider next the case of *positive correlation* $(\frac{1}{2} < \alpha < 1)$. Now, by the definition of the pivotal consumers, we find that consumers with a value of θ larger than $\max\{\theta_1(p_1), \theta_2(p_2)\}$ buy both goods, while those with a value of θ comprised between $\min\{\theta_1(p_1), \theta_2(p_2)\}$ and $\max\{\theta_1(p_1), \theta_2(p_2)\}$ buy only a single good. Whatever the ranking of $\theta_1(p_1)$ and $\theta_2(p_2)$, the monopolists' profit writes now as

$$\pi_s = p_1(1 - p_1) + p_2\left(1 - \frac{p_2 - (1 - \alpha)}{2\alpha - 1}\right).$$

The profit-maximizing prices are: $p_1^* = \frac{1}{2}$ and $p_2^* = \frac{\alpha}{2}$. At these prices, one checks that $\theta_2(p_2^*) < \theta_1(p_1^*) < 1$. For the solution to be interior, we still need that $\theta_2(p_2^*) > 0 \Leftrightarrow \alpha > \frac{2}{3}$. If the latter condition is not satisfied, we have a corner solution: $\bar{p}_2 = 1 - \alpha$, and the market is fully covered.

Collecting our previous results, we can compute the optimal profit under separate sales for all values of α:

$$\pi_s^* = \begin{cases} \frac{\alpha^2 - 4\alpha + 2}{4(1 - 2\alpha)} & \text{for } 0 \leq \alpha \leq \frac{1}{3}, \\ \alpha + \frac{1}{4} & \text{for } \frac{1}{3} < \alpha \leq \frac{1}{2}, \\ 1 - \alpha + \frac{1}{4} & \text{for } \frac{1}{2} < \alpha \leq \frac{2}{3}, \\ \frac{\alpha^2 + 2\alpha - 1}{4(2\alpha - 1)} & \text{for } \frac{2}{3} < \alpha \leq 1. \end{cases} \tag{6.3}$$

6.3.1.2 Pure Bundling

Let p_b denote the price of the bundle (which is the only available good in the present case). Consumer θ's net utility is given by $u_b(\theta) - p_b = (1 - \alpha) + 2\alpha\theta - p_b$. Consider first the special case of *perfect negative correlation* $(\alpha = 0)$. In that case, all consumers have the same utility for the bundle: $u_b(\theta) = 1 - \alpha = 1$. The monopolists will thus set $p_b = 1$ and sell the bundle to the whole population of consumers, achieving a profit of $\pi_b = 1$. For $\alpha > 0$, we can identify the consumer who is indifferent between buying the bundle or not as $\theta_b(p_b) = \frac{p_b - 1 + \alpha}{2\alpha}$. The monopolists' profit-maximization program is given by

$$\max_{p_b} \pi_b = p_b\left(1 - \frac{p_b - 1 + \alpha}{2\alpha}\right) \quad \text{s.t. } 1 - \alpha \leq p_b \leq 1 + \alpha. \tag{6.4}$$

Solving for the first-order condition, we find $p_b^* = \frac{1+\alpha}{2}$. This solution meets the constraints if and only if $\alpha \geq \frac{1}{3}$. Otherwise, we have a corner solution: $\bar{p}_b = 1 - \alpha$ and the market is fully covered. In sum, the optimal profit under pure bundling is equal to

$$\pi_b^* = \begin{cases} 1 - \alpha & \text{for } 0 \le \alpha < \frac{1}{3}, \\ \frac{(1+\alpha)^2}{8\alpha} & \text{for } \frac{1}{3} \le \alpha < 1. \end{cases} \tag{6.5}$$

Note that the optimal profit under pure bundling is a decreasing function of α.

6.3.1.3 When Is Pure Bundling More Profitable than Separate Sales?

From the previous analysis, we observe that, as α increases, bundling becomes less profitable for two reasons. First, we have just shown that because the demand for the bundle rotates, lower profits are obtained when selling the bundle. Second, for larger values of α, there is a smaller proportion of consumers who buy a single good when sold separately but who buy the bundle when it is offered. These two effects are illustrated in table 6.1 where we compute the change in profit that bundling (B) yields compared to separate sales (S) for $\alpha = 0.2$ and $\alpha = 0.4$.

More precisely, comparing expressions (6.3) and (6.5) for all values of α, we find the following (see figure 6.2):

Table 6.1
Change in profit: bundling vs. separate sales

$\alpha = 0.2$	Purchasing decision	Change in profit
$0 \le \theta \le 1/2$	(S) buy 2 at $p_2 = 0.4$ (B) buy bundle at $p_b = 0.8$	+0.2
$1/2 \le \theta \le 2/3$	(S) buy 1 and 2 at $p_1 + p_2 = 0.9$ (B) buy bundle at $p_b = 0.8$	−0.0167
$2/3 \le \theta \le 1$	(S) buy 1 at $p_1 = 0.5$ (B) buy bundle at $p_b = 0.8$	+0.1
TOTAL		**+0.2833**
$\alpha = 0.4$	Purchasing decision	Change in profit
$0 \le \theta \le 1/8$	(S) buy 2 at $p_2 = 0.4$ (B) buy nothing	−0.05
$1/8 \le \theta \le 1/2$	(S) buy 2 at $p_2 = 0.4$ (B) buy bundle at $p_b = 0.7$	+0.1125
$1/2 \le \theta \le 1$	(S) buy 1 and 2 at $p_1 + p_2 = 0.9$ (B) buy bundle at $p_b = 0.7$	−0.1
TOTAL		**−0.0375**

for $0 \leq \alpha \leq \dfrac{1}{3}$, $\pi_b^* = 1 - \alpha > \pi_s^* = \dfrac{\alpha^2 - 4\alpha + 2}{4(1 - 2\alpha)}$;

for $\dfrac{1}{3} < \alpha < \sqrt{\dfrac{1}{7}}$, $\pi_b^* = \dfrac{(1 + \alpha)^2}{8\alpha} > \pi_s^* = \alpha + \dfrac{1}{4}$;

for $\sqrt{\dfrac{1}{7}} \leq \alpha < \dfrac{1}{2}$, $\pi_b^* = \dfrac{(1 + \alpha)^2}{8\alpha} < \pi_s^* = \alpha + \dfrac{1}{4}$;

for $\dfrac{1}{2} < \alpha \leq \dfrac{2}{3}$, $\pi_b^* = \dfrac{(1 + \alpha)^2}{8\alpha} < \pi_s^* = 1 - \alpha + \dfrac{1}{4}$;

for $\dfrac{2}{3} < \alpha \leq 1$, $\pi_b^* = \dfrac{(1 + \alpha)^2}{8\alpha} < \pi_s^* = \dfrac{\alpha^2 + 2\alpha - 1}{4(2\alpha - 1)}$.

We therefore conclude

Result 6.3   Profits are higher under bundling than under separate sales if and only if the correlation between the distributions of consumer utilities for the two goods is sufficiently negative, that is, if and only if $\alpha \leq \sqrt{\tfrac{1}{7}} \simeq 0.38$).

The intuition for this result has been explained. By selling a bundle at a lower price, the monopolists attempt to attract consumers who place a relatively low value on either of the two goods but who are

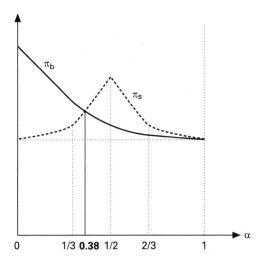

Figure 6.2
Comparison of profits under separate sales and pure bundling

willing to pay a reasonable sum for the bundle. When the two goods are sold separately, these consumers would buy a single good, but if the goods are sold as a bundle, they would buy the bundle and, therefore, acquire a good they would not have purchased otherwise. This strategy works, however, provided that willingnesses to pay for the individual products are sufficiently different. In their discussion of bundling, Evans, Hagiu, and Schmalensee (chapter 3) propose a similar intuition by pointing out that bundling reduces variation in reservation prices and, thereby, enables the seller to capture more of the product's value.

6.3.2 Functional Degradation

We now examine the logic behind a practice that becomes increasingly common nowadays: *functional degradation* of computer software. Well-known examples of this practice are software such as *Acrobat Reader*, *RealPlayer*, *Mathematica Reader*, and various *Microsoft Office (Word, Excel, PowerPoint) Viewers*. These software are designed to view and print (or play) contents written in a specific format, but are not capable of producing the contents in the specific format. The software manufacturers typically provide two different versions of a product, the read-only (or play-only) version and the full version. They offer the viewer or player almost free of charge by allowing consumers to download it on the Internet. However, the viewer (or player) is viewing and printing (or playing) only. To be able to create and edit contents (as well as view or play them), users need to purchase the corresponding full version, which is of course sold at a positive price. In the following simple model, based on Csorba and Hahn (2003), we show that this practice is based on a mixture of economic motivations: versioning, damaged good strategy, network building through free versions, and unbundling.

Suppose a firm is the sole supplier of a software that combines a read and a write function: the write function is required to produce documents that can be read using the read function. Since not all consumers are interested in writing documents, it is natural to offer the software under two versions: a *full* (write and read) version and a *read-only* version.[12] As before, we assume that there is a continuum of potential consumers who buy at most one unit of the good. Consumers are identified by a parameter θ (drawn from a uniform distribution on the unit interval), which indicates their valuation for the two functions of the good. More precisely, the valuations for the two functions are assumed to be proportional: θ is the valuation for the *write* function, while $\beta\theta$ (with $\beta > 0$) is the valuation for the *read* function. That is, we restrict the attention to cases where users who value highly one function also value highly the other function (and *vice versa*).[13]

The software exhibits *two-sided network effects*, insofar as the users' utility from reading (respectively writing) increases with the number of writers (respectively readers).[14] Letting p_f and p_r denote the prices of the full and the read-only versions, and n_f and n_r denote the numbers of consumers who buy the full and the read-only versions, we can express the (net) utility of consumer θ as follows:

$$U(\theta) = \begin{cases} \theta(n_f + n_r) + \beta\theta n_f - p_f & \text{if buying the full version,} \\ \beta\theta n_f - p_r & \text{if buying the read-only version,} \\ 0 & \text{if not buying.} \end{cases}$$

Let us detail this utility function. The full version can be seen as a bundle combining the two functions. Utility is assumed to be additively separable in the two functions. The first term is the utility from the write function: users owning the full version enjoy a network effect exerted by the users able to read the documents they produce (that is, those users who own either version of the good). The second term is the utility from the read function: the network effect, here, is exerted by the users able to write documents and is valued at $\beta\theta$ (instead of θ for the write function). Naturally, utility from owning the read-only version is limited to the latter term.

Because the firm cannot observe the consumers' types, it cannot resort to personalized or group pricing. Two options are available: either sell the full version only (which can be seen as pure bundling), or sell the two versions (which is a form of versioning or of mixed bundling). We consider the two options in turn.

6.3.2.1 Sell the Full Version Only When selling only the full version, the firm is in the position of monopolists pricing a good that exhibits network effects. If the read-only version is not available, n_r is necessarily equal to zero and the consumer θ's options are restricted to buying the full version (which yields a net utility of $[1 + \beta]\theta n_f^e - p_f$) or not buying the product. Note that n_f^e denotes the *expected* number of consumers buying the good: as choices are simultaneous, consumers base their purchasing decision on the expectations they form about future network sizes. The consumer who is indifferent between the two options is thus identified by θ_f, with

$$(1 + \beta)\theta_f n_f^e - p_f = 0 \Leftrightarrow \theta_f = \frac{p_f}{(1 + \beta)n_f^e}.$$

We suppose that consumers form rational expectations. Therefore, we have in equilibrium that $n_f^e = 1 - \theta_f$ (because all consumers with a higher valuation than θ_f decide to buy the full version), which means that

$$p_f = n_f^e(1 + \beta)(1 - n_f^e). \tag{6.6}$$

Because of the presence of network effects, there may exist more than one n_f (that is, more than one quantity) that satisfies the equilibrium condition (6.6) for a given price. For instance, $p_f = 0$ for $n_f^e = 0$ and $n_f^e = 1$. We thus need a rule to choose between multiple solutions. We apply the *Pareto criterion*: if, at a certain price, there exist more than one number of consumers ("quantity") that satisfies the equilibrium condition and one of these "quantities" Pareto-dominates (that is, makes everyone better off than) the other quantities, consumers expect this allocation to prevail in equilibrium. In the present case, the larger n_f (which corresponds to the lower θ_f) that satisfies (6.6) gives a larger value to the network good, so everyone would be better off by coordinating on this solution. This is thus the value we pick when following the Pareto criterion.

We can now express the firm's problem as

$$\max_{n_f} \; p_f n_f = n_f^2(1 + \beta)(1 - n_f).$$

The first-order condition for profit maximization is $n_f(2 - 3n_f) = 0$, which admits two roots: $n_f = 0$ and $n_f = \frac{2}{3}$. Checking for the second-order condition, we find that the former corresponds to a minimum while the latter corresponds to a maximum. It follows that, when selling the full version, the firm's optimal network size, price, and profit are given by (with the superscript F meaning "full version only"):

$$n_f^F = \frac{2}{3}, \quad p_f^F = \frac{2(1 + \beta)}{9}, \quad \pi^F = \frac{4(1 + \beta)}{27}. \tag{6.7}$$

6.3.2.2 Introducing the Read-Only Version The introduction of the read-only version aims to achieve versioning. The idea is to segment the market into two groups: the full version is targeted toward consumers with a high valuation, and the read-only version toward consumers with a low valuation. We can therefore follow the same methology as in section 6.2.1. We identify two pivotal consumers. Let θ_{fr} denote the consumer who is indifferent between the two versions. That is,

$$\theta_{fr}(n_f^e + n_r^e) + \beta\theta_{fr}n_f^e - p_f = \beta\theta_{fr}n_f^e - p_r \Leftrightarrow \theta_{fr} = \frac{p_f - p_r}{n_f^e + n_r^e}.$$

Similarly, let θ_{ro} denote the consumer who is indifferent between the read-only version and no purchase:

$$\beta\theta_{ro}n_f^e - p_r = 0 \Leftrightarrow \theta_{ro} = \frac{p_r}{\beta n_f^e}.$$

To achieve the desired segmentation, the firm must choose p_f and p_r so that $0 \leq \theta_{ro} < \theta_{fr} < 1$. Suppose for now it is the case. Because consumers form rational expectations, the expectations about the respective network sizes must be fulfilled at equilibrium. It follows that $n_f = 1 - \theta_{fr}$ and $n_r = \theta_{fr} - \theta_{ro}$. Plugging the values of θ_{fr} and θ_{ro} into the latter two expressions, we can solve for the prices and derive the following two equilibrium conditions:

$$p_f = (n_f + n_r)(1 - n_f) + \beta n_f(1 - n_f - n_r), \tag{6.8}$$

$$p_r = \beta n_f(1 - n_f - n_r). \tag{6.9}$$

As before, there can be multiple pairs of (n_f, n_r) that meet the two conditions for a given pair (p_f, p_r). It can be shown, however, that different equilibrium pairs always can be ordered, in the sense that a larger value of n_f always corresponds to a larger value of n_r.[15] Since larger network sizes confer higher utility to all consumers, the Pareto criterion tells us that consumers expect the largest pair (n_f, n_r) satisfying (6.8) and (6.9) to be the equilibrium.

We can now write the firm's profit-maximization problem in the case where the read-only version is used as a versioning device:

$$\max p_f n_f + p_r n_r = n_f(n_f + n_r)((1 + \beta)(1 - n_f) - \beta n_r)$$

subject to $0 \leq \theta_{ro} < \theta_{fr} < 1$.

To find the (unconstrained) profit-maximizing values of n_f and n_r, we proceed in three steps. First, solving for the FOC with respect to n_r, we find that

$$n_r = \left(\tfrac{1}{2}\beta\right)\left(1 + \beta - (1+2\beta)n_f\right). \tag{6.10}$$

Second, we plug this value into the FOC with respect to n_f, which then rewrites as

$$\left(\tfrac{1}{4}\beta\right)(n_f - 1 - \beta)(3n_f - 1 - \beta) = 0.$$

Third, we consider the two possible roots of the latter equation. Either $n_f = 1 + \beta$ or $n_f = \frac{1+\beta}{3}$. Using expression (6.10), we observe that for $n_f = 1 + \beta$, $n_r = -(1+\beta)$, while for $n_f = \frac{1+\beta}{3}$, $n_r = \frac{1-\beta^2}{3\beta}$. Since we impose $\theta_{ro} < \theta_{fr}$ (that is, $n_r > 0$), we can reject the former solution. As for the latter solution, it satisfies the constraints providing (1) $n_r > 0 \Leftrightarrow \beta < 1$, and (2) $n_f + n_r = \frac{1+\beta}{3\beta} \le 1 \Leftrightarrow \beta \ge \tfrac{1}{2}$. Therefore, there are three cases to consider according to the value of β (that is, the ratio between the valuations of the reading and writing functions).

1. *If the reading function is valued relatively higher than the writing function* $(\beta \ge 1)$, *there is no interior solution to the above problem.* The firm does not find it profitable to introduce the read-only version (which amounts to set $n_r = 0$) and there is *no versioning*.

2. *If the reading function is valued relatively lower than the writing function* $(\beta < 1)$, *versioning is profitable.* Two cases of interest appear.
(a) For $\tfrac{1}{2} < \beta < 1$, $n_f = \frac{1+\beta}{3}$ and $n_r = \frac{1-\beta^2}{3\beta}$ meet the constraints. The corresponding optimal prices are both strictly positive and are given by (with the superscript V for "versioning")

$$p_r^V = \frac{(1+\beta)(2\beta - 1)}{9}, \quad p_f^V = p_r^V + \frac{(1+\beta)(2-\beta)}{9\beta}.$$

We compute the resulting profit as

$$\pi^V = \frac{(1+\beta)^3}{27\beta},$$

and we check that $\pi^V > \pi^F \ \forall \left(\tfrac{1}{2}\right) < \beta < 1$.
(b) For $0 < \beta \le \tfrac{1}{2}$, the valuation for the reading function becomes relatively very small and the firm finds it optimal to cover the whole market (that is, the constraint $n_f + n_r \le 1$ is binding). Since $n_f + n_r = 1$, it follows from (6.9) that $p_r = 0$: *the read-only version is introduced for free.* It also follows from (6.8) that $p_f = 1 - n_f$, meaning that the firm maximizes $\pi = n_f(1 - n_f)$ by choosing $n_f = \tfrac{1}{2}$ (which implies that $n_r = \tfrac{1}{2}$ too). In sum, the optimum when $0 < \beta \le \tfrac{1}{2}$ is (with the superscript 0 for "versioning with a free read-only version")

$$p_r^0 = 0, \quad p_f^0 = \tfrac{1}{2}, \quad \pi^0 = \tfrac{1}{4}.$$

Again, it is easily checked that $\pi^0 > \pi^F \ \forall 0 < \beta \leq \tfrac{1}{2}$.

The latter result shows that the seller might find it profitable to give away a degraded version of the software in order to build the network of the full version. In their analysis of digital piracy, Gayer and Shy (chapter 8) reach a similar conclusion. They show a case where, in the presence of network effects, a copyright-owner's losses from piracy diminish when moving from nondigital to digital copying technologies. Because the quality of copies is enhanced, more (illegitimate) users copy the product, which generates larger network effects and thereby raises the price paid by legitimate users.

To conclude, we summarize our findings.

Result 6.4 Consider a software that combines a read and a write function. Suppose that consumers' valuations for the two functions are proportional. As long as the reading function is valued relatively lower than the writing function, the seller finds it profitable to engage in versioning by selling a read-only version along with the full (read and write) version of the software. If the relative valuation of the reading function is sufficiently low, it is even profitable to give away the read-only version for free.

6.3.3 Conditioning Prices on Purchase History

In the ecommerce world, sellers are able to monitor consumer transactions, typically through the use of *cookies*. A cookie is a unique identifier that is sent by a website for storage by the consumer's Web browser software. The cookie contains information about the current transaction and persists after the session has ended. As a result, for the next visit to the website by that consumer, the server can retrieve identification and match it with details of past interactions, which allows the sellers to condition the price offers that they make today on past behavior.

In other words, cookies make price discrimination on an individual basis feasible. Note that other technologies can be used toward the same objective: static IP addresses, credit card numbers, user authentication, and a variety of other mechanisms can be used to identify user history. Of course, users can take defensive measures. No one is forced to join a loyalty program, and it is possible to set one's browser to reject cookies or to erase them after a session is over.[16]

In sum, online technologies allow e-commerce sellers to post prices, observe the purchasing behavior at these prices, and condition future prices on observed behavior. Yet consumers are free to hide their previous behavior (possibly at some cost) and can always pretend that they visit a website for the first time. Therefore, as usual in versioning, sellers are bound to offer buyers some extra benefits to prevent them from hiding their identity.

We now extend the model of section 6.2.1 to investigate this type of strategic interaction between buyers and sellers in an e-commerce environment.[17] A single profit-maximizing seller provides a good at constant marginal cost (which, for simplicity, is set to zero). The seller can set cookies for recording consumers' purchase history. However, consumers can delete cookies at some cost (and inconvenience) denoted by $\gamma > 0$. Consumers can visit the seller's online store in two consecutive periods. In period $i = 1, 2$, the utility from purchasing one unit of the good is described as in expression (6.1):

$$U(\theta, s_i) = k + \theta s_i - p_i$$

(where, as assumed before, $0 < k < s_i$). We assume that $s_2 > s_1$ to capture the idea that the second unit of consumption is more valuable than the first. This might occur because the second visit to the online store is more efficient than the first one (for example, it is easier to find one's way through the Web pages), or because the seller offers enhanced services to second-time visitors (such as one-click shopping, loyalty rewards, and targeted recommendations).

Let us first examine the benchmark case where the seller sets a *flat price each period*, denoted by p. In period i, the consumer who is indifferent between buying the good and not buying is identified by $\theta_i(p) = \frac{p-k}{s_i}$. The seller thus chooses p to maximize

$$\pi_F = p(1 - \theta_1(p)) + p(1 - \theta_2(p)) = \frac{p}{s_1 s_2}(2s_1 s_2 + k(s_1 + s_2) - p(s_1 + s_2)).$$

The optimal price and profit are found easily as

$$p_F = \frac{k}{2} + \frac{s_1 s_2}{s_1 + s_2} \quad \text{and} \quad \pi_F = \frac{[2s_1 s_2 + k(s_1 + s_2)]^2}{4s_1 s_2(s_1 + s_2)}.$$

Naturally, the seller will try to take advantage of cookies and *condition prices on purchase history*. To do so, the seller designs the following pricing scheme:

(1) the price p_0 is charged to consumers having no cookie indicating a prior visit;

(2) the price p_b is charged to consumers with a cookie indicating that they made a purchase on a prior visit;

(3) the price p_n is charged to consumers with a cookie indicating that they did not make a purchase on a prior visit.

We investigate how to implement a solution where consumers with a high θ consumes in both periods (and do not delete their cookies) and consumers with a lower θ consume only in the first period. We identify two pivotal consumers:

• consumer θ_0 is indifferent between buying in the first period only and not buying at all: $k + \theta_0 s_1 - p_0 = 0 \Leftrightarrow \theta_0(p_0) = \frac{p_0-k}{s_1}$;
• consumer θ_b is indifferent between buying in both periods (and keeping the cookie) and buying in period 1 only: $2k + \theta_b(s_1 + s_2) - p_0 - p_b = k + \theta_b s_1 - p_0 \Leftrightarrow \theta_b(p_b) = \frac{p_b-k}{s_2}$.

If the proposed pricing scheme is correctly designed, the seller's profit writes as

$$\pi_C = p_0(\theta_b(p_b) - \theta_0(p_0)) + (p_0 + p_b)(1 - \theta_b(p_b))$$

$$= p_0\left(1 - \frac{p_0 - k}{s_1}\right) + p_b\left(1 - \frac{p_b - k}{s_2}\right).$$

Solving for the first-order conditions, one computes the optimal prices as

$$p_0^* = \frac{k + s_1}{2} \quad \text{and} \quad p_b^* = \frac{k + s_2}{2}.$$

Our assumption of enhanced services at the second visit $(s_2 > s_1)$ guarantees that $\theta_b(p_b^*) = \frac{s_2-k}{2s_2} > \theta_0(p_0^*) = \frac{s_1-k}{2s_1}$. We still need to check, however, that all consumers behave rationally.

• Consider first the consumers with $\theta \geq \theta_b(p_b^*)$ who are supposed to prefer buying in both periods and are not deleting their cookies. From the definition of θ_b and θ_0, we know already that these consumers are worse off if they buy in period 1 only, or if they do not buy at all. There remain two options. First, they could buy in both periods but delete their cookies, securing a net utility of $2k + \theta(s_1 + s_2) - 2p_0 - \gamma$ (that is, by hiding their prior purchase, they continue to pay the low price p_0 but have to incur the cost γ). This option is dominated if and only if

$$p_b^* \le p_0^* + \gamma \Leftrightarrow \gamma \ge \frac{1}{2}(s_2 - s_1). \tag{6.11}$$

Second, consumers could buy in the second period only and obtain a net utility of $k + \theta s_2 - p_n$. This option is dominated if and only if $\theta s_1 \ge p_0^* + p_b^* - p_n - k$, or

$$\theta \ge \frac{s_1 + s_2}{2s_1} - \frac{p_n}{s_1}.$$

The latter condition always is satisfied for these consumers if

$$\theta_b(p_b^*) = \frac{s_2 - k}{2s_2} \ge \frac{s_1 + s_2}{2s_1} - \frac{p_n}{s_1} \Leftrightarrow$$

$$p_n \ge \frac{s_2^2 + s_1 k}{2s_2} = p_0^* + \frac{(s_2 - k)(s_2 - s_1)}{2s_2}. \tag{6.12}$$

• Consider next the consumers situated between $\theta_0(p_0^*)$ and $\theta_b(p_b^*)$ who are supposed to buy in period 1 only. Again, the definition of the two pivotal consumers guarantees that these consumers are worse off if they buy in both periods (and keep their cookies) or if they do not buy at all. We still need to check whether they are also worse off in the same two remaining options as above. First, consuming in both periods and deleting the cookies leaves them worse off if and only if $k + \theta s_1 - p_0^* \ge 2k + \theta(s_1 + s_2) - 2p_0^* - \gamma$, or

$$\theta \le \frac{p_0^* - k + \gamma}{s_2} = \frac{s_1 - k + 2\gamma}{2s_2}.$$

This inequality always is satisfied for these consumers if

$$\theta_b(p_b^*) = \frac{s_2 - k}{2s_2} \le \frac{s_1 - k + 2\gamma}{2s_2} \Leftrightarrow \gamma \ge \frac{1}{2}(s_2 - s_1),$$

which is equivalent to condition (6.11). Second, consuming in period 2 only is dominated if and only if $k + \theta s_1 - p_0^* \ge k + \theta s_2 - p_n$, or

$$\theta \le \frac{p_n - p_0^*}{s_2 - s_1}.$$

Again, all consumers in the range satisfy this condition if

$$\theta_b(p_b^*) = \frac{s_2 - k}{2s_2} \leq \frac{p_n - p_0^*}{s_2 - s_1} \Leftrightarrow p_n \geq p_0^* + \frac{(s_2 - k)(s_2 - s_1)}{2s_2},$$

which is equivalent to condition (6.12).

So, as long as the cost of deleting cookies is large enough (that is, as long as condition [6.11] is met), conditioning prices on purchase history is feasible (and thus profitable). The seller sets a low price for (genuine or pretended) first visitors, $p_0^* = \frac{k+s_1}{2} < p_F$, and a higher price for identified second-time buyers, $p_b^* = \frac{k+s_2}{2} > p_F$. The difference between this price and the first-visitor price is, however, inferior to the cost of deleting cookies. Finally, the price for consumers who visit the website for a second time but who have not purchased earlier, p_n^*, is set high enough (that is, in accordance with condition [6.12]) to discourage such behavior. As the seller keeps the possibility of setting $p_0^* = p_b^*$, fixing different prices must be profit-enhancing. We check indeed that

$$\pi_C = \frac{(k^2 + s_1 s_2)(s_1 + s_2) + 4k s_1 s_2}{s_1 s_2} = \pi_F + \frac{1}{4} \frac{(s_2 - s_1)^2}{s_1 + s_2}.$$

Note that conditioning prices on past purchase behavior would not be feasible if the second unit of consumption (or the second visit to the website) did not provide consumers with a higher value than the first unit. Indeed if $s_2 = s_1$, then $\theta_b(p_b^*) = \theta_0(p_0^*)$ and the market cannot be segmented.[18]

We can summarize our findings as follows.

Result 6.5   If the second visit to an online store is more valuable than the first visit, and if the cost of deleting cookies is large enough, conditioning prices on purchase history is feasible (and thus profitable). The seller sets a low price for (genuine or pretended) first visitors, and a higher price for identified second-time buyers; the difference between this price and the first-visitor price is inferior to the cost of deleting cookies. The price for consumers who visit the website for a second time but who have not purchased earlier is set high enough to discourage such behavior.

6.4   Conclusion

Price discrimination consists of selling the same product (or different versions of it) to different buyers at different prices. When sellers cannot relate to some observable characteristics a buyer's willingness to pay, price discrimination can be achieved by targeting a specific package (that is, a selling contract that includes various clauses in addition to price) for each class of buyers. The seller faces then the problem of designing the menu of packages in such a way that consumers indeed choose the package targeted for them. This practice, known as versioning (or as second-degree price discrimination), is widespread in the information economy: it is not only particularly well-suited for information goods (for which consumers' valuations might differ widely), but it is also facilitated by the use of information technologies (which allow the creation of different versions of the same good at very low cost and along many possible dimensions).

In this chapter, we have used a simple unified framework to expose the general theory behind versioning, and to consider a number of specific applications. In the general exposition, we have studied how to implement versioning and when it is optimal to do so. Applying the general analysis to information goods, we have shown that when the consumers' utility for an information good can be separated along two dimensions (a "key dimension" for which consumers have different valuations, and a "secondary dimension" for which all consumers have the same valuation), versioning the information good along the key dimension is the most profitable option for the monopolists.

We then extended our theoretical framework to shed light on three specific versioning strategies used in the information economy: bundling, functional degradation, and conditioning prices on purchase history. *Bundling* consists in selling different products as a combination package (like a word processor and a spreadsheet sold in an "office suite"). It is more profitable than separating sales if the correlation between the distributions of consumer utilities for the various goods comprised in the bundle is sufficiently negative. Under this condition, bundling induces a sufficient number of consumers to acquire a good they would not have purchased otherwise. *Functional degradation* is a practice by which a software firm removes some functions of its original product and sells the degraded version at a lower or zero price. For instance, Adobe sells Acrobat Reader along with Adobe Acrobat. The former software, available free of charge, is designed to view and print contents written in PDF format, but is not capable of producing the contents in this format. To be able to create and edit contents, users need to purchase the latter software, which is sold at a positive price. In a model involving two-sided network effects, we have shown the following: As long as the reading function is valued (by all users) relatively lower than the writing function, the seller finds it profitable to engage in versioning by selling a read-only version along with the full (read and write) version of the software. If the relative valuation of the reading function is sufficiently low, it is even profitable to give away the read-only version for free. Finally, we have considered the practice of *conditioning prices on purchase history*. Indeed online technologies allow e-commerce sellers to post prices, observe the purchasing behavior at these prices, and condition future prices on observed behavior. Yet consumers are free to hide their previous behavior (possibly at some cost) and can always pretend that they visit a website for the first time. Not surprisingly, the analysis revealed that the profitable use of such practice is conditional on the cost of hiding previous purchasing behavior being sufficiently large.

Notes

Useful comments and suggestions by Martin Peitz and two anonymous referees are gratefully acknowledged.

1. This definition is adapted from Phlips (1983, p. 6). As Phlips argues, this definition seems more acceptable than the standard definition, which identifies price discrimination as the practice of setting different prices for the same good. Indeed one often observes that it is not the same product, but differentiated products, that are sold at discriminatory prices.

2. As Tirole (1988) points out, arbitrage costs might be associated either with the *transferrability of the good itself* (for example, it is too time-consuming to unbundle a "3-for-the-price-of-2 package" in order to resell individual units), or with the *transferrability of demand* between different packages aimed at different consumers (see section 6.2).

3. See Ulph and Vulkan (2000) for a study of personalized pricing in a duopoly setting.

4. These two examples present, however, the following difference: the home and office products are generally the same, but the student version of Mathematica lacks some features with respect to the nonstudent version. We return to this practice of *functional degradation* in sections 6.2.2 and 6.3.2.

5. For an economic analysis of DRM, see Bomsel and Geffroy (2005).

6. This problem was initially examined by Mussa and Rosen (1978). We use here the results of the extended analysis of Bhargava and Choudhary (2001).

7. However, if $k = 0$ and $c_1 = c_2$, condition (B') cannot be met and the monopolists will prefer to offer the high quality only. This is the result reached by Salant (1989) under the assumption that the marginal cost function for quality is linear.

8. See the discussion of functional degradation in section 6.3.2 for further examples.

9. For related literature, see Adams and Yellen (1976), Schmalensee (1984), or McAfee, McMillan, and Whinston (1989).

10. Three papers addressing this topic are Whinston (1990), Choi and Stefanidis (2003), and Nalebuff (2004).

11. Regarding tying, let us simply mention that it can be viewed as a price-discrimination device because it enables the monopolists to charge more to consumers who value the good the most. Here, the value consumers place on the primary product (for example, the printer) depends on the frequency with which they use it, which is itself measured by their consumption of the tied product (for example, the ink cartridges). Those who most need the primary product will consume more of the secondary product and, thereby, pay a higher effective price.

12. A "write-only" version does not make much sense, as it seems hard to write a document without being able to read it.

13. In other words, there is positive correlation between the distribution of utilities for the two functions. Applying the analysis of the previous section, we can anticipate that this positive correlation is likely to drive the monopolists to "unbundle" the two functions.

14. For more on two-sided or multi-sided markets, see the analyses by Evans, Hagiu, and Schmalensee (chapter 3) and by Jullien (chapter 10) in this book.

15. See Csorba and Hahn (2003).

16. According to the Jupiter Research 2004 survey, an increasing number of people are blocking cookies or deleting them to protect their privacy or security: nearly 58 percent of online users deleted the small files; as many as 39 percent may be deleting cookies from their primary computer every month. (Sharma, D.C., C|Net News.com, March 16, 2005).

17. This model is adapted from Acquisti and Varian (2004).

18. The same conclusion holds when $k = 0$, which is reminiscent of what we observed in the general model of section 6.2.2.

References

Acquisti, A., and H. R. Varian (2004). Conditioning prices on purchase history. Mimeo. University of California, Berkeley.

Adams, W. J., and J. L. Yellen (1976). Commodity bundling and the burden of monopoly. *Quarterly Journal of Economics* 90: 475–498.

Bhargava, H. K., and V. Choudhary (2001). Second-degree price discrimination for information goods under nonlinear utility functions. In *Proceedings of the 34th Hawaii International Conference on System Sciences*.

Bomsel, O., and A.-G. Geffroy (2005). Economic Analysis of Digital Rights Management systems (DRMs). Mimeo. Cerna, Centre d'économie industrielle. Ecole Nationale Supérieure des Mines de Paris.

Choi, J. P., and C. Stefanidis (2003). Bundling, entry deterrence, and specialist innovators. Mimeo. Michigan State University.

Csorba, G., and Y. Hahn (2003). Functional degradation and two-sided network effects: An application to software markets. Mimeo. Keele University.

Denekere, R. J., and R. P. McAfee (1996). Damaged goods. *Journal of Economics and Management Strategy* 5: 149–174.

Ekelund, R. B. (1970). Price discrimination and product differentiation in economic theory: An early analysis. *Quarterly Journal of Economics* 84: 268–278.

McAfee, R. P., J. McMillan, and M. Whinston (1989). Multiproduct monopoly, commodity bundling and correlation of values. *Quarterly Journal of Economics* 104: 371–384.

Meurer, M. J. (2001). Copyright law and price discrimination. 23 *Cardozo Law Review* 55.

Mussa, M., and S. Rosen (1978). Monopoly and product quality. *Journal of Economic Theory* 18: 301–317.

Nalebuff, B. (2004). Bundling as an entry deterrent. *Quarterly Journal of Economics* 119: 159–188.

Pigou, A. C. (1920). *The Economics of Welfare*. Macmillan, London.

Phlips, L. (1983). *Economics of Price Discrimination. Four Essays in Applied Price Theory*. Cambridge University Press, Cambridge.

Salant, S. W. (1989). When is inducing self-selection suboptimal for a monopolist? *Quarterly Journal of Economics* 104: 391–397.

Shapiro, C., and H. Varian (1998). Versioning: the smart way to sell information. *Harvard Business Review*, Nov–Dec.

Shapiro, C., and H. Varian (1999). *Information Rules: A Strategic Guide to the Network Economy*. Harvard Business School Press, Boston, Mass.

Schmalensee, R. (1984). Gaussian demand and commodity bundling. *Journal of Business* 57: 58–73.

Tirole, J. (1988). *The Theory of Industrial Organization*. The MIT Press, Cambridge, Mass.

Ulph, D., and N. Vulkan (2000). Electronic Commerce and Competitive First-Degree Price Discrimination. Mimeo. Department of Economics, University College London.

Varian, H. R. (1998). Markets for information goods. Mimeo. University of California, Berkeley.

Whinston, M. (1990). Tying, foreclosure, and exclusion. *American Economic Review* 80: 837–869.

7   Preannouncing Information Goods

Jay Pil Choi, Eirik Gaard
Kristiansen, and Jae Nahm

7.1   Introduction

With the advent of digital technology, information goods are increasingly composed of bits, not atoms. This has profound implications for the industry of information goods as discussed in various chapters of this book. Software companies, for instance, face a number of challenges in their business strategy. They need to protect their innovations through patents (see Fershtman and Gandal, chapter 2 of this book) and copyright protection (see Gayer and Shy, chapter 8). Versioning is another strategic instrument that plays an important role (see Belleflamme, chapter 6). Software companies are also often part of a "subeconomy," that is, they are a component of a software platform (see Evans, Hagiu, and Schmalensee, chapter 3). As such, software solutions have impacted several related markets including digital music distribution (see Peitz and Waelbroeck, chapter 4) and electronic commerce (see Dinlersoz and Pereira, chapter 9).

In this chapter, we focus on a widely practiced business strategy of *preannouncing new products* in the industry of information goods. In particular, information goods in digital form are much more durable than tangible goods that are subject to wear and tear over time. This implies that one of the most important decisions for a consumer is choosing when to buy information goods, especially when the market is characterized by switching costs (Klemperer 1995) and ongoing technological progress.

Developing a new product is a lengthy process, and the expected arrival of a new product affects consumers and rival firms. As a result, firms usually make new product announcements well in advance of actual market availability. By making preannouncements, firms can deliver information on a product while it is being developed. The announcement may influence the decisions of rival firms and consumers. In particular, a firm in the process of developing a new product could make preannouncements aimed at persuading consumers to delay their purchase until its own product is available. The announcements could also be directed at potential rival firms. For instance, if there is a high duplicated R&D cost, a firm, by announcing that it is already very close to finishing its R&D project, could discourage potential competitors from investing in a similar project. This is especially true for information goods that are characterized by large sunk costs of development, but negligible marginal costs. Thus a firm has strategic reasons to convey its private information on a new product in order to change other parties' behavior in a way that is beneficial to the firm.

However, there is an issue of credibility associated with such announcements—that is, whether the firm would have incentives to be truthful in its announcements. In fact this practice has been called *vaporware* by industry commentators since, in many instances, these promised products were significantly delayed or the promised features did not meet expectations.[1] *Wired News*, for instance, puts out an annual list of the top ten vaporware products of the past year that includes various hardware, software, and game titles. In the most recent annual list (released on January 7, 2005), Alienware's Video Array topped the list, and 3D Realms's Duke Nukem Forever received a Lifetime Achievement Award for its endless delay. Whether these delays were an honest mistake due to unforeseen difficulties in the development process or whether the firm intentionally made a false announcement is debatable.

If a firm uses preannouncement as a strategic tool to stifle market competition, it could have perverse effects on market competition. For instance, when a rival firm introduces a new product, an entrenched dominant firm, by announcing that it would introduce a better product, may induce consumers to withhold purchasing the rival's product and prevent the loss of market shares. In this way, the incumbent can maintain its dominant position by using product preannouncement as a strategic tool. Thus product preannouncement has been a contentious issue in major antitrust cases. For instance, Microsoft was recently accused of this practice concerning its MS-DOS operating system.[2] IBM's announcement of its System/360 line of computers in the 1960s is another example.[3]

In this chapter, we conduct a selective review of the literature on the effects of product preannouncement on market competition; we provide a very simple model of vaporware in the context of reputation and discuss its implications for social welfare and antitrust policy. We also discuss several open issues in need of further research.

The remainder of the chapter is organized as follows. Sections 7.2 and 7.3 constitute a selective review of the related literature that analyzes announcements as a firm strategy. The literature can be classified broadly into two categories depending on the main purpose or audience of the announcement. In section 7.2, we review models of product preannouncement directed toward rival firms to deter entry. Section 7.3 focuses on models of product preannouncement directed toward consumers to delay their purchase decisions until a new product is available.[4] In reviewing the literature in sections 7.2 and 7.3, we highlight the main differences between the existing models and our own model. In section 7.4, we present a very simple cheap-talk model of vaporware with reputational concerns. We identify conditions under which product preannouncement can be informative and explore welfare implications of such a practice. Section 7.5 concludes with the discussion of potential extensions.

7.2   Announcements Aimed toward Rival Firms

By using preannouncement as a strategic tool, firms intend to influence other economic agents' choices in the relevant market. The announcements, for instance, can be directed toward rival firms, potential consumers, or both. In this section, we review a line of research that analyzes the effects of announcements directed mainly toward rival firms to dissuade entry.

7.2.1   Cheap Talk Models of Coordination

When there is a high sunk cost of entry or of developing a new product, a market can accommodate only a few firms. Suppose there are two potential entrants and that a market can accommodate only one firm. Then one firm's optimal entry decision depends on the other firm's entry decision, and the two firms need to communicate with each other to coordinate their entry decisions. There are two approaches for modeling the communication between firms. One is a signaling model, and the other is a cheap-talk model. In a signaling model, it is assumed that making a false announcement is costly. A firm that makes a false announcement could, for example, be penalized by an antitrust investigation. On the contrary, in a cheap-talk model, communication between firms does not entail any direct costs.

The main insight of the cheap-talk literature is that cheap talk can function as preplay communication among players to achieve coordination, even though it does not involve any direct cost or benefits of communication. Farrell (1987) and Park (2002), for instance, analyze how costless and nonbinding communication can achieve coordination among potential entrants.

To illustrate the main intuition, consider the following entry game analyzed in Farrell (1987). There are two potential entrants who must decide whether or not to enter simultaneously. The market can accommodate only one firm. If both firms enter, each firm loses L; if only one firm enters, the firm earns M, and the other firm earns B, where M is larger than B. If neither firm enters, each firm earns zero. One critical assumption is that $B > 0$. That is, even if it does not enter, each firm prefers that the other firm enter. The assumption reflects the case in which the new product is complementary to the firms' existing products. The game can be described by the following matrix (table 7.1).

The Pareto optimal allocation in this game is that only one firm chooses "In." There are multiple equilibria in this game, with two asymmetric pure-strategy equilibria and one symmetric mixed-strategy equilibrium. In the two asymmetric pure-strategy equilibria, one firm chooses "In" while the other chooses "Out," and the resulting equilibrium is Pareto optimal. However, the most natural equilibrium may be the symmetric mixed-strategy equilibrium since both firms are symmetric in this game. Without communication, the unique, symmetric equilibrium is that each firm enters with probability $p = \frac{M}{B+L+M}$. With the symmetric mixed-strategy equilibrium, however, we have a coordination failure. With the probability of p^2, both firms choose "In," and with the probability of $(1 - p)^2$, both firms choose "Out" and no entry

Table 7.1
Payoff matrix of the simultaneous entry game

	In	Out
In	$-L, -L$	M, B
Out	B, M	0, 0

occurs. Thus, the overall probability of coordination failure is given by $[p^2 + (1 - p)^2]$.

Suppose the two firms can have a preplay "talk." More specifically, consider a game of preplay communication in which the two firms simultaneously announce "In" or "Out" before making their real entry decisions. If only one firm says "In," then the firm will choose "In," while the other firm stays out. If both firms say "In" or "Out," then they play the symmetric equilibrium we derived above—that is, each firm enters with the probability $p = \frac{M}{B+L+M}$. Then, in the unique symmetric equilibrium of the game with preplay communication, each firm says "In" with probability $q = \frac{M-pB}{B-2pB+B}$. Thus the probability of a failure of coordination (both enter or neither enters) is reduced from $[p^2 + (1 - p)^2]$ to $[p^2 + (1 - p)^2][q^2 + (1 - q)^2]$. Thus the communication can help the coordination problem among potential entrants.[5]

Farrell and Saloner (1985) analyze coordination under incomplete information in the context of technology adoption with network externalities. They discuss the effects of preplay communication and show that "symmetric" or Pareto inertia due to incomplete information can be eliminated with simple communication through cheap talk.[6] However, they also point out the possibility that preplay communication exacerbates inertia where the preferences differ.[7]

7.2.2 Signaling Models of Entry Deterrence

Bayus et al. (2001) develop a signaling model that analyzes how firms' announcements of new products affects other firms' entry decisions. They consider a situation in which two firms simultaneously decide whether and *when* to introduce a new product. Each firm, by spending more on R&D, can introduce its product earlier. In contrast to Farrell (1987), Bayus et al. consider an asymmetric setting in which one firm is dominant in the sense that the other firm cannot operate profitably if it enters later than the dominant firm. There are two types of firms: the R&D cost of the low-type firm is lower than that of the high-type firm. Thus the low type can develop its product earlier than the high type for the same R&D spending. By announcing an earlier release time of the new product, the firm can signal that it is of the low type. Since the entry by the follower is unprofitable when the dominant firm is of the low cost type, intentional vaporware is associated with entry deterrence. In such a setting, Bayus et al. analyze the dominant firm's incentives for intentional vaporware, that is, the firm making an announcement on the release time knowing that it could miss the date.

They show that there is a separating equilibrium in which the low-type firm engages in intentional vaporware, whereas the high-type firm announces its release time truthfully.

Penalty costs associated with false announcements are what enable separation of types in the model of Bayus et al. (2001). They assume a penalty cost function that is increasing and convex in the discrepancy between the announced time and the actual time of product introduction. They justify this assumption with potential antitrust investigation or loss in reputation associated with false announcements. Even though the assumption is reasonable, it is at best ad hoc in that there is no microfoundation for such penalty costs in their model. In particular, no one is deceived by intentional vaporware since all receivers can infer the actual timing of product introduction in equilibrium, even if it is different from the announced date. In section 7.4, we develop a model of vaporware in which the reputation cost is endogenously derived.

Haan (2003) also develops a model of premature announcements that are used strategically to deter other firms from developing a similar product. In his model, an incumbent sells a durable good in period one, but can introduce a new product in the second period. The new product makes an existing product obsolete. There is also a firm that considers entering the market. However, if the incumbent is about to introduce the new product, it is not optimal for this entrant to enter. Whether or not the incumbent has an innovation is private information. After observing the incumbent's output level, consumers in period one decide how much to pay for the incumbent product and the entrant decides whether or not to enter. The model is, technically, a two-audience signaling model in the spirit of Gertner, Gibbons, and Scharfstein (1988). The reason is that the price consumers are willing to pay in the first period depends on their beliefs about the market price in the second, which, in turn, depends on whether or not the incumbent firm introduces the drastic innovation in the future. In this setup, Haan (2003) shows that there is no separating equilibrium and that no information can be revealed in equilibrium. This is due to the incumbent's incentives to send different messages to different audiences. More specifically, the incumbent would like to have consumers believe that, in the next period, there will not be a new product that would make their purchases in the first period obsolete. In this way, the incumbent firm can sell the old technology at a higher price and have consumers make another purchase when the new product is introduced. For the potential entrant, in contrast, the incumbent would like to convince consumers that there *will* be a new product, which will make entry unprofitable. As a result, neither type has incentives to separate from the other type, and the resulting outcome is a pooling equilibrium in which neither type is revealed in equilibrium. We should mention that strictly speaking, since the means of signaling in Haan's model is the production level in the first period, he focuses on whether there is separation of types through the firm's production decision, and not on whether the firm has any incentives to make false announcements.

7.3   Announcements Aimed toward Consumers

This section describes the models that analyze the effects of announcements targeting consumers for the purpose of delaying their purchase decisions. Developing a new product usually takes time. If there is a high switching cost, consumers who buy a currently available product are locked into that product and find it difficult to switch to a new product when it is introduced. Thus consumers need to decide whether to buy currently available products or to wait for a new product. The consumers' optimal decisions depend on the expected quality of the new product. Conversely, the firm's R&D incentive to develop a new product depends on how many consumers are waiting for its product. Therefore, there are common interests between the firm and consumers, and they have incentives to "talk" to each other.

Suppose that in a two-period model, consumers can buy a currently available durable good. The currently available product provides consumers a flow consumption benefit of w per period. One firm is developing a new product and is able to introduce it in period two. The new product can provide consumers a flow benefit of $(w + s)$ per period, where s can be interpreted as the improvement of the new product over the currently available one and is assumed to be private information of the firm. For simplicity, there is no time discount between periods one and two. If consumers buy the currently available product in period one, they can enjoy $2w$ benefit for the two periods, while they can get $(w + s)$ by delaying their purchase until period two when the new product is available. Since consumers need to pay the opportunity cost of waiting w, consumers will delay their purchasing only if the additional consumer benefit from the new product is larger than w. If the firm can verify the size of s to consumers in period one, the firm's announcement can help consumers make better decisions.

By assuming that the firm can make a verifiable claim on its product quality, Farrell and Saloner (1986) provide an early analysis of how product preannouncements affect consumers' technology adoption decisions. They point out that, even though a product preannouncement helps consumers make better decisions, it could be anticompetitive in the presence of *network effects*. In particular, they construct a dynamic model of technology adoption in which consumers arrive sequentially in the market, and each decides which technology to choose given what others have done. In the model, the announcement of a new *incompatible* product can have an impact on the pattern of technology adoption, that is, whether or not the new product succeeds in replacing the existing technology. Upon hearing the announcement, some consumers decide to wait. Even if the potential users who decide to wait are well informed and their welfare is increased as a result of product preannouncement, due to the presence of network effects their adoption of the new technology may adversely affect both consumers with the old product and later adopters, who might have preferred the old technology to the new one.

Gerlach (2004) also analyzes the effects of advance announcements directed at consumers to increase their expected value of waiting and prevent the loss of potential future demand in a durable goods market with switching costs. He calls this positive effect of announcements for the firm the *demand pull effect*. Gerlach's model is noteworthy in that he allows the possibility that the advance information directed toward consumers spills over to the incumbent rival firm, which can respond preemptively to the revelation of new information on impending entry, strategically setting its price to deter the entry of the announcing firm.[8] This negative effect of announcement is called the *strategic reaction effect*.[9] Gerlach analyzes the entrant's incentive to make a preannouncement on its product and shows that entrants do not always announce in equilibrium due to the tradeoff between the positive demand pull and the negative strategic reaction effect. Gerlach further demonstrates that such an equilibrium behavior maximizes ex ante social welfare, even though consumers might be better off with a ban on announcements.

However, both Farrell and Saloner (1986) and Gerlach (2004) consider the case in which firms can make verifiable statements about their products. The studies do not allow the possibility of false announcements, and nor do they analyze consumers' inference problems from announcements.[10] In most cases, firms cannot make a verifiable statement about their product, and consumers do not know the veracity of the announcement. Consumers need to rely on the information the firm provides, but the firm has an incentive to cheat consumers with regard to quality level. Suppose that the additional consumer surplus from the new product over the old product is between zero and w. Then it is optimal for consumers to buy the current product in period one without waiting for the new product. However, if consumers are induced to wait until period two, they will choose the new product over the old product since the new one provides a higher consumer surplus than the old product does. Thus as long as the firm can induce consumers to wait until period two, the firm can sell its product to consumers in period two. The firm has an incentive to inflate (or make a false claim about) its product's quality level. Also, since a new product is still in development, it is very difficult for the firm and consumers to make a contract based on the product's quality. For instance, when a software company promises in advance features of a new software program, it could be difficult to describe them in precise terms, without any ambiguity, so that the contract could be enforceable in court.

The question, then, is: what makes a firm's preannouncements credible since every firm has incentives to make consumers wait for its product? If a firm and consumers have only a one-time interaction, then it would be difficult for a product preannouncement to be informative. However, if a firm has repeated interactions with consumers, the firm will have a reputation concern, and the firm's reputation will depend on its past behavior. Fisher et al. (1983) argue:

> [T]here is no reason to inhibit the time when a firm announces or brings products to the marketplace. Customers will be the final arbiters of the product's quality and the firm's reputation. Broken promises and unattractive products can be expected to lead quickly to a loss of credibility and sales.

Levy (1997) explores antitrust implications of vaporware and echoes the argument in Fisher et al. (1983). More specifically, he considers a situation in which consumers do not know the veracity of the firm's announcements when they are made. He concludes that vaporware should not be of concern to antitrust authorities since reputation concerns prevent firms from intentionally making false announcements. However, he does not model reputation explicitly in his paper.

Dranove and Gandal (2003), in a rare paper, provide an empirical analysis of preannouncement effects in the DVD market. Regarding the standard war between the DVD and DIVX formats, they show that the preannouncement of DIVX slowed the adoption of DVD technology, which is consistent with the theory of product preannouncements in theoretical literature.

Choi, Kristiansen, and Nahm (2004) (hereafter referred to as CKN) analyze the role of preannouncement when a firm has a reputation concern. They model explicitly the formation of reputation in a repeated product preannouncement game and characterize the equilibrium in which private information held by the firm is partially revealed. The following section describes the CKN model in more detail.

7.4   Vaporware and Reputation

In this section, we construct a simple model to answer the question of whether preannouncements of a new product can help consumers make better purchasing decisions when a firm's announcement is nonbinding and nonverifiable. Indeed, if the game is played only once, there would be no room for the product preannouncements to be informative. However, if there are repeated interactions between the firm and consumers, the firm tries to build its reputation. Thus CKN (2004) consider a scenario in which the firm and consumers interact repeatedly and develop a reputation model of vaporware. CKN derive conditions under which product preannouncements can be informative and they analyze the welfare effect of product preannouncement. Let us present a simpler version of the CKN model with only two types.

Consider a game that is played by consumers and a firm that develops a *sequence* of new products. This would be the case if the industry were characterized by a constant stream of new products.[11] For instance, consumers expect computer and video game producers to introduce new titles over time. Computer hardware and software producers are also expected to continuously develop new gadgets and software programs. For simplicity, we assume there are two sequential product cycles and a firm can introduce a new product in each cycle. Let δ denote the time discount between the first and second product cycles. In each product cycle, there are two periods. More specifically, in the first period, an existing product is competitively supplied. The firm that develops a new product introduces the new product in the second period. For simplicity, there is no time discount between periods within the same product cycle. Consumers who have unit demand for the product in each product cycle have two options in the first period: they can either purchase the existing product at the competitive price or wait until the second period for the new product. For the first period purchase decision to have dynamic implications, we assume that the good is durable. In addition, once the consumers purchase in the first period, they are locked in and cannot switch to the new product in the second period due to switching costs (see Klemperer 1995).

The quality of the new product can be either high (H) or low (L). The ex ante probability that the firm can develop a high-quality product is denoted by θ, which can be considered the firm's type. There are two types of firm, θ_1 and θ_2, $\theta_1 < \theta_2$. The firm knows its own type, but consumers know only the distribution of the firm types. The prior belief that the firm is of type θ_2 is q. The firm's type is assumed to be invariant across product cycles and represents the firm's innovativeness or research capability. The realization of quality, however, is independent across product cycles. The firm that is in the process of developing a new product knows the quality of the product in the first period of each product cycle. The firm can announce the quality of the product to consumers in period one to persuade consumers to delay their purchase. We assume that product preannouncements are cheap talk and do not entail any costs to make.

If a consumer buys the currently available product in period one, the consumer's surplus per period is w. When consumers wait, they forego the current consumption benefit that can be considered their waiting costs.[12] The new product developed by the firm is superior to the existing product, regardless of its quality realizations. Let s_H and s_L be the expected value of the indirect utility difference between the new and old products when the quality of the new product is high and low, respectively. This implies that the consumer surplus from waiting until period two is $w + s_i$, where $i = H$ or L, depending on the quality realization of the new product, while that of buying the current product in period one is $2w$.

We assume that $s_H > s_L > 0$, which implies that consumers get a higher surplus from the high-quality product than from the low-quality product and that consumers will buy even the low-quality product in period two if they wait until period two. Consumers are more willing to wait if the new product is of high quality.[13] To have a meaningful analysis of consumers' waiting decision, we assume that $s_L < w < s_H$. That is, consumers are willing to delay their purchase if and only if the new product is of high quality. We also assume that $\theta_2 s_H + (1 - \theta_2)s_L > w$ and that $\theta_1 s_H + (1 - \theta_1)s_L < w$. That is, if the firm's type is known to be θ_2, the expected quality of the new product is high enough that consumers will wait until period two. However, if the firm's type is known to be θ_1, consumers will not wait.

Let π^H (π^L) denote the profit for the firm that introduces a high-quality product and a low-quality product, respectively, when consumers wait. We assume that $\pi^H > \pi^L > 0$. Since $\pi^H > 0$ and $s_H > w$, if the new product is of high quality, it is mutually beneficial for consumers and the firm that consumers wait for the new product. We assume that if consumers do not wait, the firm profit is zero. This assumption can be justified because significant switching costs prevent consumers from buying the new product once they have purchased in the first period. This implies that if announcing a high-quality product induces consumers to wait until period two, the firm with the low-quality product has an incentive to mislead consumers and announce a high-quality product. Therefore, product preannouncements cannot impart any information to consumers if the game is played only once. Next we analyze whether or not we can have an informative equilibrium in such a situation if the announcement game is played repeatedly.

As usual, we derive an equilibrium with backward induction and analyze the second product cycle first. In the second product cycle, the firm's announcement does not convey any credible information since it is the last interaction between the firm and consumers. Consumers, thus, make their decision based only on their updated belief about the firm's type derived from its history.

Let μ denote consumers' belief that the firm has a high-quality product. Then we can define a critical level of belief $\bar{\mu}$ at which consumers are indifferent between purchasing the currently available product in the first period and waiting for the new product until the second period.

$$\bar{\mu} s_H + (1 - \bar{\mu})s_L = w$$

That is,

$$\bar{\mu} = \frac{w - s_L}{s_H - s_L} \tag{7.1}$$

Since $\theta_2 s_H + (1 - \theta_2)s_L > w$ and $\theta_1 s_H + (1 - \theta_1)s_L < w$, $\bar{\mu}$ is between θ_1 and θ_2.

Let μ_2 denote the consumers' updated belief of the firm's probability to deliver a high-quality product in the second product cycle. We interpret μ_2 as the reputation level of the firm. If μ_2 is higher than $\bar{\mu} = \frac{w - s_L}{s_H - s_L}$, consumers will wait until period two in the second product cycle.

If consumers do not wait until the second product cycle, the firm's profit is zero. However, if consumers wait, the firm's ex ante expected profit (that is, before knowing whether it has a high- or low-quality product) is $\theta \pi^H + (1 - \theta)\pi^L$, which increases in θ. That is, even though all types benefit from consumers' waiting, type θ_2 has a higher return from it than type θ_1 does. That is, type θ_2 has more reputation concerns than type θ_1 does if a higher reputation leads consumers to wait, which implies that the Spence-Mirrlees single crossing property holds.[14] Due to the single crossing property, we can get a separating equilibrium in which higher types make an honest announcement, while lower types could make an intentionally false announcement. We are interested in conditions under which the firm's reputation concerns leads the firm to make an honest announcement on the quality of its product in the first product cycle.

In particular, we are looking for an informative equilibrium with the following properties:

(1) If the firm has a high-quality product in the first cycle, both types (truthfully) announce a high-quality product. Consumers take the announcements as partially true and wait until the second period in the first product cycle. Since their beliefs are confirmed, consumers update their beliefs upward and also wait for a new product in the second product cycle.

(2) If the firm has a low-quality product in the first cycle,
(i) the θ_1-type firm makes a false announcement that its product is of high quality, and consumers are misled into waiting for the new product in the first cycle. They will revise their beliefs downward and not wait in the second cycle.
(ii) the θ_2-type firm makes a truthful announcement (or does not make an announcement), and consumers do not wait in the first cycle. However, they revise their beliefs upward and reward the firm by waiting in the second product cycle.

Knowing that a firm might make an intentionally false announcement, consumers update their beliefs about the new product's quality based on the firm's announcement strategy. Given the equilibrium strategies of the firm above, if the firm announces a high-quality product in the first cycle, the updated belief that the product is of high quality in the first cycle is given by:

$$\mu_1^H = \frac{q}{q\theta_2 + (1-q)}\theta_2 + \left(\frac{1-q}{q\theta_2 + (1-q)}\right)\theta_1 \tag{7.2}$$

For the product preannouncements to have impacts on consumers' waiting decision, we assume the following:

$$\mu_1^H > \bar{\mu} \tag{7.3}$$

That is, when the firm announces a high-quality product, consumers will wait for the new product in the first cycle. If the announcement turns out to be true, then consumers will update their beliefs about the firm's type according to the Bayes rule. The posterior probability that the firm is of high type can be derived as:

$$\Pr(\theta = \theta_2 \,|\, Quality = H)$$

$$= \frac{\Pr(\theta = \theta_2)\,\Pr(Quality = H \,|\, \theta = \theta_2)}{\Pr(\theta = \theta_2)\,\Pr(Quality = H \,|\, \theta = \theta_2) + \Pr(\theta = \theta_1)\,\Pr(Quality = H \,|\, \theta = \theta_2)}$$

$$= \frac{q\theta_2}{q\theta_2 + (1-q)\theta_1}$$

Thus μ_2 becomes $\frac{q\theta_2}{q\theta_2+(1-q)\theta_1}\theta_2 + \left(\frac{(1-q)\theta_1}{q\theta_2+(1-q)\theta_1}\right)\theta_1$. If the announcement turns out to be false, then μ_2 becomes θ_1. Since $\frac{q\theta_2}{q\theta_2+(1-q)\theta_1} > \frac{q\theta_2}{q\theta_2+(1-q)}$, equation (7.3) implies that $\frac{q\theta_2}{q\theta_2+(1-q)\theta_1}\theta_2 + \left(\frac{(1-q)\theta_1}{q\theta_2+(1-q)\theta_1}\right)\theta_1 > \bar{\mu}$. That is, if the firm introduces a high-quality product in the first cycle, consumers will wait in the second cycle as stipulated in the description of the equilibrium.

Finally, if the firm does not make an announcement in the first cycle, then consumers do not wait in the first cycle, but μ_2 becomes θ_2. Since we assume that $\theta_2 s_H + (1 - \theta_2)s_L > w$, that is, $\theta_2 > \bar{\mu}$, consumers will wait in the second cycle.

Let us check whether the firm's strategies described satisfy incentive compatibility constraints in the first product cycle. If the firm has a high-quality product in the first cycle, it is obvious that it is an optimal strategy for the firm to make an honest announcement. Now consider the case in which the firm has a low-quality product in the first cycle. If the firm makes a false announcement, consumers will wait, and the firm's profit in the first product cycle is π^L. However, the firm loses its reputation and consumers will not wait in the second product cycle. In contrast, if the firm does not make any announcement, it gets zero profit in the first product cycle whereas its expected profit in the second product cycle is $\delta[\theta \pi^H + (1 - \theta)\pi^L]$. Consumers wait in the second product cycle and the firm's expected profit in such a scenario depends on its ex ante probability that the firm can develop a high quality product, that is, the firm's type θ.

The incentive compatibility conditions for type θ_2 with a low-quality product to make a true announcement in the first cycle, while for type θ_1 with a low-quality product to make a false announcement, are satisfied if the following condition holds:

$$\theta_1 < \frac{1 - \delta}{\delta} \frac{\pi_L}{\pi_H - \pi_L} < \theta_2 \qquad (7.4)$$

Thus we can conclude that if conditions (7.3) and (7.4) are satisfied, we can have the informative equilibrium described.[15] We summarize our main result in the following proposition.

Proposition 7.1 Suppose that conditions (7.3) and (7.4) hold. Then there exists an informative equilibrium with the following properties:

7.4.1 Firm Behavior

If the firm has a high-quality product in the first cycle, both types (truthfully) announce a high-quality product. If the firm has a low-quality product in the first cycle, the low-type firm (θ_1) makes a false announcement that its product is of high quality whereas the high-type firm (θ_2) makes a truthful announcement (or does not make an announcement).

7.4.2 Consumer Behavior

When the firm makes an announcement of high quality in the first cycle, consumers take the announcements as partially true and wait until the second period in the first product cycle. If the product is of high quality and their beliefs are confirmed, consumers update their beliefs upward and also wait for a new product in the second product cycle. If the product is of low quality and consumers are misled into waiting for the new product in the first cycle, they will revise their beliefs downward and not wait in the second product cycle. If there is an announcement of low quality (or no announcement) consumers do not wait in the first cycle. However, they revise their beliefs upward and reward the firm by waiting in the second product cycle.

In this simple, twice-repeated cheap-talk game, we can also show that in any informative equilibrium, a firm's announcement always ex ante improves consumer welfare, even though a firm might make a false announcement. This implies that, as long as consumers understand the low-type firm's incentives to mislead with its announcements and take them into account in making their purchase decisions, consumers cannot be worse off with product preannouncements. Our model thus formalizes the argument in Fisher et al. (1983) and Levy (1997) that firms will refrain from making false announcements due to concerns about reputation.

Proposition 7.2 The welfare effect of product preannouncements on consumers is positive.

Proof See the appendix.

7.5   Concluding Remarks

We have conducted a selective review of the related literature and highlighted the differences between the existing models and our own. In a simplified version of the CKN model, we also show that reputational concerns can be used as an incentive device to make cheap talk *partially informative*. As a result, consumers are able to make a better intertemporal purchase decision; they are better off with the possibility of product preannouncements as long as consumers are rational and understand the incentives of low-type firms to mislead consumers. We conclude by discussing potential extensions of our chapter and several open issues in need of further research.

7.5.1   Strategic Price-Setting by the Incumbents
As in Farrell and Saloner (1986), we do not consider strategic pricing by the incumbent firms, but instead assume that the old product is competitively supplied. It would be an interesting extension of our model to allow the possibility that the incumbent firms can respond to product preannouncements by innovators of a new product, as in Gerlach (2004).

7.5.2   Network Effects
The welfare result in our model depends crucially on the assumption that there are no externalities associated with consumers' purchase decisions. However, product preannouncements have been prominent

in industries characterized by network effects, such as the computer software industry. In such a case, we cannot rule out the possibility that product preannouncements might influence which product prevails in the marketplace and lead to socially inefficient technology adoption. This may be true even if those who make purchase-or-wait decisions are better informed, with the potential source of inefficiency being incompatibility between the old and new products. Farrell and Saloner (1986) demonstrate the possibility that preannouncement can lower social welfare in a dynamic model of technology adoption. We can surely derive a similar result in our model if we introduce network effects. This possibility certainly provides a caution against blanket approval of product preannouncements.

7.5.3 Intentional versus Unintentional Vaporware
To analyze the possibility of the informativeness of product preannouncements, we focus exclusively on *intentional* vaporware, assuming that the innovating firm can predict the quality of the product or the timing of the product introduction without any error. In reality, however, such a prediction inevitably entails some error due to unforeseen events in the development process. With such a possibility, consumers' inference problem can be more complex. When there is a discrepancy between the announced timing and quality of the new product and the actual delivery, consumers have to assess the cause of the discrepancy: was the firm dishonest, or was the delay due to an honest mistake? If the consumers are lenient and give the firm the benefit of the doubt when the actual delivery does not meet expectations, the incentives to tell the truth would be destroyed. However, if the consumers are too harsh and treat any discrepancy as a proof of dishonesty, the innovating firms would refrain from providing any information for fear of a mistake. This could block a useful channel of information between producers and consumers. The optimal punishment scheme should balance these two conflicting effects, as in the design of the optimal collusive scheme under uncertainty (see Green and Porter 1984).

The possibility of unintentional vaporware also poses a problem for antitrust policymakers. If all product preannouncements can be made and ex post fact verified without any error, the best public policy would be to prohibit any false announcements. Such a policy would lead to perfect information revelation, as in Grossman (1981). In reality, however, it would be difficult to implement such a policy because of the difficulty and ambiguity associated with ascertaining whether the firm actually delivered the promised quality, especially when the features promised are something nonexistent at the time of announcement—a fact that makes direct contracting between the firm and consumers infeasible in the first place. Also, another hurdle in implementing such a policy is the difficulty of determining whether or not the firm made its product announcements in good faith.

7.5.4   The Finite Horizon versus Infinite Horizon

We develop a reputational model of a cheap-talk game with a finite number of product cycles. If we considered an infinite horizon of product cycles, we would have a similar result, with the high types always telling the truth and the low types lying when they have a low-quality product. The mechanism in the infinite horizon model through which the high types tell the truth would be similar to the one in Choi's (1998) model of brand extension. In Choi (1998), as long as all previous products with the same brand name were of high quality, consumers believe that a new product under that brand name will be of high quality, as well. Once the brand name is extended to a low-quality product, consumers ignore any signaling value of brand extension. In response, the monopolists extend brand name only to a high-quality product, and consumers' beliefs are confirmed. In our model, consumers would believe product preannouncements as long as all the previous announcements were true. Once the firm makes a false announcement, consumers will ignore any future announcement made by the firm. One major difference in Choi's brand extension model is that his model is of moral hazard, and there is no uncertainty about the firm type. In contrast, in our model there is also an adverse selection problem about the firm type, with the separation of types taking place over time.

Appendix: Proof of Proposition 7.2 The Effect of Product Announcements on Consumer Welfare

In this section, we analyze how the firm's product announcements affect consumer welfare in the simple two-type model. We refer the reader to CKN (2004) for a more detailed welfare analysis for a general setting.

When the firm is allowed to make product preannouncements, the expected total consumer welfare in the informative equilibrium is as follows,

$$W^A = W_1^A + \delta W_2^A$$

$$= (1-q)(\theta_1(s_H + w) + (1-\theta_1)(s_L + w)) + q(\theta_2(s_H + w)$$

$$+ (1-\theta_2)2w) + \delta[(1-q)(\theta_1(w + \theta_1 s_H + (1-\theta_1)s_L)$$

$$+ (1-\theta_1)2w) + q(w + \theta_2 s_H + (1-\theta_2)s_L)].$$

(where W_i^A denotes consumer welfare in period i, $i = 1, 2$ when preannouncements are allowed)

Let us analyze how prohibiting preannouncements affects consumers' welfare. First, suppose that $q\theta_2 + (1-q)\theta_1 < \bar{\mu}$. Then if the social planner prohibits preannouncements, consumers will buy the currently available product and get $2w$ in the first cycle. In the second cycle, consumers will update their beliefs about the product's quality based on whether the product in period one is of high quality. If the firm produced a high-quality product in the first cycle, then the updated belief that the product is of high quality in the second cycle is given by $\frac{q\theta_2}{(1-q)\theta_1 + q\theta_2}\theta_2 + \left(1 - \frac{q\theta_2}{(1-q)\theta_1 + q\theta_2}\right)\theta_1$. In contrast, if the firm produced a low-quality product in the first cycle, the updated belief is given by $\frac{q(1-\theta_2)}{(1-q)(1-\theta_1) + q(1-\theta_2)}\theta_2 + \frac{(1-q)(1-\theta_1)}{(1-q)(1-\theta_1) + q(1-\theta_2)}\theta_1$. By condition (7.3) and the fact that $\frac{q(1-\theta_2)}{(1-q)(1-\theta_1) + q(1-\theta_2)} < q$, consumers will wait for a new product in the second cycle only if the product in the first cycle is of high quality. The total expected consumer welfare is as follows:

$$W^{NA} = W_1^{NA} + \delta W_2^{NA}$$

$$= 2w + \delta[(1-q)((1-\theta_1)2w + \theta_1(w + \theta_1 s_H + (1-\theta_1)s_L))$$

$$+ q((1-\theta_2)2w + \theta_2(w + \theta_2 s_H + (1-\theta_2)s_L))].$$

Let us compare W^A and W^{NA}. First, $W_1^A - W_1^{NA} = ((1-q)\theta_1 + q\theta_2)s_H + (1-q)(1-\theta_1)s_L - (1-q+q\theta_2)w$. If we divide both sides by $(1-q+q\theta_2)$, we get $\mu_1^H s_H + (1-\mu_1^H)s_L - w$, where $\mu_1^H = \frac{q\theta_2}{q\theta_2 + (1-q)} + \left(\frac{1-q}{q\theta_2 + (1-q)}\right)\theta_1$. Since $\mu_1^H > \bar{\mu}$, we have that $W_1^A - W_1^{NA} > 0$. Second, $W_2^A - W_2^{NA} = q(1-\theta_2)(\theta_2 s_H + (1-\theta_2)s_L - w)$. Since $\theta_2 > \bar{\mu}$, $W_2^A - W_2^{NA} > 0$. Thus, we have $W^A > W^{NA}$.

Second, suppose that $q > \bar{\mu}$. Then, if the firm is not allowed to make product preannouncements, consumers will wait for a new product in the first cycle. Consumers will wait in the second cycle only if the product in the first cycle is of high quality, as in the previous case. In the second case, the expected consumer welfare can be written as follows:

$$\mathring{W}^{NA} = \mathring{W}_1^{NA} + \delta \mathring{W}_2^{NA}$$

$$= (w + (1-q)(\theta_1 s_H + (1-\theta_1)s_L) + q(\theta_2 s_H + (1-\theta_2)s_L))$$

$$+ \delta(1-q)((1-\theta_1)2w + \theta_1(w + \theta_1 s_H + (1-\theta_1)s_L))$$

$$+ \delta q((1-\theta_2)2w + \theta_2(w + \theta_2 s_H + (1-\theta_2)s_L))$$

Let us compare W^A and $\mathring{W}^{NA}$. First, $W_1^A - \mathring{W}_1^{NA} = q(1-\theta_2)(w - s_L) > 0$. Second, since $\mathring{W}_2^{NA} = W_2^{NA}$, we have $W_2^A - \mathring{W}_2^{NA} > 0$. Thus, we have $W^A > \mathring{W}^{NA}$.

Combining these two cases together, we can conclude that allowing preannouncements always helps consumers make a better decision, and its effect on consumer welfare is positive.

Notes

This paper was prepared for the CESifo Economic Studies Conference on "Understanding the Digital Economy" held in Munich on July 2–3, 2004. We thank Christian Wey, editor Martin Peitz, two anonymous referees, and participants in the conference for helpful and constructive comments on the previous version of the paper.

1. See Bayus et al. (2001) for the origin of the term *vaporware*.

2. Although Microsoft announced that its DOS 5.0 would be released in the first quarter of 1991, it was not released until June 1991. It was also alleged that some of the announcements about its features were spurious.

3. See Fisher et al. (1983) for details.

4. There also are papers that allow the spillover of announcement information.

5. Another efficiency argument for product preannouncements directed to business firms can be made in systems markets with complementarities. In such a market, a product's value depends on the availability of complements. An announcement by industry leaders, such as IBM or Microsoft, about the features or characteristics of the new platform product coordinates the research and development efforts of suppliers of complements. We thank our discussant Christian Wey for pointing this out.

6. Symmetric excess inertia refers to a situation in which the new technology is not adopted when adoption is favored by both firms.

7. It is a general result in the cheap talk literature that preplay communication is more effective when the players' interests are more aligned. See Farrell and Rabin (1996) for a survey of the cheap talk literature.

8. Technically speaking, Gerlach (2004) is a model of cheap talk with two audiences in which the sender's (the entrant's) preferences are aligned with one type of audience (consumers), but are opposed to the other (the incumbent). In a model of cheap talk with one

audience, Crawford and Sobel (1982) show that the sender's message can be more informative the more aligned the preferences of the sender and the audience.

9. In Farrell and Saloner (1986) and our model in section 7.4, this information spillover would not matter since the current product market is assumed to be perfectly competitive, and the prices of the products are exogenously set. Thus, the announcement of the new product does not affect pricing of the old product, and the strategic reaction effect does not exist.

10. Even though Gerlach's (2004) main analysis is of the case of verifiable announcement, he also considers the possibility of false announcements. He shows that when the entrant's claims are not verifiable, the announcements cannot be informative in equilibrium. In contrast, in our model in section 7.4, we construct a reputational model of cheap talk, and the central question is whether or not nonverifiable announcements can be informative in a sequence of announcements.

11. Our model also would apply if the firm is expected to introduce a sequence of upgrades that would render the previous generations of the product obsolete.

12. For simplicity, we assume that consumers are homogeneous in their waiting costs (w) and, therefore, make the same decision as to purchase or wait in the first period. We can relax this assumption and allow different consumption patterns according to their waiting costs without affecting the main qualitative results. See Choi et al. (2004) for more details.

13. See Choi et al. (2004) for a microfoundation of the assumptions we make.

14. See Mas-Colell, Whinston, and Green (1995) for more details.

15. It can be easily verified that the set of parameters satisfying conditions (7.3) and (7.4) is nonempty.

References

Bayus, B. L., S. Jain, and A. G. Rao (2001), "Truth or Consequences: An Analysis of Vaporware and New Product Announcements," *Journal of Marketing Research* 38, 3–13.

Choi, J. P. (1998), "Brand Extension as Informational Leverage," *Review of Economic Studies*, 655–670.

Choi, J. P., E. G. Kristiansen, and J. Nahm (2004), "Vaporware," unpublished manuscript.

Crawford, V. P., and J. Sobel (1982), "Stratgic Information Transmission," *Econometrica* vol. 50, 1431–1451.

Dranove, D., and N. Gandal (2003), "The DVD vs. DIVX Standard War: Empirical Evidence of Vaporware," *Journal of Economics and Management Strategy* 12, 363–386.

Farrell, J. (1987), "Cheap Talk, Coordination, and Entry," *Rand Journal of Economics* vol. 18, no. 1, 34–39.

Farrell, J., and M. Rabin (1996), "Cheap Talk," *Journal of Economic Perspectives* 10(3), 103–118.

Farrell, J., and G. Saloner (1985), "Standardization, Compatibility, and Coordination," *Rand Journal of Economics*, 70–83.

Farrell, J., and G. Saloner (1986), "Installed Base and Compatibility: Innovation, Product Pre-announcements, and Predation," *American Economic Review* 76, 940–955.

Fisher, F. M., J. J. McGowan, and J. E. Greenwood (1983), "Folded, Spindled, and Mutilated: Economic Analysis and U.S. vs. IBM," The MIT Press, Cambridge.

Gerlach, H. A. (2004), "Announcement, Entry, and Preemption When Consumers Have Switching Costs," *Rand Journal of Economics* 35, 184–202.

Gertner, R., R. Gibbons, and D. Scharfstein (1988), "Simultaneous Signaling to the Capital and Product Market," *Rand Journal of Economics* 19, 173–190.

Green, E., and R. Porter (1984), "Noncooperative Collusion under Imperfect Price Information," *Econometrica* vol. 52, 87–100.

Grossman, S. J. (1981), "The Informational Role of Warranties and Private Disclosure about Product Quality," *Journal of Law and Economics* 24, 461–483.

Haan, A. M. (2003), "Vaporware as a Means of Entry Deterrence," *Journal of Industrial Economics*, Volume LI, 345–358.

Klemperer, P. (1995), "Competition When Consumers Have Switching Costs," *Review of Economic Studies* (62), 515–539.

Levy, S. M. (1997), "Should 'Vaporware' be an Antitrust Concern?," *The Antitrust Bulletin*, 33–49.

Mas-Colell, A., M. D. Whinston, and J. R. Green (1995), "Microeconomic Theory," Oxford University Press.

Park, I. (2002), "Cheap-Talk Coordination of Entry by Privately Informed Firms," *Rand Journal of Economics* vol. 33, no. 3, 377–393.

8   Copyright Enforcement in the Digital Era

Amit Gayer and Oz Shy

8.1   Introduction

8.1.1   Preface

We discourage illegal copying (piracy) simply because we believe that laws must be obeyed. However, we believe that common statements made by publishers and their lawyers concerning their "losses" from piracy are heavily exaggerated and that these "reported losses" do not always exist. Moreover, recent empirical studies have shown that file sharing via the Internet has a minor impact on sales of music CDs. Rob and Waldfogel (2004) and Oberholzer-Gee and Strumpf (2004) empirically demonstrate that a free download does not imply a lost sale. Rob and Waldfogel (2004) show that students each spent $126 on the bestselling CDs without downloading and $101 with downloading. This implies that every ten downloads of music result in one to two lost sales at the most! In addition, Oberholzer-Gee and Strumpf (2004) argue that the effects of file sharing on sales is statistically indistinguishable from zero. However, the reader is referred to chapter 5 in this book where Liebowitz reads this evidence somewhat differently than we do.

Furthermore, as we demonstrate in this chapter, in the digital era publishers can be better off by using copying technologies to promote their products instead of spending resources on legal fees to bring illegal users to trial.

8.1.2   Motivation

Digital convergence of information products has generated the following consequences:

(1) Different modes of information now can be stored digitally on potentially the same storage devices.

(2) Different modes of information can now be distributed via the same distributing channels. Moreover, they can be legally or illegally copied using the same transmission channels.

Consequence (1) follows from the observations that before the introduction of digital technologies, audio recordings were played on LP (Long Play) vinyl records, and also recorded on magnetic tapes using analog protocols. In contrast, visual information was stored on photographic films. Clearly, any mixture of audio and video required the use of complicated synchronizing technologies. Printed matter was either pressed into books and journals, or duplicated using mimeograph and photocopy machines.

Consequence (2) forms the main motivation for writing this chapter, namely that in the digital era all forms of information can be legally and illegally distributed via a wide variety of easy-to-copy channels, such as burned CDs, DVDs, and of course file sharing via the Internet. This means that users of information have more to gain by investing in learning how to obtain, copy, and distribute digital material since the same channels can be used to obtain all forms of information: print, audio, as well as video. Prior to the digital era such investments where less beneficial since distributions of the different forms of information required completely different knowledge and equipment.

8.1.3 The Literature

Theoretical papers like Conner and Rumelt (1991), as well as Shy and Thisse (1999) and Peitz (2004), demonstrate that strong network externalities imply a firm's earnings need not be reduced as a result of piracy as long as the demand for legal copies is enhanced with the actual distribution of illegal copies. Other theoretical contributions include Takeyama (1994, 1997), Slive and Bernhardt (1998), Poddar (2003), Gayer and Shy (2003, 2005), and a critical review by Peitz and Waelbroeck (2003) (see also their contribution in chapter 4 of this book). The present chapter draws some ideas from this literature and presents it using simple models without using any calculus.

8.1.4 Organization of this Chapter

Section 8.2 compares the effects of digital copying with nondigital copying on the profit of publishers. Section 8.3 analyzes how the introduction of peer-to-peer distribution channels affects publishers' profits. Section 8.4 points out some conflicts of interest among artists, publishers, and lawyers who are not affected in the same way by the introduction of digital technologies. Section 8.5 concludes.

8.2 Digital versus Nondigital Copying

One of the major claims made by publishers is that digital copying increases their losses from piracy compared with nondigital copying because digital copies potentially have the same quality as the originals. Therefore, we first demonstrate the logic behind this argument. Then we demonstrate some additional arguments showing cases where piracy of digitally stored products is not always profit-damaging compared with the piracy of nondigital information products.

In this chapter we deliberately abstract from describing the process of how copies and copies of copies are made. See Shy (2000) and (2001, section 7.1) for classifications of vertical and horizontal copying mechanisms. Issman-Weit and Shy (2003) offer a methodology for computing the value of (endogenously determined) generations of copies made from nondigital information.

8.2.1 Market Segmentation

We now demonstrate how piracy of digitally stored information can be more damaging to the publishers than the piracy of nondigital information.

Suppose that an audio or video recording can be copied only once. Formally, if consumers value the information product at V, then a nondigital copy is valued at ρV, where $0 < \rho < 1$ measures the rate of quality deterioration due to the copying procedure. For simplicity, however, we assume that a copy of a copy is valued at 0 (and not $\rho^2 V$). Clearly, if the information is digitally stored, then each copy is valued the same as the original, that is, at V.

Now suppose that the consumer population of this information is divided into two groups: type H, who can better accommodate the deteriorated low quality of a copy, and type L, who "really suffers" from a low-quality copy. Formally, let there be n_H type H consumers who value a copy at $\rho_H V$, and n_L type L consumers who value each nondigital copy at $\rho_L V$, where $0 < \rho_L < \rho_H < 1$. Table 8.1 displays our simple model.

Table 8.1 illustrates that a digital copy is valued always at the same level as the original by both consumer types. However, nondigital copies are valued differently by the two user types.

Table 8.1
User (consumer) valuation of originals and copies

User type	Number	Original value	Digital copy	Nondigital copy
H	n_H	V	V	$\rho_H V$
L	n_L	V	V	$\rho_L V$

8.2.1.1 Nondigital Copying Suppose now that all copies are obtained illegally, and that all originals can be purchased only direct from a monopoly publisher at the price of p. Then table 8.1 implies that a type H user will choose to pirate a copy over purchasing an original if

$$V - p \leq \rho_H V.$$

Similarly, an L will choose buying an original over pirating a copy if

$$V - p > \rho_L V.$$

Now suppose that $(1 - \rho_L)n_L \geq (1 - \rho_H)(n_L + n_H)$. Then the monopoly publisher will choose to set the highest price in the price range given by

$$V(1 - \rho_H) \leq p \leq V(1 - \rho_L) \tag{8.1}$$

The unique profit-maximizing price and profit levels are then given by

$$p = V(1 - \rho_L) \quad \text{and} \quad p = V(1 - \rho_L)n_L > 0 \tag{8.2}$$

8.2.1.2 Digital Copying Now suppose that the "new" digital technology has replaced the "old" nondigital copying technology. Then table 8.1 implies that both types of users would always choose to pirate a copy instead of purchasing an original since $V - p < V$. Hence the monopoly publisher would set $p = 0$ and earn $\pi = 0$ profit.

We summarize our findings with the following statement.

Result 8.1 The change from nondigital to digital copying technologies reduces the profit of monopoly publishers, since publishers can no longer segment the market according to users' disutility from deteriorated quality.

Result 8.1 is important since it highlights precisely the reason why the switch to digital information may hurt publishers. Paradoxically, although digital copies are of a higher quality, publishers are worse off since they can no longer charge their buyers a premium for the quality difference between purchased information and illegally copied information.

8.2.2   Network Effects

The previous example demonstrates how the switch from nondigital to digital copying technologies generates more losses from piracy. We now give a different example showing that under network effects, losses from piracy may diminish as a result of this technology change.

Consider a market with two potential users (which we call *support-oriented* and *support-independent*). Let n denote the total number of users (the sum of those who buy and those who illegally copy this information). Thus, $n = 0, 1$, or 2. Also, we assume that copying bears a cost of $c > 0$, which reflects the value of time spent on locating the original to be copied, learning how to bypass the copy-protection devices, and learning how to install and use an illegal copy that generally comes without an operating manual. We should note that one possible extension of this model would be to assume that the cost of making a digital copy is lower than the cost of making a nondigital copy. We assume that $c < V$, so that digital copies yield a utility level exceeding the reservation level. The utility function of a support-oriented user is given by

$$
U^0 = \begin{cases}
n(V + S) - p & \text{if one buys this information product} \\
n\rho V - c & \text{if one makes an illegal nondigital copy} \\
nV - c & \text{if one makes an illegal digital copy} \\
0 & \text{does not use this information}
\end{cases} \tag{8.3}
$$

where, as before, $\rho < 1$ measures the quality deterioration of a nondigital copy. The parameter S is an additional value to support-oriented users from buying the information instead of illegally copying it. This extra value could be toll-free service helplines, extra manuals, discounts on upgrades, Internet access to retrieve some additional information, or simply extra utility gain from supporting this publisher.

The utility of a support-independent user is given by

$$
U^1 = \begin{cases}
nV - p & \text{if one buys this information product} \\
n\rho V - c & \text{if one makes an illegal nondigital copy} \\
nV - c & \text{if one makes an illegal digital copy} \\
0 & \text{does not use this information}
\end{cases} \tag{8.4}
$$

Comparing the utility of a support-oriented user (8.3) with the utility of the support-independent user (8.4) reveals the following list of observations:

(1) All users gain from the network size in the sense that their utility is enhanced with an increase in the total number of users, n.

(2) Only support-oriented users find the service provided by the publisher useful.

8.2.2.1 Nondigital Copying Suppose that digital copying technologies are not available. We make the following definition.

Definition 8.1 We say that the quality of a nondigital copy is high if $\rho \geq \frac{c}{2V}$, and is low otherwise.

Definition 8.1 can be written in an equivalent way emphasizing the cost of making a copy. That is, instead of writing low quality we can equally say that the cost of making a copy is high relative to the low quality of the copy, formally $c > 2\rho V$. Definition 8.1 implies that $c > 2\rho V$, therefore the utility functions (8.3) and (8.4) imply that *nondigital copies are never made if the quality of the copies is low*. To demonstrate our argument in the shortest way, we eliminate some cases by restricting our analysis to the following case.

Assumption 8.1 The quality of nondigital copies is low. Formally, $\rho < \frac{c}{2V}$.

Under assumption 8.1 no copies are being made, hence the number of buyers equals the number of users, n. The monopoly publisher has two options.

Setting a high price Thereby selling only to support-oriented consumers ($n = 1$).

Setting a low price Therefore selling to both consumer types ($n = 2$).

A support-oriented user will buy if $V + S - p \geq 0$, or $p \leq V + S$. In this case, the publisher sells only one unit and therefore earns a profit of $\pi = p = V + S$ (assuming zero production costs). Next a support-independent user will buy if $2V - p \geq 0$, or $p \leq 2V$. Under this low price, the publisher sells two units and earns a profit of $\pi = 2p = 4V$. Charging a high price is more profitable than charging a low price if $\pi = V + S \geq 4V$, or $S \geq 3V$. Summing up the two cases, the profit-maximizing price as a function of the quality of the copy made from the original is

$$p^{nd} = \begin{cases} V + S & \text{if } S \geq 3V \\ 2V & \text{if } S < 3V \end{cases} \tag{8.5}$$

Assuming zero cost of production, the resulting profit levels are

$$\pi^{nd} = \begin{cases} V + S & \text{if copy quality is low, and } S \geq 3V \\ 4V & \text{if copy quality is low, and } S < 3V \end{cases} \tag{8.6}$$

Note that the key feature of this example is that when the publisher sets a high price the network of users equals the number of buyers (given our assumption that the quality of copies is low), which equals to n. The small number of users hurts consumers since (8.3) and (8.4) imply that utility increases with the size of the user network. This results in a limit on how high the price could be set without losing the support-oriented buyer.

Finally, a careful reader may ask what happens if assumption 8.1 is reversed, so that nondigital copies can be of a high quality. In this case, the monopoly publisher will restrict its price so that $2(V + S) - p \geq 2pV - c$. That is, to induce the support-oriented consumer to buy rather than to copy. We use assumption 8.1 to reduce the number of cases analyzed here in order to keep this example as simple as possible.

8.2.2.2 Digital Copying Since digital information can be perfectly copied, (8.4) implies that the support-independent user will always copy, and hence will never buy. Therefore, to tempt the support-oriented consumer to buy (rather than to copy), (8.3) implies that the publisher should restrict the price so that $2(V + S) - p \geq 2V - c$, thus the monopoly publisher cannot set a price above $p^d = 2S + c$. Hence, the profit is $\pi^d = p^d = 2S + c$. Notice that although there are $n = 2$ users, only one consumer pays for the product, whereas the other copies it without paying. The copying user, however, enhances the welfare of the paying consumer by enlarging the network of users.

Our main proposition below lists the conditions under which the move from nondigital to digital technologies enhances the publisher's profit.

Result 8.2 Suppose that the quality of a nondigital copy is low (definition 8.1), and that the value of service to a support-oriented user is high ($S > 3V$). Then,

(1) the publisher earns a higher profit under the digital technology, and

(2) there are more users under the digital technology compared with the nondigital technology.

Proof (1) The condition $S > 3V$ implies that $\pi^d > \pi^{nd}$ if $S > V - c$, which must hold under the condition $S > 3V$. (2) Under the digital technology there are $n = 2$ users, as compared with $n = 1$ users under the nondigital technology. Q.E.D.

Result 8.2 resembles results from the research on piracy, where an increase in the total number of users enhances the value of the product and hence the price paid by support-oriented consumers. In the present model, no copies are made when the information is nondigital (due to the assumed low quality). However, copying (and hence piracy) always prevail under a digital technology. The increase in the user base (from $n = 1$ to $n = 2$) enhances the value of this information product and hence the price from $p^{nd} = V + S$ to $p^d = 2S + c$.

Finally, result 8.2 will not hold if we assume that service of nondigital products can be sold separately from the product itself. In this case, the publisher will sell the product bundled with service to the support-oriented consumer for the price of $p^{nd} = 2(V + S)$, and without the service for $p^{nd} = 2V$ to be purchased by the support-independent consumer. With a total profit of $(4V + 2S)$, the introduction of digital technologies reduces profit. Pricing techniques of this sort combine price discrimination, bundling, and versioning to increase the surplus extracted from buyers. Belleflamme in chapter 6 of this book analyzes versioning of information goods. Clearly, bundling, versioning, and damaging the products for price discrimination purposes are much easier for information products than for physical products.

8.3   Peer-to-Peer Distribution Channels

The Internet provides a low-cost channel to distribute a wide variety of digitally stored products. The digital bits transferred over the Internet include computer software, music, artworks, books, video clips, and movies.

Digitally stored products can be downloaded from fixed Internet sites that specialize in storing these products. In addition, digitally stored products can be obtained using a variety of peer-to-peer (P2P or Gnutella) Internet distribution channels. Each channel allows a group

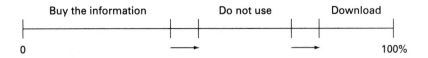

Figure 8.1
The effect of P2P on sales. Top: Partially served market. Bottom: Fully served market.
Remark: Arrows indicate introduction of P2P.

of users with the same networking program to connect with each
other, and directly retrieve files from another's hard drives.

Following Gayer and Shy (2003), figure 8.1 illustrates how the introduction of digital P2P distribution channels may affect sales.

Figure 8.1 indicates there are two possible market configurations:

Partially served market, where the introduction of P2P distribution
channels increases the number of users who copy, and does not decrease the number of buyers. In fact, this figure shows that the number
of buyers may rise as a result of an increase in the popularity of this
network (information) product.

Fully served market, where all users either buy or copy. In this case,
P2P distribution reduces the number of buyers. However, we must
point out that this reduction is partially offset by an increase in the
popularity of the product, which may enhance buyers' willingness to
pay.

Formally, let n^b denote the number of users who buy, and let n^c denote the number of users who copy. We assume that the number of
buyers is given by

$$n^b = \alpha - \beta n^c + \gamma n^c, \quad \text{where } \alpha, \beta, \gamma > 0 \tag{8.7}$$

Thus α measures the number of support-oriented consumers who always will buy (assuming that the price falls below a certain level). The
parameter β measures the substitution between those who copy and
those who buy. For example, if $\beta = 1$ then every additional consumer
who copies implies a loss of one additional buyer. If $\beta = 0$, then the
market is only partially served, hence the introduction of P2P does not

hurt sales. Finally, γ is the network effect (popularity) parameter. When more people copy the product, more people then will buy the product.

Assuming that the publisher's profit is $\pi = pn^b$, we can state the following result.

Result 8.3 The publisher's profit is enhanced (reduced) with the introduction of digital P2P distribution channels if the network effect is stronger than (weaker than) the substitution effect; that is if $\gamma \geq \beta \ (\gamma < \beta)$.

8.4 Conflict of Interests

It is commonly argued that digital convergence and the emergence of the Internet as a key distribution channel enhance the incentives to take legal measures against those who illegally copy digital material. These claims generally do not consider the fact that the incentives to litigate are not the same among all participating agents. Lawyers always gain from increased litigations, but it is not clear whether the creators of intellectual properties (for example, artists) benefit from increased litigations. This conflict of interest was first formally analyzed in Gayer and Shy (2005).

The massive number of highly publicized lawsuits in the past two years initiated by the Recording Industry Association of America (RIAA) against individuals who downloaded music files via the Internet, and the recent declaration by the Motion Picture Association of America (MPAA) to follow the RIAA's massive lawsuits, raise the question of who really benefits and who loses from these court cases.

An interesting clue for this question that hints that these lawsuits may damage artists comes from a recent survey by the Pew Internet & American Life Project (2004) (see Zeller 2004). The survey finds that 43 percent of paid artists in the music industry agree that, "file-sharing services are not really bad for artists, since they help to promote and distribute an artist's work to a broad audience." The same survey also found that 37 percent of all artists and 35 percent of paid artists in the music industry say that file sharing of music and movies should be legal. The purpose of this chapter is to investigate whether artists gain or lose from file sharing and compare it with their publishers' incentives to reduce or eliminate file-sharing activities over the Internet.

The main result obtained in Gayer and Shy (2005) shows that lawsuits against users who infringe on artists' copyrights may in practice hurt the artists who are the original creators of this information product. In fact the publishers who act as the artists' agents, as well as the lawyers who work for the publishers, do not protect the artists' interests under network effects in digitally distributed information. This conflict arises because artists gain parts of their profits from other sources such as musical performances, television and radio shows, and even ringtones for mobile phones. In contrast, publishers earn their profits from selling CDs, DVDs, and audio and video cassettes.

It is clear that these conflicts arise since the contracts do not take into account the artist's gain from popularity from nonrecording activities. However, there are a few exceptions. The *BBC* (2003) reported that the singer Robbie Williams signed what is believed to be an 80-million-pound contract with EMI Records in what could be the UK's biggest record deal. The deal means EMI will take an unusually high share of profit from touring, publishing profits, and merchandise areas where the artists themselves usually make more money. His representatives called the new deal a "multi-platform" approach to the respective elements of recording, live work, film, and television. Clearly, this "new" type of contract "internalizes" the conflict of interest between publishers and artists.

8.5 Conclusions

Digital convergence of information products potentially can increase copyright violation by adding very efficient distribution channels. However, this chapter demonstrates that the potential profit gain from "becoming digital" may outweigh the losses, provided publishers allocate resources to segment the market between buyers and users who copy without paying.

Our main recommendation is that publishers should attempt to fully utilize the digital distribution technologies instead of resisting it and lobbying for stricter enforcement of copyright laws.

The increase in the efficiency, quality, and speed of distribution of digitally stored information increases the potential conflict of interest among the creators (artists), the publishers (distributors), and their attorneys. Attorneys may feel that digital distribution generates more opportunities and cases to deal with.

The creators may have the opposite incentives since their popularity depends on the size of the entire market, which includes those users who do not pay for it.

References

BBC News (2003), "Music Piracy 'Great', Says Robbie," posted on: http://news .bbc.co.uk/2/hi/entertainment/2673983.stm.

Conner, K., and R. Rumelt (1991), "Software Piracy: An Analysis of Protection Strategies," *Management Science* 37, 125–139.

Gayer, A., and O. Shy (2003), "Internet and Peer-to-Peer Distributions in Markets for Digital Products," *Economics Letters* 81, 51–57.

Gayer, A., and O. Shy (2005), "Publishers, Artists, and Copyright Enforcement," working paper, Department of Economics, University of Haifa.

Issman-Weit, E., and O. Shy (2003), "Pricing of Library Subscriptions with Applications to Scientific Journals," *Journal of Economics & Business* 55(2), 197–218.

Oberholzer-Gee, F., and K. Strumpf (2004), "The Effect of File Sharing on Record Sales," Harvard Business School.

Peitz, M. (2004), "A Strategic Approach to Software Protection: Comment," *Journal of Economics & Management Strategy* 13, 371–374.

Peitz, M., and P. Waelbroeck (2003), "Piracy of Digital Products: A Critical Review of the Economics Literature," CESifo Working Paper 1071, electronic document available at www.ssrn.com.

Pew Internet & American Life Project (2004), posted on: http://www.pewinternet.org/ press_release.asp?r=94.

Poddar, S. (2003), "On Software Piracy when Piracy is Costly," Working Paper, Department of Economics, National University of Singapore.

Rob, R., and J. Waldfogel (2004), "Piracy on the High C's: Music Downloading, Sales Displacement, and Social Welfare in a Sample of College Students," NBER Working Paper W10874.

Shy, O. (2000), "The Economics of Copy Protection in Software and Other Media," in B. Kahin and H. Varian (eds.), *Internet Publishing and Beyond: The Economics of Digital Information and Intellectual Property*, 99–113, The MIT Press.

Shy, O. (2001), *The Economics of Network Industries*, Cambridge University Press.

Shy, O., and J. Thisse (1999), "A Strategic Approach to Software Protection," *Journal of Economics & Management Strategy* 8, 163–190.

Slive, J., and D. Bernhardt (1998), "Pirated for Profit," *Canadian Journal of Economics* 31, 886–899.

Takeyama, L. (1994), "The Welfare Implications of Unauthorized Reproduction of Intellectual Property in the Presence of Network Externalities," *Journal of Industrial Economics* 62, 155–166.

Takeyama, L. (1997), "The Intertemporal Consequences of Unauthorized Reproduction of Intellectual Property," *Journal of Law and Economics* 40, 511–522.

Zeller, T. (2004), "Pew File-Sharing Survey Gives a Voice to Artists," *New York Times*, December 6, 2004.

9

Diffusion of Electronic Commerce

Emin M. Dinlersoz and Pedro Pereira

9.1 Introduction

The e-commerce technology can be defined broadly as a technology that allows business transactions to be carried out through processing and transmission of digital data on the Internet, in contrast to the traditional business technology, whose logistics are based on the laws of the physical environment. Since the early 1990s, this new technology has been adopted extensively by traditional firms and also by new, entirely Internet-based firms. Yet these two types of firms have exhibited different tendencies in embracing the new technology, and their rates of adoption have varied considerably by industry. Table 9.1 provides a list of major adopters of e-commerce by retail sector. In most sectors, a new firm emerged as an early adopter, such as Amazon.com in books or Netflix.com in movies. In other sectors, established firms such as Gap.com in clothing, Tesco in grocery, or Charles Schwab in brokerage, were quick in adoption. In some sectors, established firms took much longer to adopt, such as Blockbuster in movies and Borders in books. The main observation from table 9.1 is that new firms usually came first, and established firms followed.

The observed adoption patterns pose several questions regarding the nature of the diffusion of e-commerce technology: How do traditional and new firms differ in their incentives to adopt e-commerce? In what type of market environments are we likely to observe early adoption by new, Internet-based firms versus established, traditional firms? Are adoption patterns systematically related to the main differences between traditional and virtual markets? What can be said about interindustry differences in the diffusion of e-commerce? These questions retain their importance as new firms and new industries continue to embrace e-commerce, as consumer learning takes place, and as

Table 9.1
Adoption dates of major early and late movers in online retailing

Category	Major early adopter(s)	Major late adopter(s)
Books	Amazon.com (July 1995)	**Barnes & Noble** (May 1997), **Borders** (May 1998)
Clothing and apparel	**Gap** (November 1997) **Recreational Equipment Inc.** (September 1996)	**JCPenney** (1998)
Movies	Netflix.com (1999)	**Walmart** (January 2000), **Blockbuster** (2004)
Grocery	Peapod.com (1996), Webvan.com (1996), **Tesco** (November 1996)	Homegrocer.com (1997), **Sainsbury** (March 1997), Freshdirect.com (2002)
Electronics	Value America Inc.com (February 1998)	**Circuit City** (July 1999), **Radio Shack** (May 1999), **Best Buy** (1999)
Pet supplies	Petstore.com (October 1998)	**Petsmart** (June 1999), **Petco** (December 2000), Petopia.com (July 1999)
Toys	Etoys.com (1997)	**Toys "R" Us** (June 1998), Smarterkids.com (1998)
Drugs	Planetrx.com (1997), **Drug Emporium** (May 1997)	Drugstore.com (February 1999), **CVS** (August 1999) **Eckerd** (1999)
Software	Egghead.com/Onsale.com (May 1994), Buy.com (June 1997)	**Circuit City** (July 1999), **Best Buy** (1999)
Stock trading	**Charles Schwab** (January 1996), Datek.com (February 1996), Etrade.com (October 1995)	**Merrill Lynch** (November 1998) **Paine Webber** (1999)

Source: Authors' own documentation based on phone calls and using company histories available online. Company names including ".com" refer to pure Internet-based companies. Bold indicates an established traditional firm that diversified into online retailing.

consumer confidence in the Internet medium grows. Improvements in Internet access and connection speed also continue to open new opportunities for better interfacing between sellers and consumers, and enhance the diffusion of e-commerce into new goods and services that were previously thought of as unsuitable for online trading.

This chapter seeks to put into perspective the patterns of retailers' adoption of e-commerce across product categories and firm types. The focus is on understanding how consumer loyalty, differences in firms' technologies and consumers' preferences across the traditional versus the virtual market, and expansion in market size made possible by the

Internet affected the timing and sequence of adoption by firms, as well as the postadoption evolution of prices. For this purpose, a dynamic model of technology adoption is proposed and its implications are compared with the empirical patterns observed. The theoretical analysis presented here is based on a more comprehensive model developed by Dinlersoz and Pereira (2004). In a two-firm, continuous-time technology adoption game, firms decide whether to adopt the e-commerce technology and then compete by choosing prices, given the adoption decisions. The implications of the model for the timing and sequence of adoption by firms are used to understand which firm type is more likely to adopt first, whether the gap between adoption times of firms is large, and how the adoption times depend on the parameters characterizing the traditional and virtual market environments. The predictions of the model are consistent with the observed adoption patterns across firm types and product categories.

The design of the model reflects important differences between traditional and virtual markets, as well as between traditional and Internet-based firms. While a long list of such differences can be made, the model includes those that have high empirical relevance and analytical tractability. First, firms' costs and consumers' utility across traditional and virtual markets differ. Potential cost savings in the virtual market can arise from low-cost electronic transactions and reduced need for inventory, retail space, and labor, as well as from the elimination of some traditional intermediaries. For some goods, convenience of online transactions and savings in shopping time and transportation costs may enhance utility, but for others, delayed consumption or the inability to inspect the good physically may result in a utility loss. Second, some consumers have a preference for the good sold by the established firm, resulting from the established firm's reputation or from consumers' trust in an established brand name built during the firm's long presence in the traditional market. The importance of such reputation and brand name effects in online markets has been emphasized in recent empirical literature.[1] Such brand preference by consumers can be broadly termed as "loyalty." Third, the Internet can increase an established firm's market size by extending its geographic reach or by expanding hours of shopping. This expansion in the market reach of a firm has been generally recognized as one of the major changes introduced by the Internet to the way markets are defined.

The analysis of the model reveals that either firm can lead in adoption, depending on the parameters. The new firm tends to be a leader in adoption when it faces an established firm with low levels of loyalty in an environment where the physical shop of the established firm has low marginal cost, the virtual market provides low incremental profit over the traditional one, and the market has little opportunity for expansion through e-commerce. On the other hand, the established firm always leads in adoption if it enjoys relatively high loyalty, its physical shop has relatively high marginal cost, the incremental profit from e-commerce is high, and the market expansion effect is significant. The relevance of these predictions is assessed by examining the entry patterns in various industries. The model also has implications for the adoption patterns in growing markets for digital and information goods, which are further analyzed by Peitz and Waelbroeck and by Belleflamme in chapters 4 and 6, respectively, of this volume.

The theoretical framework discussed here is related to earlier models of technology adoption, such as Fudenberg and Tirole (1985), Quirmbach (1986), Jensen (1982), and Reinganum (1981). The approach differs, however, from the earlier literature in certain ways. In earlier models, the payoff-relevant consequences of competition between firms at any point in time generally are summarized by an exogenously given reduced-form profit function. Here the market game at any time, and the resulting profit functions, are endogenously determined by the adoption decisions, as well as by the fundamentals of the model. This allows for the investigation of the sensitivity of the results to the parameters of the market game. In addition, while previous models assume a stationary demand, the present framework accounts for non-stationary demand by allowing for growth in market size, which corresponds to the diffusion of Internet access among consumers. As in Baye, Kovenock, and deVries (1992), Narasimhan (1988), and Varian (1980), mixed-strategy pricing emerge naturally. Recent empirical evidence suggests the relevance of mixed-strategy pricing in online markets.[2] Mixed-strategy equilibria also lead to simpler period payoff structures for firms and make the dynamic model tractable, compared to the complicated payoff structures in pure-strategy equilibria that arise in many commonly used product differentiation models, such as the horizontal differentiation model of Salop (1979) and the quality differentiation model of Shaked and Sutton (1982).

The rest of the chapter is organized as follows. Section 9.2 discusses major factors influencing adoption. Section 9.3 provides some empirical evidence motivating the model. Section 9.4 presents the model, followed by the characterization of equilibrium in section 9.5. In section 9.6, the model is analyzed and its empirical implications are derived. Section 9.7 reconciles the model with the empirical evidence. Section 9.8 concludes. The reader is referred to Dinlersoz and Pereira (2004) for technical details.

9.2   Important Factors in Adoption Decision

This section discusses three influential factors in the adoption decision of firms that motivate the theoretical setup.

9.2.1   Incremental per Consumer Profitability

The *incremental per consumer profitability* refers to the difference, negative or positive, in per consumer profit in the virtual market with respect to the physical market, which results from changes in firms' costs and consumers' utility introduced by the e-commerce technology. If the virtual market is less profitable per consumer, an established firm may choose not to adopt because of the possibility of *cannibalization*: if the firm sells to only some of its existing consumers through the virtual shop at a lower profit per consumer than the physical shop, the net effect is a loss. In the early days of e-commerce, the possibility of cannibalization was thought of as a potential deterrent for adoption by established firms. However, an implicit assumption behind the cannibalization effect is that the virtual market does not create any new sales. It is quite possible that the profit per consumer may be higher in the virtual market and/or a firm's market size may increase beyond its local physical market.

Relative profitability depends on both the technology and the preference structures of the two markets. There are many ways the virtual market can be more cost effective compared to the traditional market. First, the e-commerce technology can reduce the cost of retail transactions, such as making payments, keeping records, managing inventory, ordering, invoicing, and exchanging information with customers, employees, and suppliers. Second, the technology can reduce the dependence on traditional inputs of retail technology, such as physical space and sales force, which tend to constitute a large fraction of traditional retailers' costs.

While systematic evidence is not yet available, efficiency gains made possible by the Internet are believed to be widespread. Litan and Rivlin (2001) provide several examples and case studies supporting this view. Garicano and Kaplan (2001) find important transaction and process cost reductions in business-to-business automobile auctions. Lucking-Riley and Spulber (2001) discuss further evidence on declining transaction costs.[3] Humphrey et al. (2001) estimate large cost savings from electronic transactions in banking, which replaced paper transactions in many European banks.

The evidence on reductions in transaction costs is accompanied by reductions in inventory and distribution costs, especially for pure Internet-based firms. Many such firms have wholesalers and manufacturers handling the inventory and shipping services for them, a method called *drop-shipping*. This cuts costs significantly (see Randall, Netessine, and Rudi 2002). Overall, for tangible goods, the Internet channel is estimated to reduce distribution costs by more than 25 percent (Geyskens et al. 2002). The accumulating evidence on the effects of e-commerce on firms' cost structure is summarized below.

Observation 9.1 The e-commerce technology generates important cost reductions in many stages of retail trade. Such reductions can be substantial especially for traditional inputs of retail trade, such as labor and space.

Online shopping can also affect consumers' utility. For instance, for products whose features cannot be inferred without a physical inspection or for which shipping delay can be substantial, consumers may have to forego some utility. For other products, such concerns may be less of an issue, and the convenience of online shopping can result in higher utility compared to the physical market.[4] A category of products that are especially suitable for e-commerce is digital goods, as they can be delivered and returned easily in electronic form. Virtual product demos on websites enable consumers to explore and verify the features of the product. In fact digital products are such an integral part of e-commerce activity that most of this volume—chapters 2 through 8—focus on the economic issues surrounding the sale of such goods on the Internet. The effect of e-commerce on consumers' utility can be summarized as follows.

Observation 9.2 Internet shopping enhances consumers' utility by increasing convenience of shopping and variety available to consumers. However, it potentially can reduce utility in purchases where quality verification and physical inspection are prominent concerns.

9.2.2 Loyalty

The consumers' loyalty to the established firm can result from consumer trust and brand recognition, both of which are tied to the firm's long presence in the traditional market. Loyalty creates an important asymmetry between an established firm and a new firm, and may have been especially relevant in the early phases of e-commerce when consumers were reluctant to experiment with new, purely Internet-based firms and release personal information to relatively unknown websites. The emergence of third-party certification of trust by intermediaries, for examples, Trust-E.com or BBBonline.com, highlights the importance of such intangible assets.[5] A loyal customer base confers two advantages to the established retailer. First, the firm can serve its loyal customers with Internet access through a virtual shop without the fear of losing them to competition. Second, loyalty allows the firm to charge higher prices to its captive consumers.

Recent empirical evidence suggests the importance of loyalty in online markets. Smith and Brynjolfsson (2001) document the importance of brand recognition for homogeneous products among users of price-comparison search engines, who are presumably the most price-sensitive consumers online. Using data on searches for book prices conducted at Dealtime.com in late 1999, we find that while price is the strongest predictor of customer choice, only 49 percent of customers choose the cheapest vendor. Among consumers who do not choose the cheapest offer, the average selected offer was 20 percent higher than the cheapest offer. Consumers were willing to pay 5 percent more to purchase from Amazon, rather than from the lowest-priced vendor, and 3 percent more to purchase from Barnes & Noble or Borders. Johnson et al. (2001), using data from Media Metrix from July 1997 through June 1998, report that 70 percent of CD shoppers, 70 percent of book shoppers, and 42 percent of travel shoppers were observed as being loyal to just one site through the duration of the data. Households that browsed a category initially visited, on average, only 1.2 CD sites, 1.1 book sites, and 1.8 travel sites. Shankar, Rangaswamy, and Pusateri (2001) also find that consumers with prior positive experience with an established brand in the physical market had lower price sensitivity in online markets, where it may be difficult to evaluate a retailer's reliability. These findings collectively suggest that brand awareness, loyalty, and trust potentially can speed adoption of e-commerce by established retailers.

Observation 9.3 Consumers' loyalty to traditional firms played an important role in the early stages of e-commerce during which trust, security, and brand-awareness were relatively more important. Loyalty seems to have facilitated traditional firms' adoption of e-commerce in certain product categories. Creating and maintaining customer loyalty continues to be an important concern for Internet retailers.

In the theoretical model presented in this chapter, loyalty is treated as exogenous and constant for the established firm. This simplification is appropriate for a short-run analysis. Over time, the number of loyal consumers for the established firm can grow, and the new firm can also develop loyalty. The latter possibility is investigated in Dinlersoz and Pereira (2004), where a fraction of consumers that are not loyal to any firm become loyal to the new firm according to an exogenous process.

9.2.3 Market Expansion

The expansion in the market size made possible by the Internet encompasses not only the geographic space, but also other dimensions, such as the window of time consumers can shop, or the demographic dimension.[6] Market expansion can in principle alleviate the cannibalization problem for an established firm. If the market expansion effect is large enough, the firm can go online even when the incremental per consumer profitability of the virtual market is negative. Established firms, such as Nike, initially emphasized that market expansion was one of their primary motives in opening an Internet-based store. The evidence is scant, however, on how important this market expansion effect might have been quantitatively. An early investigation by Jupiter Communications estimated that only 6 percent of online sales in 1999 were incremental and therefore noncannibalizing (see Sgoutas 2000).

Observation 9.4 E-commerce expands the market size for all retailers by increasing the geographic and demographic reach, and by extending the shopping hours.

In addition to the three influential factors discussed, other factors may also have played an important role in the adoption decisions, but the analysis here abstracts from them to highlight the role of the three main factors introduced. For instance, it is well known that financial constraints tend to be less binding for established firms. While such constraints can delay adoption, the capital markets actually favored

Internet-based start-ups, at least initially.[7] Another factor is the *organizational inertia* of established firms because of bureaucratic resistance to new technologies (see Henderson 1993).[8] *Channel conflict* that arises from the resistance of intermediaries to a new, direct channel of sale can also delay adoption. However, this conflict especially applies to manufacturers that bypass wholesalers and retailers by offering direct sales through the Internet, and it is less of a concern in retailers' adoption.

9.3   Some Evidence on Adoption Patterns

The share of e-commerce in total retail sales is still small. The most recent estimate from the U.S. Census Bureau's E-stats Program at the time of this writing was around only 2 percent. The share of e-commerce in any product category is in fact not high enough to generate perceptible differences across broadly defined product categories. Table 9.2 presents the percentage of sales accounted for by e-commerce for several categories, considering only the firms classified in the

Table 9.2
Fraction of sales accounted by e-commerce in electronic and mail order houses (NAICS 454110)

Category	Fraction of total sales accounted by e-commerce					
	1999	2000	2001	2002	Average	% growth
Books and magazines	0.43	0.44	0.45	0.46	0.44	7.5
Electronics	0.19	0.32	0.39	0.46	0.34	145.7
Office equipment and supplies	0.08	0.21	0.30	0.40	0.25	377.2
Music and videos	0.18	0.27	0.33	0.37	0.29	106.4
Toys, hobby goods, and games	0.18	0.26	0.31	0.36	0.28	104.0
Sporting goods	NA	0.24	0.28	0.34	0.29	44.2
Food, beer, and wine	0.16	0.30	0.24	0.34	0.26	110.8
Furniture	0.06	0.16	0.25	0.34	0.20	473.1
Computer software	0.29	0.31	0.30	0.33	0.31	15.3
Clothing	0.07	0.14	0.21	0.30	0.18	354.4
Computer hardware	0.18	0.23	0.26	0.27	0.24	46.7
Drugs, health, and beauty aids	0.02	0.05	0.06	0.07	0.05	231.1

Notes: The data source is U.S. Census Bureau E-stats Program.
Percent growth is the percentage growth rate between 1999 and 2002.

"Electronic and Mail Order Houses" industry. The electronic and mail order industry (industry code NAICS 454110) includes catalog and mail order houses and other direct retailers, many of which sell in multiple channels, as well as pure Internet-based firms and "brick and click" retailers, if the e-commerce group operates as a separate unit and is not engaged in the online selling of motor vehicles. One expects the diffusion of e-commerce sales to be relatively rapid and widespread in this more narrowly defined industry. Therefore, differences across product categories in shares of e-commerce in sales should be more visible. As of 2002, the latest year for which data is available, the highest share was in books and magazines (46 percent), followed by electronics and appliances (46 percent) and office equipment (40 percent).

Important observations from tables 9.1 and 9.2 can be summarized as follows:

Observation 9.5 The nature of the product is an important determinant of the extent of e-commerce diffusion in the market for that product.

Observation 9.6 The timing of adoption varies considerably depending on product category and a firm's presence in the traditional market.

Observation 9.7 New, Internet-based firms usually tended to enter Internet retail markets first, and established, traditional firms followed.

The following examples from selected retail industries clarify the relevance of the major factors (identified in section 9.2) in explaining the adoption patterns.

9.3.1 Books
In this category, Amazon.com was the first major adopter, whereas Barnes & Noble, an established traditional firm, came much later.[9] Books are relatively homogenous and noncustomized products. There is little need to inspect the product, and consumers can enjoy the conveniences of online shopping, such as ease of ordering a locally unavailable book or saving in transportation costs, which can be high relative to the value of a book. These benefits may result in a net utility gain for consumers shopping online. Marginal cost for firms selling books online may be lower, as firms can economize on costs of labor, inventory, and real estate, which must be borne by physical shops.

Loyalty appears to be important for established firms even for homogenous goods such as books, but its effect may not have been as pronounced as in the case of a good that requires physical inspection or service, both of which tend to increase the importance of trust and reputation.

Overall, then, early emergence of Amazon.com can be attributed to the convenience of online shopping for books and/or lower marginal costs, which resulted in high incremental profitability for the virtual market, and to the relative homogeneity of books as a product category, which may have rendered loyalty less influential. The reasoning in the case of book retailing may also apply to CD and movie retailing. In movies, Netflix.com, an early Internet-only adopter, leads online sales followed by Walmart. Blockbuster, the largest traditional retailer of movies, adopted e-commerce in 2004, several years after Netflix.com (see Tedeschi 2003).

9.3.2 Clothing and Apparel

Clothing and apparel represent a category of products for which the Internet might be relatively less suitable as a sales channel. Established firms such as Gap, JCPenney, and Recreational Equipment Inc. were early adopters. In clothing, Internet retail sales are much more concentrated in traditional retailers than pure Internet-based ones (see Ramanathan 2000). In many ways, such concentration is not surprising. Clothing products are generally heterogeneous and customized. Since a product is fit to personal taste, and good service, such as convenient return policies and alteration possibilities, are more serious concerns for these goods, a physical market presence, reputation, and trust are likely to be more important.

The case of Gap highlights how product type and customer loyalty can play a role in adoption. According to McIntyre and Perlman (2000), the following reasons were important in giving an advantage to an established retailer such as Gap: return policy, that is, the product could be returned to the physical stores; services, for example, alterations could be done at the nearest physical store; loyalty to a trusted brand name; preshopping; and instore promotions. Of these advantages, loyalty and promotions are quite general and may apply to other product categories. The first two emphasize how product type and synergies between traditional and online operations could matter. Convenience of return and alteration services provided by physical stores can reduce the marginal cost, and enhance consumers' utility.

The case of Recreational Equipment Inc., REI, a traditional retailer of outdoor gear and apparel, and an early adopter, is similar. Kaufman (1999) argues that loyalty was crucial, as most of REI's web customers were familiar already with its name. Market expansion opportunity was also taken by REI, as it launched a website in Japanese.[10] In summary, product type, loyalty, and market expansion effect may have each played some role in early adoption by Gap and REI.

9.3.3 Digital Products

Digital products, such as software, MP3 music, stocks, and downloadable movies, is a class of goods particularly well suited for e-commerce.[11] Mortgage and insurance can also be included in this category, as they are now conveniently traded in electronic form. A large portion of this volume is dedicated to the study of such goods, especially chapters 4 through 8. For digital goods, online product demonstrations and easy delivery and return may increase consumers' utility. Reductions in marginal cost also can be large, as a digital product requires much less physical storage space and does not need to be transported in a physical medium.

As an important case of adoption patterns in digital goods, consider brokerage. Pure Internet-based firms, such as Datek.com, Ameritrade.com, and E-trade.com, as well as Charles Schwab, an established, traditional discount broker, adopted early. Other established firms, such as Merrill Lynch, Morgan Stanley Dean Witter, and Paine Webber were late. As discussed in Mendelson, Techopitayakul, and Meza (2000), there are a number of important reasons why Internet-only firms adopted early. First, the Internet appears to have decreased both the fixed and variable costs of brokerage. Second, the composition of consumers in this industry reveals significant heterogeneity in terms of price sensitivity. The authors report that about 40 percent of all investors are highly price sensitive, whereas a majority of the rest exhibit low sensitivity and loyalty. New Internet-only brokers charged low prices and targeted highly price-sensitive investors. Thus early adoption by new firms in this sector was made possible by lower costs and the existence of a relatively large set of price-sensitive consumers. In particular, early adoption by Charles Schwab can be explained by its emphasis on low cost trading, which was further reinforced by the convenience of online shopping for price-sensitive consumers and the availability of a large pool of such consumers. On the other hand, the Internet, at least initially, was not an ideal medium for loyal consumers who value full-service and personalized advice. This is one reason why full-service brokers such as Merrill Lynch adopted e-commerce relatively late.

9.4 Theory

This section presents a model stylized to highlight how the main factors outlined here can together generate the observed variation in adoption patterns. The model is available in its entirety in Dinlersoz and Pereira (2004).

Consider a retail market in which a single firm initially can sell to consumers through a physical shop. The physical shop operates in a traditional physical environment: consumers can visit the shop, physically inspect the good, and interact with a sales person. The firm with the physical shop is called the "old firm," to emphasize that it has been in the market for a while before the e-commerce technology arrives. There is also a "new firm," which has no physical market presence, but can enter the market by adopting the e-commerce technology.

The e-commerce technology enables any firm to operate a virtual shop. A virtual shop consists of a website through which consumers potentially can learn about the details of the product, and place and track orders. After this new technology arrives, the new firm can open a virtual shop and compete with the old firm for consumers with Internet access.[12] The old firm also has the option of opening a virtual shop, in addition to its physical shop.

Time, t, is continuous on $[0, \infty)$ and the e-commerce technology arrives at $t = 0$. Every period t consists potentially of two stages. In the first stage, firms simultaneously decide whether to adopt the new technology, if they have not already done so before time t. In the second stage, firms choose prices simultaneously for their open shops and consumers make their decisions.

9.4.1 Consumers
There is a continuum of identical risk-neutral consumers with unit demands. Each consumer holds a reservation price of 1 for the good sold in the physical shop, and a reservation price of $1 - v$ for the good sold in a virtual shop, where v is in $[0, 1]$. This specification represents physical goods for which delays in consumption due to waiting for shipment, or the consumer's inability to physically inspect the good to infer its features, may cause some loss in surplus. Examples are books

and CDs, for which v may be small, or apparel and furniture, for which v may be large. The case of v in $[-1, 0]$ is representative of digital goods, such as software, for which easier delivery and return via the Internet may result in higher utility.

There are three types of consumers. Some consumers, called "loyals," have access to the physical shop and always prefer buying from the old firm. In other words, loyal consumers view the product of the new firm as an unacceptable substitute for the product of the old firm. Loyalty may result from the old firm's reputation or from trust in an established brand name built during the old firm's long presence in the traditional market. Loyalty is assumed to be an asset specific to the old firm and cannot be imitated easily by the new firm. Let λ in $(0, 1)$ denote the measure of loyal consumers in the market.

Another set of consumers are called "local switchers." These consumers have access to the physical shop, and view the products of the two firms as perfect substitutes. Let σ in $(0, 1)$ be the measure of such consumers in the market. Assume that $\lambda + \sigma = 1$, so that the size of the "local market" for the old firm's physical shop is normalized to one. Thus a larger λ corresponds to a larger established firm with a higher market share.

Finally, another set of consumers are referred to as "distant switchers." Just as local switchers, these consumers view the products of the two firms as perfect substitutes. However, they are unable to buy from the old firm's physical shop due to high transportation costs or inconvenient shopping hours. These consumers can be reached only via a virtual shop. Let α in $(0, 1)$ denote the measure of distant switchers. The magnitude of α gives the strength of the market expansion effect made possible by the Internet. The rest of the chapter assumes $\alpha < \lambda$, that is, the market expansion is small relative to the size of the loyals. Theoretical results are not substantially different when $\alpha > \lambda$.

At the beginning of each period, a cohort of consumers enters the market and then leaves at the end of the period to be replaced by a new cohort of consumers in the next period. Each cohort has the same proportion of loyals, local switchers, and distant switchers. Loyalty is assumed to persist across cohorts through some mechanism like word-of-mouth communication or reputation effects that persist over generations. The assumption of full consumer turnover each period simplifies the analysis by removing the possibility of intertemporal substitution by consumers.[13]

At any time, only a fraction of consumers have access to the Internet. Having access implies that the consumer has the relevant equipment to buy at a virtual shop if desired. Access diffuses across consumers gradually according to an exogenous, deterministic process.[14] All consumers gain access at the same rate, regardless of their type. Let $a(t)$ denote the fraction of consumers with Internet access at time t, such that $a(0) = 0$, $a(t)$ is differentiable on $(0, \infty)$, $a'(t) > 0$, $a(t) < 1$ for t in $(0, \infty)$, and $\lim_{t \to \infty} a(t) = 1$. These assumptions allow for many types of growth processes, including the common S-shaped diffusion of technology. Note that it is possible to specify a different access rate $a(t)$ for different types of consumers. For instance, it may be argued that distant consumers might have higher incentives to gain access, which can be represented by a steeper $a(t)$ than that of the local consumers. Technological improvements in access, such as broadband technology, can be represented also as a steeper $a(t)$ or possibly as a discontinuous jump in the process $a(t)$ at the time the technological refinement arrives. These considerations can be embedded into the analysis with some complication in the tractability. To summarize, a consumer's preferences can be compactly stated as follows:

$$U(p) = \begin{cases} 1 - p - \gamma, & \text{if the consumer purchases from the physical shop at price } p, \\ 1 - v - p - \delta, & \text{if the consumer purchases from a virtual shop at price } p, \\ 0, & \text{if the consumer does not purchase at all,} \end{cases}$$

where $\gamma = 0$ for local switchers and for loyals, and $\gamma = +\infty$ for distant switchers; $\delta = 0$ for local and distant switchers and for loyals who buy at the old firm's virtual shop, and $\delta = +\infty$ for consumers without access to the Internet or for loyals that buy from the new firm's virtual shop.

9.4.2 Firms

Let $i = $ "n" or "o" index, the new and the old firm, respectively. Similarly, let $j = $ "p," "vo," or "vn" denote the physical shop, the old firm's virtual shop, and the new firm's virtual shop, respectively.

Opening a virtual shop entails an entry cost of $K > 0$. This cost includes any investment to implement the e-commerce technology, including the costs of website design and new distribution and warehousing systems. The physical shop has a marginal cost of c in $(0, 1)$.

The marginal costs of virtual shops are both equal to $c - \Delta$, where Δ in $(0,1)$ is the reduction in marginal cost made possible by the e-commerce technology.

Let $\rho = \Delta - v$ be the incremental per consumer profit of a virtual shop relative to the physical shop. We assume that $\rho > 0$, which means that the virtual shop is more profitable per consumer compared to the physical shop. This is the case if $v < \Delta$, that is, if the disutility is small compared to the cost reduction. Examples could be books and CDs, for which there is little inconvenience to consumers shopping online and for which there may be important reductions in costs from online operations. Dinlersoz and Pereira (2004) analyze also the case $\rho < 0$, which corresponds to an environment where the Internet market can be relatively less profitable per consumer compared to the physical market.

Let s_{it} be the indicator of adoption by firm i, that is, $s_{it} = 1$, if firm i has adopted the technology at or before time t, and $s_{it} = 0$ otherwise. The state of adoption by firms at time t is given by the pair $s_t = (s_{nt}, s_{ot})$. A firm's pricing strategy is a rule that indicates the cumulative distribution function, $G_{s_t}^j(.)$, according to which each of its open shops chooses prices at any time given s_t.[15] Also, let $D_{s_t}^j(.)$ be the demand function for shop j, given s_t. Finally, let $V_{s_t}^i(t)$ be the maximum instantaneous profit of firm i, given a pricing strategy by its rival. This profit is simply the sum of the maximum instantaneous profits of a firm's shops.

An adoption strategy is a rule that indicates, for each period, whether firm i should adopt the new technology if it has not adopted yet, conditional on whether its rival has adopted already. Denote firm i's adoption time by t_i. Let $r > 0$ be the market interest rate. The total payoff for the old firm as a leader and a follower are given by

$$L^o(t_o, t_n) = \int_0^{t_o} V_{00}^o(t)e^{-rt}\, dt + \int_{t_o}^{t_n} V_{01}^o(t)e^{-rt}\, dt + \int_{t_n}^{\infty} V_{11}^o(t)e^{-rt}\, dt - Ke^{-rt_o},$$

$$F^o(t_o, t_n) = \int_0^{t_n} V_{00}^o(t)e^{-rt}\, dt + \int_{t_n}^{t_o} V_{10}^o(t)e^{-rt}\, dt + \int_{t_o}^{\infty} V_{11}^o(t)e^{-rt}\, dt - Ke^{-rt_o}.$$

Similarly, the payoff functions for the new firm are

$$L^n(t_n, t_o) = \int_{t_n}^{t_o} V_{10}^n(t)e^{-rt}\, dt + \int_{t_n}^{\infty} V_{11}^n(t)e^{-rt}\, dt - Ke^{-rt_n},$$

$$F^o(t_n, t_o) = \int_{t_n}^{\infty} \dot{V}_{11}^n(t) e^{-rt} \, dt - K e^{-rt_n}.$$

9.5 Characterization of Equilibrium

The equilibrium concept is *subgame perfect Nash equilibrium*. Because firms are asymmetric, there are equilibria in pure-adoption strategies, different from previous studies, which focused mainly on mixed strategies, as in Fudenberg and Tirole (1985). In what follows, a ∗ will denote equilibrium variables and functions.

First, the price equilibria are characterized at a given time for a given state of adoption. Then using the instantaneous profits in these equilibria, the equilibrium adoption times are determined.

9.5.1 Price Equilibria
From the definition of consumer's utility function, equilibrium behavior of different consumer types can be described as follows. Loyals buy from the old firm's shop that offers the highest utility. Local switchers buy from the shop that offers the highest utility. Finally, distant switchers buy from the cheapest of the virtual shops. Given this behavior, we can proceed to characterize the price equilibria conditional on the state of adoption.

9.5.1.1 No Firm Has a Virtual Shop Consider first the case $s_t = (0,0)$, where no firm has adopted yet. Since the physical shop is a monopoly, the old firm's equilibrium pricing strategy is to charge the consumers' reservation price of 1. The old firm sells to all consumers but distant switchers, making a profit of

$$V_{00}^{*o}(t) = (1 - c).$$

9.5.1.2 Only the Old Firm Has a Virtual Shop Next, consider the case $s_t = (0,1)$, where only the old firm has a virtual shop. Denote by p_j the price charged by shop $j = p, vo$. Assume that, when indifferent between the two shops, a consumer buys from the virtual shop. The demand functions for the two shops are given by

$$D_{01}^p(p) = \begin{cases} 1, & \text{if } p < p_{vo} + v,\ p \le 1 \\ 1 - a(t), & \text{if } p_{vo} + v \le p \le 1 \\ 0, & \text{if } 1 < p \end{cases}$$

$$D_{01}^{vo}(p) = \begin{cases} a(t)(1+\alpha), & \text{if } p < p_p - v, \ p \leq 1 - v \\ 1 - a(t), & \text{if } p_p - v \leq p \leq 1 - v \\ 0, & \text{if } \max\{1, p_p\} < p \end{cases}$$

The old firm chooses its prices so that it serves all consumers with Internet access through its virtual shop, and all consumers without Internet access through the physical shop. The equilibrium pricing strategies for the physical shop and the old firm's virtual shop are to charge the consumers' reservation prices, 1 and $1 - v$, respectively. The old firm's profit is

$$V_{01}^{*o}(t) = (1 - c) + a(t)[\alpha(1 - c) + (1 + \alpha)p].$$

The old firm's incremental instantaneous profit from operating a virtual shop is then

$$V_{01}^{*o}(t) - V_{00}^{*o}(t) = a(t)[\alpha(1 - c) + (1 + \alpha)p].$$

9.5.1.3 Only the New Firm Has a Virtual Shop Next, turn to the case $s_t = (1, 0)$, where only the new firm has adopted. The demand functions are

$$D_{10}^{p}(p) = \begin{cases} 1, & \text{if } p < p_{vn} + v, \ p \leq 1 \\ 1 - a(t)\dfrac{\sigma}{2}, & \text{if } p_{vn} + v = p \leq 1 \\ \lambda, & \text{if } p_{vn} + v < p \leq 1 \\ 0, & \text{if } 1 < p \end{cases}$$

$$D_{10}^{vn}(p) = \begin{cases} a(t)(\sigma + \alpha), & \text{if } p + v < p_p, \ p + v \leq 1 \\ a(t)\left(\dfrac{\sigma}{2} + \alpha\right), & \text{if } p_p = p + v \leq 1 \\ 0, & \text{if } \max\{p_p, 1\} - v < p \end{cases}$$

In this case, there exists no Nash equilibrium in pure strategies, as shown in Dinlersoz and Pereira (2004). To characterize the equilibrium mixed strategies, a range of prices needs to be identified for each shop so that a shop is indifferent between charging any price in the corresponding range. This process is carried out in Dinlersoz and Pereira (2004). The equilibrium pricing strategies for the firms can be characterized as follows:

Proposition 9.1 When only the new firm has a virtual shop, the equilibrium prices are drawn from the distributions

$$G_{10}^{*p}(p) = \begin{cases} 0, & \text{if } p < b^p \\ \left(\dfrac{\alpha + \sigma}{\sigma}\right)\left(1 - \dfrac{(1-c)[1-a(t)\sigma] + \rho}{p - c + \rho}\right), & \text{if } b^p \leq p < 1 \\ 1, & \text{if } p \geq 1 \end{cases}$$

$$G_{10}^{*vn}(p) = \begin{cases} 0, & \text{if } p < b^p - v \\ 1 - \left(\dfrac{1 - a(t)\sigma}{a(t)\sigma}\right)\left(\dfrac{1 - v - p}{p + v - c}\right), & \text{if } b^p - v < p < 1 - v \\ 1, & \text{if } p > 1 - v \end{cases}$$

where $b^p = c + (1-c)[1 - a(t)\sigma]$.

The intuition behind proposition 9.1, proved in Dinlersoz and Pereira (2004), is as follows. Both shops compete for local switchers with Internet access. Only the physical shop sells to consumers with no Internet access. For the new firm, charging a price lower than $1 - v$ entails both an expected marginal benefit associated with more sales to local switchers with Internet access and a marginal loss due to smaller per-consumer profit on distant switchers with Internet access. Similarly, for the old firm charging a price lower than 1 entails an expected marginal benefit associated with increased sales to local switchers with Internet access, and a marginal cost associated with a smaller per-consumer profit on loyals and local switchers without Internet access. Since the measure of distant switchers is smaller than the measure of loyals, $\alpha < \lambda$, the opportunity cost of charging lower prices is higher for the old firm than the new firm. As a consequence the physical shop charges stochastically higher prices. The physical shop charges $p = 1$ with positive probability. This price can be interpreted as its regular price, and lower prices can be viewed as discounts to attract local switchers.

As the Internet access $a(t)$ increases over time, both prices stochastically decrease, in a first-order sense. For the physical shop, a higher Internet access rate for local switchers implies a higher opportunity cost of charging high prices. Therefore, it has more incentive to charge lower prices. Consequently, the new firm's virtual shop also has to charge a lower price to attract these consumers. However, a higher λ leads to stochastically higher prices for both firms. When the fraction of loyals is higher, the old firm has less incentive to lower its price and compete with the new firm for local switchers with Internet access. This leads to higher prices by the new firm as well. An increase in α implies stochastically lower prices for the old firm, but does not change the new firm's prices.

Finally, the equilibrium instantaneous profits in this case are given by

$$V_{10}^{*o}(t) = [1 - a(t)\sigma](1 - c),$$

$$V_{10}^{*n}(t) = (\sigma + \alpha)a(t)[(1 - c + p) - \sigma(1 - c)a(t)].$$

9.5.1.4 Both Firms Have Virtual Shops The demand functions for the case $s_t = (1,1)$ can be obtained as before and are omitted. In this case, there exists no equilibrium in which virtual shops play pure-pricing strategies, as argued in Dinlersoz and Pereira (2004). The old firm has a dominant strategy of charging the monopoly price $p = 1$ in its physical shop. At this price, the physical shop sells to all local consumers without Internet access.

The equilibrium mixed strategies can be characterized for this case following a similar approach as in the case $s_t = (0,1)$. Dinlersoz and Pereira (2004) establish the following result:

Proposition 9.2 When both firms have virtual shops, in equilibrium the physical shop charges $p^p = 1$, and the virtual shops charge prices according to the distributions

$$G_{11}^{*vo}(p) = \begin{cases} 0, & \text{if } p < b^{vo} \\ \left(1 - \left(\dfrac{\lambda}{1+\alpha}\right)\left(\dfrac{1-c+p}{p-c+\Delta}\right)\right), & \text{if } b^{vo} < p < 1 - v \\ 1, & \text{if } p \geq 1 - v \end{cases}$$

$$G_{11}^{*vn}(p) = \begin{cases} 0, & \text{if } p < b^{vo} \\ \left(1 - \left(\dfrac{\lambda}{\sigma+\alpha}\right)\left(\dfrac{1-v-p}{p-c+\Delta}\right)\right), & \text{if } b^{vo} < p < 1 - v \\ 1, & \text{if } p \geq 1 - v \end{cases}$$

where $b^{vo} = c - \Delta + \left(\dfrac{\lambda}{1+\alpha}\right)(1 - c + p)$.

Note some important features of the firms' pricing strategies. First, prices do not depend on $a(t)$ unlike in the case of $s_t = (1,0)$. The old firm serves consumers with and without Internet access through two different shops. Therefore, the physical shop does not compete directly with the new firm's virtual shop for local switchers with Internet access. Only the virtual shops compete for local and distant switchers with Internet access, and their prices depend on only the relative measure of loyals and switchers. Second, the old firm's virtual shop charges stochastically higher prices compared to the new firm's virtual shop. This follows because the loyals with Internet access always buy from the old firm's virtual shop and this reduces the incentives for the old firm to charge lower prices to attract the switchers with Internet access. As a consequence, the old firm's virtual shop charges $p = 1 - v$ with positive probability. Third, an increase in λ leads to stochastically higher prices for both virtual shops, as in proposition 9.1. Fourth, the prices for both virtual shops are stochastically lower for higher α. The larger the measure of distant switchers with Internet access, the larger is the marginal return for both virtual shops to charge a price lower than $1 - v$.

The equilibrium profits as a function of time are given by

$$V_{11}^{*o}(t) = (1 - a(t)\sigma)(1 - c) + a(t)\lambda p,$$

$$V_{11}^{*n}(t) = a(t)\lambda \left(\frac{\sigma + \alpha}{1 + \alpha}\right)(1 - c + p).$$

Note that the old firm's incremental instantaneous profit from opening a virtual shop is then

$$V_{11}^{*o}(t) - V_{10}^{*o}(t) = a(t)\lambda p.$$

Observe that the physical shop's profit decreases to zero in the limit as $a(t)$ increases, because the physical shop sells only to local consumers without Internet access. In the presence of fixed costs, the old firm eventually shuts down the physical shop. However, if the diffusion of access is never complete, that is, $\lim_{t \to \infty} a(t) < 1$, or if fixed costs are not too high, the physical shop always remains open.[16]

9.5.2 Adoption Equilibria
To analyze adoption equilibria, assume that $K < \frac{1}{r} \min\left\{\lambda\left(\frac{\sigma + \alpha}{1 + \alpha}\right) \cdot (1 - c + p), \lambda p\right\}$. This assumption ensures that the entry cost is low enough so a firm can open a virtual shop eventually, regardless of whether it is a leader or a follower, preventing the uninteresting case where a firm never adopts because the entry cost is very high. Because

$K > 0$ and $a(0) = 0$, the possibility of immediate adoption by firms at time $t = 0$ is also ruled out.

Let $\theta = (r, K, c, \rho, \lambda, \alpha)$ be the vector of parameters. It is straightforward to show that the functions L^i and F^i, $i = $ "o," "n" are strictly quasiconcave in their first arguments, and admit unique interior maxima, independent of their second arguments. Denote these maximizers by $t_i^L \equiv t_i^L(\theta)$ and $t_i^F \equiv t_i^F(\theta)$, $i = $ "o," "n." For the old firm, t_o^L and t_o^F are the solutions, respectively, to the first-order conditions pertaining to the value functions L^o and F^o

$$-V_{01}^{*o}(t_o^L) + V_{00}^{*o}(t_o^L) + rK = 0$$

$$-V_{11}^{*o}(t_o^F) + V_{10}^{*o}(t_o^F) + rK = 0.$$

Similarly, for the new firm t_n^L and t_n^F are characterized, respectively, by the first-order conditions pertaining to the value functions L^n and F^n

$$-V_{10}^{*n}(t_n^L) + rK = 0$$

$$-V_{11}^{*n}(t_n^F) + rK = 0.$$

Given the ranking of the functions $V_{s_t}^{*i}$, it is easy to see that $t_o^L < t_o^F$ and $t_n^L < t_n^F$.

Let $t_i^c \equiv t_i^c(\theta)$ be the earliest time for which firm i is indifferent between being a leader and a follower, that is, $L^i(t_i^c, t_j^F) \equiv F^i(t_i^F, t_j^L)$. Obviously, $t_i^c < t_i^L$. Let Φ^n be the set for parameter values for which $t_n^L < t_o^c$:

$$\Phi^n \equiv \{\theta : L^o(t_o^L, t_n^F) < L^o(t_o^c, t_n^F)\}.$$

For θ in Φ^n, the old firm does not gain from preempting the new firm. The pure-strategy equilibrium adoption dates can then be characterized as follows:

Proposition 9.3 If θ belongs to Φ^n then the pure strategy equilibrium adoption dates are $\{t_o^*, t_n^*\} \equiv \{t_n^L, t_o^F\}$.

Proposition 9.3 follows from the observation that each firm's prescribed strategy is a best response to the others. By the definition of Φ^n, if θ is in Φ^n and the new firm adopts at t_n^L, the old firm has no incentive to deviate and preempt the new firm. Therefore, it adopts at the unique date t_o^F that maximizes its payoff as a follower. Given that the old firm adopts at date t_o^F, t_n^L is the unique optimal response for the new firm, because t_n^L maximizes its payoff as a leader.

Besides the equilibrium described in proposition 9.3, the model has two other types of adoption equilibria. In one, firms play pure strategies and the old firm adopts first. In the other, firms play mixed strategies as in Fudenberg and Tirole (1985), in which a follower always has an incentive to preempt its rival and become a leader in adoption. The empirical evidence reviewed in section 9.2 suggests, however, that typically new firms adopted first, as indicated in observation 9.7. Therefore, the focus of the rest of the paper is on pure-strategy equilibrium where the new firm adopts first. In other words, the focus on set Φ^n is based on its empirical relevance.

9.6 Analysis

A full analytical characterization of set Φ^n is complex. In Dinlersoz and Pereira (2004), simulations characterize this set. The analysis there suggests that the new firm is always a leader in adoption when it faces an established firm with low levels of loyalty in an industry where the physical shop has low marginal cost, the e-commerce technology brings low incremental profit, and the opportunity for market expansion is little. However, the established firm always leads in adoption if it enjoys relatively high loyalty, its physical shop has relatively high marginal cost, the incremental profit from e-commerce is relatively high, and the market expansion effect is relatively high.

The next proposition summarizes the comparative statics of the equilibrium adoption dates with respect to the important parameters. The proposition follows directly from applying the implicit function theorem to the first-order conditions.

Proposition 9.4 In the pure-strategy equilibrium in which the new firm always adopts first,

(1) An increase in the per-consumer incremental profit, ρ, decreases both adoption dates.

(2) An increase in the proportion of loyals, λ, decreases the old firm's adoption date.

(3) An increase in the marginal cost, c, increases the new firm's adoption date, and does not change the old firm's adoption date.

(4) An increase in the measure of distant switchers, α, decreases the new firm's adoption date and does not change the old firm's adoption date.

Table 9.3
The effect of parameters on adoption dates

		Effect of the parameter			
		ρ	λ	c	α
Adoption date of the new firm as a leader:	(t_n^L)	$\downarrow$	$\updownarrow$	$\uparrow$	$\downarrow$
Adoption date of the old firm as a follower:	(t_o^F)	$\downarrow$	$\downarrow$	0	0

Table 9.3 contains the results of proposition 9.4 in compact form. If incremental profitability, ρ, increases, both firms adopt sooner. An increase in the measure of loyals, λ, has a potentially ambiguous effect on the new firm's adoption date, but always leads to earlier adoption by the old firm. Higher λ implies a higher measure of captive consumers for the old firm's virtual shop and allows the old firm's virtual shop to charge higher prices, implying higher profit and earlier adoption. Higher λ has two effects on the new firm's profit. First, it implies a decrease in the measure of local switchers. Second, it leads the old firm to charge higher prices, allowing the new firm to charge higher prices. These two effects work in opposite directions. For low levels of λ, the net effect of an increase in λ is an increase in profit, whereas for high levels of λ the net effect is a decrease in profit. When the measure of distant switchers, α, is small, the first effect dominates the second effect, and the new firm adopts later.

An increase in the marginal cost, c, increases the new firm's adoption date, but has no effect on the old firm's adoption date. Except for distant switchers, the old firm can sell either through its virtual shop or its physical shop. Thus it only cares about the per-consumer incremental profit, ρ, whereas the new firm cares about the total per-consumer profit, $1 - c + \rho$.

Finally, an increase in the measure of distant switchers, α, decreases the new firm's adoption date, but has no effect on the old firm's adoption date. When only the new firm has a virtual shop, it is the only firm that sells to distant switchers with Internet access. An increase in the measure of distant switchers means an increase in the measure of its captive consumers, which increases the new firm's profit, and leads the new firm to adopt sooner. When both firms have adopted, the old firm also can sell to distant switchers through its virtual shop. However, since the old firm's virtual shop charges stochastically higher prices than the new firm's virtual shop, the old firm, on average, does not sell to distant consumers, hence the independence of its adoption date from α.

Note that the effect of a change in fixed costs has not been considered, because lower fixed costs trivially imply sooner adoption by both firms. Therefore, lower fixed costs cannot explain changes in the adoption sequence. Thus it is not obvious that early entry by new firms is necessarily a result of low fixed costs of setting up a virtual shop.

9.7   Reconciling Theory with Empirical Evidence

While the estimation of the model's parameters by retail sector is difficult, it is possible to put the observed patterns of adoption into perspective using the model's implications. In this section, the industries and adoption patterns discussed in section 9.3 are reconsidered and tied more closely to the model.

9.7.1   Books

For books, it can be argued that homogeneity of the product, relatively less need for verification of product features, and availability of a wide selection and online search for titles might have resulted in low or little utility loss for consumers, that is, low $v > 0$. Physical bookstores make significant investments in inventory, real estate, and personnel for each location. These investments were less relevant for an online book retailer, such as Amazon.com, resulting in potentially high cost savings. Altogether, this may have resulted in a moderate, or even high, level of incremental profitability, ρ, in the virtual market for books. Furthermore, the relative homogeneity of these products may have rendered any advantages of loyalty for traditional firms less influential. Cassidy (2002) reports that, shortly before Amazon.com was founded, Barnes & Noble and Borders shared close to a quarter of the market in book retailing. How much of that market share was loyal customers is unknown, but the combined market share of the two firms was not very high and the extent of loyalty may not have been overwhelming. In fact the book retailing industry remains relatively fragmented in the traditional market and there are "no eight-hundred-pound gorillas in book publishing and distribution," unlike the music industry (see Martin 1996). The adoption patterns for books can be generated by parameter configurations that involve moderate ρ and low λ.

9.7.2   Clothing and Apparel

Recall that in clothing and apparel most early adopters were established firms. This dominance can be explained by a combination of relatively high loyalty and relatively high incremental profitability for established retailers. The importance of loyalty in this product category gave a potential advantage to traditional retailers such as Gap and REI. This is so even though overall this category may not be well suited for online shopping for consumers, high $v > 0$, compared to products such as books and CDs. For traditional firms, synergies between online and in-store operations (such as alteration and return policies) may have resulted in lower marginal cost, high Δ, and relatively higher utility for consumers, negative v. This implies a potentially high, positive ρ for these firms. However, this was not the case for new firms, which did not enjoy any loyalty. Furthermore, for these firms, lack of physical stores was probably a source of inconvenience for customers in returns and alterations, high $v > 0$. Such lack of synergies between the two channels of sales may also have limited the realization of cost advantages, low Δ. Overall, these considerations resulted in an environment conducive for early adoption by established firms, rather than new ones. The adoption patterns in apparel and clothing can be represented by parameter configurations corresponding to high λ – high ρ pairs.

9.7.3   Brokerage

Brokering service is essentially a digital good, that is, $v < 0$. Stocks are convenient to trade online, which means that v is large in absolute value. Cost savings are likely to be significant, which means that Δ is large. Altogether this means that the incremental profitability ρ is positive and high. The Internet is also an ideal medium for searchers who look for cheap deals with little or no service quality. As pointed out by Mendelson, Techopitayakul, and Meza (2000), the fact that a sizeable fraction of consumers are searchers in this market, low λ, may have promoted entry by new firms. Early entry by the established firm Charles Schwab also can be explained within the model's framework. Charles Schwab is a discount broker. Its clients are interested mostly in executing trades at a low cost. For this purpose only, the Internet is more convenient for consumers and cheaper for firms. This means that Charles Schwab had a high, positive ρ, which could explain why it adopted e-commerce very quickly. On the other hand, Merrill Lynch is a full-service broker. Its clients demand a wide range of services that go beyond simply executing trades. For these types of services, the Internet is less convenient for consumers and less cost-effective for firms. This means that Merrill Lynch had a smaller ρ than Charles Schwab, which could explain its late adoption despite the loyalty exhibited by its customers who value full-service.

9.7.4 Jewelry

Initially, the Internet may not have been considered a suitable sales channel for jewelry. However, online retailing recently started to take off for this product category.[17] Internet-based startups, such as Blue Nile, Ice.com, and now Amazon.com, are slowly taking over this category, especially in diamonds. The main reason for the success of Internet-based firms appears to be the substantial cost savings for on-line retailers in selling diamonds, for which sales traditionally have involved several stages before the item reaches the customer. These layers of middlemen, experts, appraisers, and sales force are dramatically reduced by online sellers.[18] Such savings imply a high $\Delta > 0$. Together with a focus on standardized diamonds and a money-back guarantee, Blue Nile reduced the inconvenience of buying diamonds without inspecting them. This implies a low disutility v for consumers, which, together with cost savings, amounts to a high $\rho > 0$. Since Blue Nile focuses on standardized diamonds, customer loyalty for established firms, such as Zales, was not a major factor in hindering its emergence. Therefore, Blue Nile's dominance in this category can be explained by a combination of the factors mentioned in the model. As diamond sales on the Internet increases, some traditional retailers that specialize in standard diamond types such as Zales, may lose their market share. Yet, some traditional retailers, such as Tiffany, rely more on image and brand so that loyalty for its brand name make it relatively less vulnerable to growing online retailers. In the meantime, many other small traditional retailers appear to be facing a choice between focusing on more specialized diamonds, instead of the standardized ones, so that they can avoid a direct competition with online retailers. This behavior of traditional retailers is a good example of how retail industries reorganize in response to the emergence of e-commerce, similar to the way local markets once were reshaped by the entry of Walmart stores and other dominant chains.

Overall, the discussion above suggests that early adoption by new firms can be explained by a combination of factors included in the model, depending on product category and firm type. To what extent each factor plays a role in a given case is an empirical question. Further work is needed for an empirical analysis of adoption dates by product category and estimates of at least some of the parameters. Lieberman (2002) is a recent step toward understanding environments conducive for adoption by new firms.

9.8 Conclusion

This chapter seeks to understand retailers' incentives to adopt electronic commerce, emphasizing the effect of technology, preferences, consumer inertia, and market expansion on entry decisions and post-entry dynamics of prices. While other explanations, such as favorable financial markets, ample venture capital, and irrational behavior by entrepreneurs, can account for early adoption by new firms, the model here focuses on important differences between the traditional and virtual markets, and between established and new firms. The results provide a simple characterization of market environments conducive for adoption of e-commerce by new versus established firms. The observed adoption patterns in the early days of e-commerce can be explained by the adoption equilibria resulting from the model under different parameter configurations. The analysis also demonstrates that the simple technology adoption framework can be extended to analyze entry decisions in more complicated market environments. Similar applications can be made in other settings where it is important to recognize the features of the market environment in the stage game.

An important issue we have not explored is consumer welfare consequences of adoption and diffusion. The changes in welfare depend on the strength of different effects presented in the model, such as the extent of the distant market—because consumers who were not previously able to purchase can do so after adoption, the magnitude and direction of change in the utility of consumers as a result of Internet shopping, and the change in firms' costs as a result of adoption. Analysis of welfare can be done for each adoption state as in section 9.5.1, and the changes in welfare over time can be assessed.

With the continuing adoption of e-commerce by new retail sectors, the consequences of entry by new and established firms remain important. New Internet markets are becoming feasible in at least two ways. First, consumer learning and experimentation with e-commerce lead to opening of markets for products that have not been initially thought of as good candidates for e-commerce. Second, technological advances in Internet download speed and capacity, such as cable modem and

DSL, help new applications of e-commerce develop and be put to commercial use. Clearly, with early e-commerce, the online players were mostly selling commodities: books, music, or stock trades. Consumers didn't need to see or feel the products and they mostly focused on price. Recently launched Internet firms use new techniques to make consumers purchasers of a broader array of products. In real estate, for instance, use of software to show potential homebuyers photos and floor plans of houses has been revolutionary. Because such web services reduce, though do not necessarily eliminate, the need for a real estate agent, Internet-based firms can save consumers substantial commissions. In the jewelry business, websites of Internet-based firms offer educational information on diamonds so that consumers can feel comfortable in purchasing based on ratings on several aspects of jewelry, such as color and shape. Consumers can now handle much larger loads of information released recently by Internet firms. All these advances suggest that the diffusion of e-commerce is spreading to new goods and markets rapidly, and that the issue of who adopts and when, and in what type of markets, maintains its importance to understanding the ultimate structure of an Internet market.

Notes

1. See Smith and Brynjolfsson (2001).

2. See Iyer and Pazgal (2002), Baye, Morgan, and Scholten (2001), and Arbatskaya and Baye (2002).

3. For example, Lehman Brothers estimate that banking transaction costs are an average of one cent on the Internet compared to twenty-seven cents at an ATM and $1.27 at a teller. British Telecom estimates that moving external procurement functions to electronic commerce has reduced its costs from $113 to $8 per transaction. MasterCard estimates that the cost of processing purchase orders has fallen sharply.

4. See Litan and Rivlin (2001) for a discussion of the convenience of Internet shopping.

5. See Jullien in chapter 10 of this volume for more on electronic intermediaries.

6. In 1999, while 90 percent of Victoria's Secret's store customers were women, 60 percent of its Internet buyers in the last holiday season were men (see Kaufman 1999).

7. See Cassidy (2003) for a good account of the attitude of venture capital and the stock market toward pure Internet-based firms.

8. There have been some recent attempts to analyze inertia in the context of retailers' adoption of e-commerce. For instance, Lasry (2002) relates inertia to firm size and age, and finds that larger and younger firms have lower levels of inertia and are more willing to change to accommodate e-commerce. Lieberman (2002) investigates the role of first mover advantages in the adoption of e-commerce across several business sectors.

9. See Mendelson and Meza (2001) for details on the history of Amazon.com.

10. REI also opened a physical store in Tokyo so that products could ship from within the country. However, the store and the website closed in 2001 (see Mulady 2001).

11. As Pogue (2003) reports, two Internet-only firms, Movielink.com and Cinemanow .com, are competitors in the downloadable movies category. This category is an example of how the future of e-commerce might be if the technology to download digital information improves. As of this writing, downloadable movies is a struggling category awaiting progress in speed and quality of downloads.

12. We preclude the possibility that the new firm also opens a physical shop due to empirical irrelevance.

13. In a dynamic setting like the one studied here, consumers can engage in intertemporal substitution if they are long-lived. A consumer can wait to buy at possibly lower future prices if the current lowest price is too high. Such tendency is reinforced in the presence of mixed-strategy equilibria that emerge in the model presented here, since prices change continuously over time. However, if the consumer discount factor is high, or if there is a high penalty for postponing consumption, this concern becomes less of an issue. It is not difficult to introduce dynamics to consumer behavior. As it is well known, in such an environment (for example, Sargent and Ljungqvist 2000), a consumer faces a buy-or-wait problem, and follows a reservation price strategy. The reservation price depends on time, as price distributions change over time. Firms adjust their strategies in response to the consumers' behavior.

14. For simplicity, we assume that the adoption of e-commerce by firms has no effect on the diffusion of access across consumers. Since we focus on a single industry among many others in which e-commerce diffuses, the assumption that firms in that industry take the overall diffusion process as exogenous is plausible.

15. For simplicity, we do not allow firms' pricing strategies to depend on the history of prices. Precluding such dependence rules out collusive equilibria, among others. We believe there is no strong empirical evidence of collusive equilibria in online markets so far.

16. Consumers' preferences for traditional shopping experience also can lead to the same result.

17. Amazon.com announced on its website in April 2004 that it was entering the jewelry market with an open letter to customers signed by the founder Jeff Bezos.

18. The leading Internet seller, Blue Nile, has only 115 full-time staff and a single 10,000-square-foot warehouse. Mullaney (2004) reports that Rapoport Research estimated that a physical chain would need 116 stores and more than 900 workers to match the sales of Blue Nile in the traditional market.

References

Alba, Joseph, et al. (1997), "Interactive Home Shopping: Consumer, Retailer and Manufacturer Incentives in Participating in Electronic Market Places," *Journal of Marketing*, 61: 38–53.

Arbatskaya, Maria, and Baye, Michael (2004), "Sticky Prices Online: Rate Rigidity and Asymmetric Responses to Cost Shocks in Online Mortgage Markets," *International Journal of Industrial Organization*, 22: 1443–1462.

Baye, Michael, D. Kovenock, and C. deVries (1992), "It Takes Two to Tango: Equilibria in a Model of Sales," *Games and Economic Behavior*, 4: 493–510.

Baye, Michael, John Morgan, and Patrick Scholten (2004), "Price Dispersion in the Small and in the Large: Evidence from an Internet Price Comparison Site," *Journal of Industrial Economics*, 52: 463–496.

Brown, Jeffrey, and Austan Goolsbee (2002), "Does the Internet Make Markets More Competitive? Evidence from the Life-Insurance Industry," *Journal of Political Economy*, 110: 481–507.

Cassidy, John (2003), "Dot.con: How America Lost Its Mind and Money in the Internet Era," HarperCollins.

Dinlersoz, Emin, and Pedro Pereira (2004), "On the Diffusion of Electronic Commerce," Working Paper, University of Houston and Portuguese Competition Authority.

Fudenberg, Drew, and Jean Tirole (1985), "Preemption and Rent Equalization in the Adoption of New Technology," *Review of Economic Studies*, 52: 383–401.

Garicano, Luis, and Steven Kaplan (2001), "The Effects of Business-to-Business E-commerce on Transaction Costs," *Journal of Industrial Economics*, 49: 463–485.

Geyskens, I., K. Gielens, and M. Dekimpe (2002), "The Market Valuation of Internet Channel Additions," *Journal of Marketing*, 66: 102–119.

Henderson, Rebecca (1993), "Underinvestment and Incompetence as Responses to Radical Innovation: Evidence from the Photolithographic Alignment Equipment Industry," *Rand Journal of Economics*, 24: 248–270.

Humphrey, David, M. Kim, and B. Vale (2001), "Realizing the Gains from Electronic Payments: Costs, Pricing, and Payment Choice," *Journal of Money, Credit and Banking*, 33.

Iyer, Ganesh, and Amit Pazgal (2003), "Internet Shopping Agents: Virtual Co-location and Competition," *Marketing Science* 22 (1), 85–106.

Jensen, Richard (1982), "Adoption and Diffusion of an Innovation of Uncertain Profitability," *Journal of Economic Theory*, 27: 182–193.

Johnson, E., W. Moe, P. Fader, S. Bellman, and J. Lohse (2001), "On the Depth and Dynamics of On-line Search Behavior," Working Paper, Wharton School of Business.

Kaufman, Leslie (1999), "A Behind-the-Screens Glimpse of an Internet Retailer," *The New York Times*, May 24.

Lasry, Eytan (2002), "Inertia.com: Rates and Processes of Organizational Transformation in the Retail Industry," *Quarterly Journal of Electronic Commerce*, 3: 287–305.

Lieberman, Marvin (2002), "Did First Mover Advantage Survive the Dot.com Crash?" Working Paper, University of California, Los Angeles.

Litan, Robert, and Alice Rivlin (2001), "Beyond the Dot.coms: The Economic Promise of the Internet," Brookings Internet Policy Institute.

Lucking-Riley, David, and Daniel Spulber (2001), "Business-to-Business Electronic Commerce," *Journal of Economic Perspectives*, 15: 55–68.

Martin, Michael H. (1996), "The Next Big Thing: A Bookstore?" *Fortune*, December 9.

McIntyre, Katherine, and Ezra Perlman (2000), "Gap.com," Stanford University Graduate School of Business Case Number EC-9A.

Mendelson, Haim, Daricha Techopitayakul, and Phillip Meza (2000), "Broker.com," Stanford University Graduate School of Business Case Number EC-13.

Mendelson, Haim, and Philip Meza (2001), "Amazon.com: Marching towards Profitability" Stanford University Graduate School of Business Case Number EC-25.

Mulady, Kathy (2001), "REI to Close Tokyo Store," *Seattle Post-Intelligencer*, June 20.

Mullaney, Timothy (2004), "E-Biz Strikes Again!" *Business Week*, May 10.

Narasimhan, Chakravarty (1988), "Competitive Promotional Strategies," *Journal of Business*, 61: 427–449.

Osborne, Martin, and Carolyn Pitchik (1986), "Price competition in a capacity constrained duopoly," *Journal of Economic Theory*, 38: 238–260.

Pogue, David (2003), "Film Rentals, Downloaded to Your PC," *The New York Times*, May 15.

Quirmbach, Herman (1986), "The Diffusion of New Technology and the Market for an Innovation," *Rand Journal of Economics*, 17: 33–47.

Ramanathan, Lavanya (2000), "Retail Sector Analysis. Hoover's Online," www.hoovers.com.

Randall, Taylor, Serguei Netessine, and Nils Rudi (2002), "Inventory Structure and Internet Retailing: An Empirical Examination of the Role of Inventory Ownership," Working Paper, The Wharton Scool.

Reinganum, Jennifer (1981), "On the Diffusion of New Technology: A Game-Theoretic Approach," *Review of Economic Studies*, 48: 395–405.

Salop, Steven (1979), "Monopolistic Competition with Outside Goods," *Bell Journal of Economics*, 10: 141–156.

Sargent, Thomas, and Lars Ljungqvist (2000), *Recursive Macroeconomic Theory*, The MIT Press.

Sgoutas, Kostas (2000), "Pricing and Branding on the Internet," Stanford University Graduate School of Business, Case Number: EC-8.

Shaked, Avner, and John Sutton (1982), "Relaxing Price Competition through Product Differentiation," *Review of Economic Studies*, 49: 3–13.

Shankar, Venkatesh, Arvind Rangaswamy, and Michael Pusateri (2001), "The On-line Medium and Customer Price Sensitivity," Working Paper, University of Maryland.

Smith, Michael, and Erik Brynjolfsson (2001), "Consumer Decision-Making at an Internet Shopbot: Brand Still Matters," *Journal of Industrial Economics*, 49: 541–558.

Tedeschi, Bob (2003), "Blockbuster Decides to Go Online," *The New York Times*, April 28.

Varian, Hall (1980), "A Model of Sales," *American Economic Review*, 70: 651–659.

Zettelmeyer, Florian (2000), "Expanding to the Internet: Pricing and Communication Strategies When Firms Compete on Multiple Channels," *Journal of Marketing Research*, 37: 292–308.

10   Two-Sided Markets and Electronic Intermediaries

Bruno Jullien

10.1   Introduction

Some of the major innovations associated with digital communication technologies concern the process of intermediation (see Dinlersoz and Pereira, chapter 9 of this book).[1] Traditional brick-and-mortar intermediation provides several services in an integrated system. It manages various information flows. It provides physical facilities for the exchange process (transport, storage, and exhibition). Digital technologies separate these two types of functions, exploiting the drastic reduction in the cost of information processing and telecommunications associated with information and communication technologies (ICT). It thus becomes important to understand how a sector specialized in information management can organize itself. We refer to this activity as infomediation. A key characteristic of online infomediation is that it incurs very small variable costs.

Considering at a general level the intermediation activity online, one finds two main functions being performed: intermediaries identify profitable trade opportunities, and they help determine the precise terms of trade. There are also numerous other information services that the intermediary can propose and that are derivatives of these two base functions (advice, billing, accounting, stock/flow management, etc.). To this respect, online intermediation offers a wide range of possibilities. Some sites such as ZDNet are specialized in providing information on products, sellers, or prices: they assist clients in selecting a product and/or a seller, but don't intervene on the transactions.[2] In business-to-business (B2B), one tendency is to offer a particular industry a simple matching service to help them move toward offering a full-supply chain management service. Examples are SciQuest for life sciences, or eSteel for steel constructions. Verticalnet is an example of online supply management not specialized for a particular industry.

The most known and successful intermediation website is probably eBay, which manages millions of items every day. One key to the success of eBay is their ability to provide an efficient rating system based on customers' satisfaction reports, improving greatly the quality of the match in terms of reliability. Typically eBay performs both the matching and the pricing services at once, using rather sophisticated devices: not only does it perform online auctions but it also provides the sellers with some flexibility in choosing the auction format with a nonlinear pricing scheme. Another website offering the two services at a disaggregated level is Priceline, an airline ticket reservation service that allows clients to post a destination and a desired price, letting the airlines react to the clients' offers.

Despite their diversity, most of these activities have in common that a key determinant of the value of the service is the number of potential trading partners that an agent can reach.[3] We refer to a two-sided market when this externality occurs between two different identified types of agents, with a differential treatment. For instance, the participation of potential buyers on eBay is determined by the large portfolio of goods auctioned; the willingness of sellers to use the service is directly related to the participation level of buyers. Although there was already some consideration about these aspects in the analysis of traditional intermediation,[4] recent works on various related domains have highlighted the two-sided nature of the intermediation activities (see Rochet and Tirole 2004a for a general presentation).

At the intuitive level, the concept of two-sided markets refers to situations where one or several competing platforms provide services used by two types of trading partners to interact and operate an exchange.

It is interesting that this view of intermediation seems to have been central to the successful development of Amazon. Indeed Jeff Bezos (Amazon's CEO) described its activity as one of an "information broker," helping readers and books find each other.[5] This view underlies one key to the success of using online information processing to provide clients with advice and targeted information. More recently Amazon has introduced Amazon Marketplace, allowing its clients to sell or buy used products. While it is more specialized than eBay or Yahoo services, it provides some specific services, such as the ability to use Amazon's payment service.[6]

Examples of two-sided markets that differ from online intermediation include:

Payment card systems[7]   Here the two sides of the markets are merchants and buyers who conduct a transaction and use the card as a means of payment.

Software platforms   These are discussed by Evans, Hagiu, and Schmalensee in chapter 3.

Video games   These are also discussed in chapter 3. The seller of the technology offers a platform (the console) on which developers offer video games to consumers. Consumers pay for the console, and developers pay royalties on games.

Music platforms   These are discussed by Peitz and Waelbroeck in chapter 4 of this book.

The literature then emphasizes the indirect network effects[8] involved in these activities. These effects generate a well-known chicken-and-egg problem: customers on one side of the market will be willing to participate in the platform activity only if they expect sufficient participation from the other side. In such a context platforms are going to develop specific strategies intended to "bring the two sides on board."[9] In particular, firms offer a price structure that may include fees agents must pay if they want to participate in the platform activity (registration or membership fees), as well as fees related to the level of activity on the platform such as transaction fees that are paid when an exchange takes place. The platform will need to account for the demand externalities when designing the price structure. To this extent, the literature on monopoly platforms is related to the literature on the multiproduct firm, where the goods are complements. Although, the literature on competing platforms is more related to the literature on competing networks.

The objective of this chapter is to build a simple model of the intermediation activity of trading partners involved in a commercial relationship and to use the model to illustrate some of the results that emerge in the two-sided market literature, as well as to discuss some new aspects. The first part concentrates on a monopoly intermediation service and discusses both efficient pricing and monopoly pricing. The second part builds on Caillaud and Jullien (2003) to discuss the nature of competition between platforms. The conclusion summarizes the main insights.

10.2   The Model

The model is adapted from one introduced in Gaudeul and Jullien (2001). Consider a service provider that intermediates the transactions between consumers and producers. A mass of consumers can buy electronic goods from independent producers on the Web. There is a continuum of producers that potentially can sell these products through the Web. Each producer is seen as selling a different product.

The intermediary provides a service that helps consumers find a product. Firms and consumers register to the intermediary. Then consumers can get access to the list of products, characteristics, and prices, and the service assists them in identifying their match if it is registered. Accessing this search technology involves an opportunity cost for the consumer (because of complexity, inadequate search process, and delay). This cost also can be seen as the value for the consumer of using an alternative technology to find a trading partner. Let $F(c)$ be the mass of consumers with an opportunity cost less than c. Each firm faces a fixed cost of providing the good through the platform. The products are ranked by increasing order of fixed cost and the mass of producers with a fixed cost below some level k is $H(k)$. Normalize by assuming that the total population is one on each side and that all other costs are zero. In what follows, it most often will be assumed that these distributions are continuous with corresponding densities $h(k)$ and $f(c)$, although the key results hold for arbitrary distributions.

Let m be the mass of producers on the intermediary service, and n be the mass of consumers. Assume that each consumer has a probability to have a trading partner on the platform equal to the mass m of producers. Let P be the probability that a trade occurs between two trading partners when they are both active on the platform (this requires that the two partners are matched and find an agreement). The total volume of transactions generated by the platform is $V = mnP$, where mn is the number of potential pairs of partners. Denote by s the expected surplus of a consumer conditional on having a potential trading partner on the platform; then the expected surplus that a consumer derives from participating on the platform process is $ms - c$.[10] The expected surplus s accounts for both the probability that a trade occurs (P), and the expected value generated by the exchange. Similarly, π is the expected profit per consumer (ignoring the fixed cost k) that producers derive from their participation, so that the surplus of the producers is $n\pi - k$. Again π is the product of P and the expected profit per transaction.

10.2.1 The Instruments of the Intermediary

In this setup, the prices that the intermediary uses to finance its activities depend on what is observed.

Registration Fees The intermediary may impose registration fees p for consumers and q for the producers. This requires that participation be monitored at a low cost, and that micropayments not be too costly. This is satisfied in most B2B activities, but in some business-to-consumer (B2C) or consumer-to-consumer (C2C) activities it is too costly to charge the participation of consumers—at least before a match is performed.

Transaction Fees The intermediary may charge transaction fees t_C and t_P for, respectively, the consumers and the producers. This requires monitoring transactions. In some cases only one side of the market is charged. When intermediation leads to some commercial transactions with a transfer negotiated between the two parties and only transactions can be monitored (not matches), only the total fee $t = t_C + t_P$ matters. Indeed the producer will adjust its price to any rebalancing of the fees between the two parties. Thus in this case again only one fee can be considered. Denote by T the set of feasible transaction fees. The expected surplus of producers is then $\pi = \pi(t)$, while the consumers surplus is $s = s(t)$, and the volume of transactions is $mnP(t)$.[11] Typically $\pi(t) + s(t)$ decreases with t.

To give an example, eBay charges only sellers. There is an "insertion fee" (ranging from $0.25 to $4.80 depending on the starting price of the auction, as of January 2005) plus a "final value fee," paid only if the item is sold, which depends on the closing value (the marginal rates are 5.25 percent below $25, 2.75 percent between $25 and $1,000, and 1.5 percent above $1,000).

Advertising Advertising is a way to finance the activity, which can be analyzed using the multi-sided market approach.[12] It will not be considered here.

Bundling with Information Goods One way to attract customers is to bundle the intermediation service with other information services that are not affected by network externalities. This includes the activities of portals, but also billing, accounting, or any other information services for B2B.

10.3   Externalities and Surplus

10.3.1   Registration Fees and Participation Externalities

Assume for the moment that the intermediary just uses registration fees, so that $T = \{0\}$. The surplus s, the profit π, and P are thus exogenous. The profit of a producer with an entry cost k is $n\pi - q - k$ and the expected surplus of a consumer with an opportunity cost c is $ms - p - c$. A producer joins the platform if $k \leq n\pi - q$, while a consumer joins if $c \leq ms - p$. We thus obtain

$$m = H(n\pi - q),$$

$$n = F(ms - p).$$

The two-sided nature of the market is embedded in the fact that the demand addressed by one side of the market depends on the demand from the other side. Combining the two equations we find that the mass of consumers joining the platform is the solution of the reduced form equilibrium condition:

$$n = F(H(n\pi - q)s - p).$$

The volume of trade V is then proportional to the product of the market shares on the two sides: $V = mnP = H(n\pi - q)nP$.

The model thus involves an indirect network externality between consumers: although consumers are not directly affected by other consumers, in equilibrium, each consumer creates a positive externality on the others through its impact on the producers' participation.[13] The reduced form is then similar to a model of network externality. This type of externality is referred to as "membership externalities" in Rochet and Tirole (2003).

The model may thus exhibit multiple equilibria and inefficiencies. In what follows we focus on stable equilibria where stability refers to a dynamic adjustment process where the two sides alternate in their registration choice and respond myopically to the other side's market share.

As this is not the object of the chapter we shall assume that there exists at most one equilibrium with a positive level of activity. This is the case if F and H are concave and bounded on $[0, +\infty)$. This is also the case if the two distributions H and F are Dirac, with $H(\pi) = F(s) = 1$. In both cases, there can be at most one equilibrium with positive activity as $F(H(n\pi - q)s - p)$ can cross the diagonal with a slope less than one (stability) only once.

With positive prices p and q, there always exists an equilibrium where no agents register. This is because no agents would pay to register if they anticipated that the other side would refuse to get "on board."

A key point for what will follow is that for negative consumer registration fee p, and provided that $q < F(-p)\pi$, no activity is not an equilibrium. Thus there exists a unique equilibrium allocation and it involves a positive activity on the platform.

Consider now an allocation with positive demands on both sides. Denote

$$\theta = \pi s f(ms - p)h(n\pi - q).$$

Assuming differentiability, the system of demand functions verifies

$$\frac{dm}{dq} = -\frac{h(n\pi - q)}{1 - \theta}, \tag{10.1}$$

$$\frac{dn}{dp} = -\frac{f(ms - p)}{1 - \theta}, \tag{10.2}$$

$$\pi \frac{dn}{dq} = s\frac{dm}{dp} = -\frac{\theta}{1 - \theta}. \tag{10.3}$$

An increase in the price q leads to a direct reduction h of the mass of producers. This induces an adverse effect on the participation of consumers, and through the externality a further reduction θh of m, and so on. The overall multiplier effect associated with this feedback effect is $\frac{1}{1-\theta} = \sum_{r=0}^{+\infty} \theta^r$. The coefficient θ thus captures the feedback effect. Total surplus then writes as

$$W = \left(mns - \int_0^{ms-p} c\,dF(c) \right) + \left(mn\pi - \int_0^{n\pi-q} k\,dH(k) \right).$$

The brackets separate the consumers' surplus and the producers' surplus. The link between the two sides of the market is captured first by the product term mn in both surpluses. Thus,

$$W = mn(s + \pi) - \int_0^{ms-p} c\,dF(c) - \int_0^{n\pi-q} k\,dH(k).$$

The term $\pi + s$ is the total expected surplus per pair of partners, while mn is the number of pairs. The other two terms are the opportunity costs of the agents joining the platform. Differentiating the surplus yields after some computation

$$\frac{dW}{dq} = (q + ns)\frac{dm}{dq} + (p + m\pi)\frac{dn}{dq}$$

$$\frac{dW}{dp} = (q + ns)\frac{dm}{dp} + (p + m\pi)\frac{dn}{dp}.$$

To understand the formula, consider first the term $q + ns$. For a fixed demand size n, subsidizing the entry of producers creates a distortion as in a competitive market: this is captured by the term q equal to the gross surplus of the marginal producer. This distortion vanishes at $q = 0$. Therefore for a fixed consumers' participation the optimal price would be equal to the marginal cost of servicing producers. But inducing more entry of producers also benefits directly to consumers since it increases their chance to find their desired product. The value of this externality is s per consumer, hence the term $ns\frac{dm}{dq}$. The last term then accounts for the demand externalities and the fact that reducing the price q also raises the participation of consumers.

Result 10.1 Starting from marginal cost pricing, a small subsidy to any side of the market is welfare improving.

To interpret further the results denote

$$x = ms - p; \quad y = n\pi - q$$

the surplus gross of opportunity cost of a participant on each side of the market. Then

$$W = F(x)H(y)(\pi + s) - \int_0^x cdF(c) - \int_0^y kdH(k).$$

From this formula it is evident that welfare maximization requires that $x = H(y)(\pi + s) = m(\pi + s)$ and $y = n(\pi + s)$. The interpretation is straightforward. Consumers should participate as long as their opportunity cost is smaller than the total surplus generated by their participation, which includes their surplus ms but also the positive externality on the other side of the market $m\pi$ (π for each of the m producers).

Thus welfare-maximizing prices will not coincide with marginal costs and account for externalities. Indeed optimal pricing will call for subsidies. More precisely, provided that demands are not inelastic, welfare-maximizing prices verify (using $p = ms - x$ and $q = n\pi - y$)

$$q = -ns$$

$$p = -m\pi.$$

Proposition 10.1 The welfare-maximizing registration subsidy to producers is equal to the total consumers' surplus per producer; the welfare-maximizing registration subsidy to consumers is equal to the total expected producers' profit per consumer. (Armstrong 2004)

One view about this result is that one should subsidize more the less profitable side of the market.

Notice that the producers have a collective interest in subsidizing the entry of consumers. So even in the absence of government intervention, the market may organize to provide incentives to entry. In particular, when introducing intermediation, intermediaries may internalize this effect through their pricing policies. The question will then be whether intermediaries have proper incentives to do so.

10.3.2 Transaction Fees

Let us now allow for transaction fees. To simplify, tax neutrality is assumed so that only the total transaction fee is allowed. Let $s(t)$ be the per-producer expected surplus of a consumer, and $\pi(t)$ be the per-consumer expected profit of a producer.

For a given price structure the allocation now verifies

$$m = H(n\pi(t) - q)$$

$$n = F(ms(t) - p)$$

while the volume of trade is $V = mnP(t)$.

An increase in the transaction fee has two effects. First, for a given volume of trade it affects negatively the trading parties' surplus. Here this is captured by the fact that $\pi'(t) \leq 0$ and $s'(t) \leq 0$. Second, it affects the volume of trade on the platform for a given participation level: $P'(t) \leq 0$. Denote

$$S(t) = s(t) + \pi(t) + P(t)t$$

the expected total surplus from a pair of partners. Then typically $S(t)$ is nonincreasing in t in the range of positive transaction fees.

An increase in the transaction fee leads to a reduction in participation as the net profit and the net consumers surplus decrease:

$$\frac{dm}{dt} \leq 0; \quad \frac{dn}{dt} \leq 0.$$

Let us now consider welfare maximization when transaction fees are used. Welfare writes as

$$W = mnS(t) - \int_0^{ms(t)-p} cdF(c) - \int_0^{n\pi(t)-q} kdH(k).$$

Using as before $x = ms(t) - p$ and $y = n\pi(t) - q$ we find that

$$W = mnS(t) - \int_0^x cdF(c) - \int_0^y kdH(k).$$

Notice that for any t, the platform can control the surpluses x and y through an adequate choice of registration fees. Thus the platform has enough instruments to control for both the volume of trade and the participation levels. Welfare-maximizing prices must then verify

$$t^W \in \arg\max_{t \in T} S(t)$$

$$x^W = m^W S(t^W)$$

$$y^W = n^W S(t^W).$$

The transaction fee should be used to correct for the inefficiency in the trading process. Typically, in the case of commercial transactions, there is a suboptimal level of trade so that the fee should be negative, inducing efficient trade whenever this is feasible.[14] A particular case is one where the total surplus per match is not affected by the transaction fee, $S(t) = S$ for all $t \in T$ (this is the case, for instance, if the trading parties share a fixed surplus S and $T = [0, S]$). Then the level of transaction fee can be anything provided that registration fees are adjusted consequently.

The last equations have the same interpretation as before: x is the opportunity cost of the marginal consumer and should be equal to the total surplus generated by its participation. Then, using the definition of x and y, we see that optimal registration fees verify

$$q^W = -n^W(s(t^W) + P(t^W)t^W)$$
$$p^W = -m^W(\pi(t^W) + P(t^W)t^W).$$

Typically, the registration fees are negative to induce adequate internalization of the network effects by the participants.

To conclude this section we should point out that, as discussed in Rochet and Tirole (2004a), while we focus here on participation externalities, the level of activity may also involve some two-sided externalities.[15] For instance, this may occur in our setup if the intermediary intervenes on the terms of trade either directly or through sophisticated tariffs such as a nonlinear fee. Suppose for instance that in addition to set transaction fees, the intermediary can monitor the transaction price $\hat{p}$ between the trading parties. Then it is optimal for the intermediary to use direct control of the price $\hat{p}$ to raise the surplus from trade, as in Wright (2003), and then to use transaction fees t_C and t_P to recoup the profit and to control for the participation levels of both side. In this case usage will be two-sided, as for a fixed $\hat{p}$, raising t_P and reducing t_C to modify the willingness of the parties to trade.

10.3.3 Ramsey Pricing

Notice that at the welfare-maximizing prices the profit $\Pi = -mnS(t^W)$ is negative. The platform thus runs a deficit and should be subsidized. Consider now the case where the platform is benevolent but subject to a nonnegative profit condition. Here we may think of the platform as a cooperative jointly owned by the community of consumers and producers.

The profit of the platform is

$$\Pi = mnP(t)t + pn + qm$$

$$= mnS(t) - xn - ym.$$

Maximizing total surplus under zero profit yields the constrained optimal allocation. Optimal Ramsey prices are such that the transaction fee t is set at the level that maximizes the surplus generated by each match $S(t)$, as before, while registration fees are used to cover the fixed cost.

To see this, let γ be the shadow value of the budget constraint; the optimal allocation is the solution of

$$\max_{t,x,y}\left(mnS(t) - \int_0^x cdF(c) - \int_0^y kdH(k) + \gamma(mnS(t) - xn - ym)\right)$$

st $n = F(x)$; $y = H(y)$.

It is then clear that the optimal transaction verifies as before

$$t^R \in \arg \max_{t \in T} S(t).$$

In any case, transaction fees should maximize the total surplus per match. The reason is that all efficiency gains in the trading process can be recouped through the transaction fees.[16]

The participation levels are then given by

$$x^R = m^R S(t^R) - \frac{\gamma}{1+\gamma} \frac{F(x^R)}{f(x^R)},$$

$$y^R = n^R S(t^R) - \frac{\gamma}{1+\gamma} \frac{H(y^R)}{h(y^R)},$$

corresponding to registration fees

$$p^R = -m^R (\pi(t^R) + P(t^R)t^R) + \frac{\gamma}{1+\gamma} \frac{F(x^R)}{f(x^R)},$$

$$q^R = -n^R (s(t^R) + P(t^R)t^R) + \frac{\gamma}{1+\gamma} \frac{H(y^R)}{h(y^R)}.$$

Result 10.2 In order to balance the budget it is optimal to use the transaction fee to maximize the surplus conditional on participation and to rely on fixed payments for the financing. The registration fee faced by one side decreases with the elasticity of participation with respect to the registration fee (for a fixed participation of the other side), and it decreases with the value attached to the participation of a (marginal) member by the other side and the platform.

The result of transaction fees is similar to an optimal two-part tariff rule and it is related to the fact that apart from the fixed cost of participation, all individuals are identical ex ante. In a more general setup, one would rely on all the prices so that transaction fees would be larger. Notice that in our model this implies that the platform runs a deficit on transactions.

A second consequence is that whether the consumers or the producers will be subsidized depends on two considerations: how much surplus they create for the other side, and the elasticity of their demand.

For instance, suppose that there are no transaction fees, $T = \{0\}$. This corresponds to the situation discussed in Armstrong (2004). The same logic applies where the benefits from trade are computed for $t = 0$. Optimal registration fees are given by

$$p = -m\pi + \frac{\gamma}{1+\gamma}\frac{F}{f}$$

$$q = -ns + \frac{\gamma}{1+\gamma}\frac{H}{h}$$

$$0 = pn + qm.$$

A simple computation would show that p is negative if $sn\frac{n}{f} < \pi m \frac{m}{h}$; thus if a consumer exerts a relatively high externality compared to a producer, consumers' participation is very sensitive to the price. In this case, a slight reduction of the price p is very beneficial as it leads to a large increase in the participation level of consumers and a high externality on producers.

10.4   Monopoly Pricing

Let us now consider the case of a monopoly intermediary. We shall contrast the case where the monopoly has access to a full set of instruments to various relevant scenarios. Unless stated, we assume there is no coordination problem, so that the equilibrium with positive participation of both sides emerges.

The monopoly profit is equal to $\Pi = mnP(t)t + pn + qm$. When maximizing its profit, the monopoly will account for externalities through the impact of the participation level of one side on the willingness to pay on the other side. To follow the welfare analysis, denote as before $x = ms(t) - p$ and $y = n\pi(t) - q$. Then profit is given by $\Pi = mnS(t) - xn - ym$. Let us view the monopoly as choosing x, y, and t. Then the condition for t writes

$$t^M \in \arg\max_{t \in T} S(t).$$

Thus transaction fees should be set at a level that maximizes the total surplus generated by the transactions of a pair of customers. This is similar to the conclusion derived by Rochet and Tirole (2004a) for the case where parties bargain over a transaction price.

Result 10.3 As in the case of Ramsey pricing, transaction fees serve the purpose of enhancing the surplus while the registration fees are used to share this surplus.

The participation levels are then given by

$$x^M = m^M S(t^M) - \frac{n^M}{f(x^M)}; \quad y^M = n^M S(t^M) - \frac{m^M}{h(y^M)},$$

$$n^M = F(x^M); \quad m^M = H(y^M),$$

leading to registration prices

$$p^M = \frac{n^M}{f(x^M)} - m^M(\pi(t^M) + P(t^M)t^M),$$

$$q^M = \frac{m^M}{h(x^M)} - n^M(s(t^M) + P(t^M)t^M).$$

For instance, if the value of m and q were fixed, and $t = 0$, the monopoly price on consumers would be $p = \frac{n}{f(x)}$. The monopoly price internalizes two other effects. First, for t different from zero, each new participant generates an additional income $mP(t)t$. Second, each new participant creates an externality that allows the price to rise on the other side of the market, by an amount $m\pi(t)$ for a constant in the other side's participation.

The result is related to the two-part tariff literature and the fact that faced with a homogenous population, a monopoly would set a two-part tariff with a unit price equal to marginal cost (which maximizes the total surplus from consumption). Building on this literature, one can then anticipate factors that would raise the transaction fee. For instance, consumer or producer heterogeneity, or risk aversion,[17] may lead to higher transaction fees. Similarly, if the surplus from trade is affected by the quality of intermediation, a positive transaction fee may help in providing adequate incentives to the intermediation platform.[18]

Positive transaction fees also could be motivated by some failure to charge registration fees. This is clearly the case if registration fees are too costly to implement on both sides. In other cases, one side of the market is not charged at all (this is the case for portals or eBay). Now suppose that it is too costly to charge consumers (because they face transaction costs), but that transactions can be monitored ($p = 0, t \neq 0$). Then $x = ms(t)$, and it is no longer possible to separate the determination of the surplus per match and the participation decision of consumers. Given that a positive transaction fee is passed to the consumers, it is a way to force consumers to participate in the financing of the activity. Thus transaction fees may be substitutes for registration fees.

10.5   Competing Intermediaries

From the preceding section, it appears that neither marginal-cost pricing nor monopoly pricing would achieve an efficient allocation. One then wonders whether competition between two or more platforms can generate a more efficient allocation. So suppose now that there are two identical intermediation platforms, 1 and 2, that compete on the market.

A specificity of competition between platforms is that the attractiveness of a platform for one side of the market is directly related its success on the other side of the market. As discussed in Jullien (2000), each user of a platform is both a consumer of the service and an input in the process. Platforms' pricing strategies then reflect the competition to sell the service, but also the competition to buy the input. As we shall see, this dual nature of competition may generate very aggressive strategies using cross-subsidies and prices that depart significantly from marginal costs.

A key determinant of the competitive process is whether platforms obtain exclusivity from their clients or not. For instance, most auction websites require the sellers to commit to deliver the good to the winning bidder, so that the same unit of good cannot be placed to sell on several websites. In many cases, however, exclusivity is either not required or simply impracticable because of monitoring issues. Customers can then register with several platforms. This practice is referred to as *multihoming*. A simple example is the use of several search engines or portals. In discussing the competitive outcome, we must distinguish the two cases. In the next section I devote the first part to the case of exclusivity, and then discuss multihoming. But the reader should keep in mind that the latter will be the relevant case for many applications.

10.5.1   Competition with Exclusivity
For the moment we concentrate on the case where consumers or producers can register with only one intermediary.

Notice that an efficient allocation in this setup requires that all agents register with the same intermediary. Moreover, because of network effects, the competitive pressure tends to favor the concentration of the activity on a single intermediation platform.

Caillaud and Jullien (2001, 2003) study a simplified version of this model. Their setup assumes that the transaction fees are nondistortionary. In the present setup, transaction fees are nondistortionary if there exist constants S and P such that

$$S(t) \equiv S \quad \text{and} \quad P(t) \equiv P.$$

Thus neither the total surplus nor the probability of trade is affected by transactions fees. In this case, both the optimal Ramsey transaction fee and the monopoly transaction fee are indeterminate. Their model also assumes that full taxation is possible, namely that $T = \left[0, \frac{S}{P}\right]$. Then by setting the maximal transaction fee the platform can appropriate the full surplus S. This provides a competitive benchmark in which the equilibrium involves zero profits.[19]

Proposition 10.2 Assume that transaction fees are nondistortionary and that full taxation is feasible. Then any equilibrium involves a single active intermediary with zero profits. (Caillaud and Jullien 2003)

To understand the result, consider an equilibrium where all active agents register to the same platform, say platform one.[20] Let us denote as before $x = ms(t) - p$ and $y = n\pi(t) - q$ the total expected gross surplus and profit for each side of the active platform. We thus have $n = F(x)$, $m = H(y)$ and $\Pi = mnS - xn - ym$. Now suppose that $\Pi > 0$. Then the inactive platform could simply set t so that $Pt = S$ (full taxation) and price $p = -x(-\varepsilon)$, $q = -y(-\varepsilon)$, where ε is small and positive. Given that all the surplus from trade is taxed away, consumers would receive a utility from this competing platform independent of the other side's participation level—$x(+\varepsilon) - c$ and larger than the equilibrium surplus with the other platform. With these prices it is dominant for an agent to join the second platform if it registers somewhere.[21] Thus $F(x)$ consumers would join, as well as $H(y)$. By doing so, the inactive intermediary could obtain the intermediary profit Π. Thus it must be the case that the profit vanishes in equilibrium.

The second question is whether the equilibrium is efficient. In Caillaud and Jullien (2003) this is indeed the case as neither consumers nor producers face an opportunity cost to join the platform. F and H are just Dirac distributions so that a single platform with the whole population is efficient. Whether efficiency extends to the case of an elastic participation remains an open question. Clearly, the efficient allocation will be one equilibrium, but it has to be shown whether it is the unique one.

10.5.2 Distortionary Transaction Fees: Divide and Conquer

The above reasoning depends on the assumption that transaction fees are nondistortionary, which is very peculiar. Indeed the idea is that an intermediary can use the transaction fee to capture the full surplus generated by the platform, and can use the (negative) registration fees to redistribute this surplus and control for participation. For this type of strategy, it is essential to dispose of a nondistortionary pricing instrument. So the relevance of the result may be somewhat limited in practice. One may then conjecture that as soon as $S(t)$ decreases with t, equilibria may involve positive profits.

To illustrate this, let us assume that transaction fees are not available (Caillaud and Jullien 2001). Then the most efficient competitive strategy takes the form of *divide and conquer*. Again suppose that platform 1 serves the market alone at price p and q. Suppose that the masses n and m of consumers and producers are fixed, $n = m = 1$ (zero participation costs). Then a strategy that allows platform 2 to capture the market takes the following form:

Divide   Platform 2 sets a price $p_2 = -x = p - s < 0$.

Conquer   Platform 2 sets a price $q_2 = \pi + \inf\{0, q\}$.

A symmetric strategy can be used reversing the role of the two sides. The idea of the strategy is that the platform subsidizes the consumers (or the producers) to convince them to join. Once the participation of one side of the market is obtained, a bandwagon effect allows the platform to recoup the subsidy through the registration fees payed by the other side of the market. At prices p_2, it is dominant for consumers to join platform 2. But, observing that, producers have the choice between buying from platform 1 at price q (if $q < 0$), staying out (if $q > 0$), or joining platform 2 and getting $\pi - q_2$.

These types of divide-and-conquer strategies are particular instances of more general strategies that emerge when networks compete and are able to price discriminate between users with different valuations of network effects.[22] The networks will "buy" the participation of some types of users to create value for other users.

It is clear that in the context of competing intermediaries, the choice of the best target for the subsidy accounts for two aspects:

1. The group must be easy to divide, meaning that it is willing to separate from the others for a smaller subsidy than others;

2. The group must be attractive for other participants, meaning that other agents are willing to pay a relatively large amount to join this group.

Thus consumers will be the natural target if $s < \pi$, so that they have less to gain than producers in the interaction.

These types of strategies show that despite network effects, there is limited scope for market power. Indeed in the simple case where F and H are Dirac at zero, if platform 1 is active in equilibrium, it must be the case that $p_2 + q_2 \leq 0$ or

$p + \inf\{0, q\} < s - \pi.$

Still, there is the possibility of market power and positive profits for the active platform.

Result 10.4 When transactions are not feasible, there may exist equilibria with positive profits.

From this we see that the profitability for platform 2 under the divide-and-conquer strategy is independent of the registration fee paid by producers whenever it is positive, $q > 0$. The reason is that once platform 2 has convinced consumers to join, producers are no longer willing to pay this fee. The active platform may as well set q large.[23] Based on these arguments, Caillaud and Jullien (2001, 2003) show that there exist equilibria with a single active platform and positive profits. The result relies on very little restrictions being imposed on the way consumers and producers coordinate. One way out is to limit the potential extent of coordination failure due to network externalities by imposing additional restrictions on the process governing the allocation of consumers and producers between the two intermediation platforms. For instance, Ambrus and Argenziano (2004) restore zero profit for a homogeneous population by imposing some conditions limiting the extent of coordination failure. Gabszewicz and Wauthy (2004) reach a similar conclusion assuming passive expectation.[24]

In the most reasonable case where transaction fees induce distortions or cannot be implemented and preferences are nonlinear, one can hardly expect competition to fully discipline the market. Interestingly, Ambrus and Argenziano (2004) exhibit in the case of heterogeneous populations asymmetric equilibria that involve positive profits and two active platforms. There seems to be some connection between their result and the analysis of quality choice in vertical differentiation models. In the latter case, one firm chooses a high quality, and the other chooses a low quality. In two-sided markets, one can view the mass of producers as a vertical quality parameter for consumers, since increasing m raises the value for all consumers. Similarly, n is a vertical differentiation parameter for producers. One difference is that these vertical dimensions are concomitant with demand formation. In their equilibrium, one platform chooses a high quality and high price on consumers (m high) and a low quality and low price on producers (n low), while the other chooses the symmetric strategie. The platforms then achieve an endogenous vertical differentiation and, therefore, positive profits. The same phenomenon is discussed in the case of multihoming.

10.5.3 Product Differentiation

Product differentiation is addressed in Jullien (2000) and Armstrong (2002). In particular, Armstrong extends the analysis by allowing horizontal differentiation. He assumes that for each side the two platforms are differentiated à la Hotelling, with the "transportation cost" being additive to the utility from transactions.

Assuming no transaction fees, and that the unit transportation costs are high enough so that both platforms are active, Armstrong concludes that equilibrium prices on both sides are below the standard Hotelling equilibrium prices (marginal cost plus unit transport cost). The interpretation of monopoly pricing extends to this case. The standard Hotelling equilibrium prices are adjusted to include a "subsidy" for the two-sided network effects. Hence a consumer receives a subsidy π corresponding to the price increase that its inclusion in the network of the intermediary allows it to charge the producers. The reverse holds for producers.

This corroborates Jullien (2000) finding that two-sided network externalities reduce the equilibrium profits. In particular, intermediation platforms would benefit by being compatible as this would eliminate the two-sided network effects.

10.5.4 Multihoming

In many cases, participants to an intermediation market need not deal with only one intermediary. For instance, Web surfers usually "surf" by using the services of several search engines or information services. By analogy with website hosting, let us refer to the fact that agents use the services of several intermediaries as multihoming. Notice that it is more difficult to impose exclusivity in the online intermediation activity compared with the brick-and-mortar situation, as it is easier to monitor the use of physical goods. Thus multihoming is more likely online.

Caillaud and Jullien (2003) analyze the outcome of Bertrand-type competition with transaction fees in this context. The main insights from the exclusivity case extend to this case. Competitive strategies can be analyzed as divide-and-conquer strategies, as discussed. The difference is that it is easier to divide since agents may join two platforms, and need not unregister from the first platform to register with the second platform. But in this context, the number of possible profitable strategies increases. Indeed a platform may try to corner the market, but it may also opt for a less aggressive strategy by inducing multihoming: the two intermediation platforms are then active and some agents register with both. Several aspects are worth mentioning.

Result 10.5 With positive transaction fees, multihoming agents will try to concentrate their activity on the low transaction fee platforms. This creates two levels of competition. Intermediaries compete to attract the registration, and in a second stage they compete to attract transactions of multihomers. This competition tends to reduce transaction fees. One should thus expect platforms to charge less in transaction fees if there is a large extent of multihoming.

Result 10.6 With imperfect intermediation activities, multihoming may be efficient as it allows the use of a second intermediation service when one has failed to perform. Efficiency may be obtained with a single active platform or two active platforms. In Caillaud and Jullien (2003), there always exists an efficient equilibrium, but profits are positive unlike the exclusivity case.

Result 10.7 When some agents are multihoming, platforms do not really compete for their registrations since the price of one platform does not affect the net gains of the agent on the other platform. Competition for these agents is then transferred either to the internal market for transactions (if the other side also multihomes), or to the other side registration market (as increased participation of the other side allows a price increase for the multihoming side). Some "semicollusive" equilibria may emerge in which one side of the market multihomes and the other side does not. Part of the profit is competed away on single-homers, but it is recouped by large registration fees for multihomers. This type of situation, although the least efficient, may generate the highest industry profit. This is referred to as "competitive bottleneck" by Armstrong (2005) and studied in Armstrong and Wright (2004).

The case where two platforms are active is also interesting as it involves some type of endogenous vertical differentiation. In such a scenario, the platforms set different transaction fees. All agents register to both platforms and try to use the low transaction fee platform to operate their trade (the first source). They then use the service of the high transaction fee and low registration fee platform (the second source) only when they don't find trading on the other platform. This is reminiscent of Ambrus and Argenziano's (2004) analysis. Gabszewicz and Wauthy (2004) reach a similar conclusion on endogenous vertical differentiation in a model where producers multihome but consumers register with one platform only. There are no transaction fees but populations are heterogeneous, and differentiation comes from having a different mass of agents on each platform.

10.6   Tying as a Coordination Device

Before concluding, let us now return to the assumption that consumers coordinate on the positive participation equilibrium allocation for all prices.

Consider the case of a monopoly platform. For nonnegative prices, there exists an allocation where no side registers. Whether agents will coordinate on the positive participation level or not depends on their beliefs about what the other side is doing. Thus beliefs matter, and agents participate only if they are confident in the participation of the others. This can be interpreted as a *reputation effect*. Such an interpretation in terms of reputation is developed, for instance, in Jullien (2000). The paper examines the optimal pricing strategy of an incumbent network challenged by a competing network, and analyzes the effect of price discrimination. The privileged position of the incumbent in the market is modeled as a reputation effect, based on the idea that each agent anticipates that others will coordinate on the incumbent or at least on the most favorable allocation for the incumbent. This is referred to as *domination in beliefs*. Assuming that agents coordinate on the positive demand equilibrium amounts to the same assumption.

Suppose that the intermediary has no reputation. If it wants to be sure that the consumers and the producers will join the network, it needs to set prices such that $q < F(-p)\pi$ or $p < H(-q)s$. Assume it does the former and sets the registration fees in such a way that a large enough population of consumers are willing to join even if there is no producer on the platform. Thus the intermediary has to incur significant *acquisition costs* for consumers, inducing a loss that is recouped with the revenue derived from the registration fees of producers or the taxation of transactions.

This strategy is thus a divide-and-conquer strategy (see Innes and Sexton 1993 for an application to monopoly pricing with economies of scale). One difficulty with this concept is that it leads to paying consumers and thus may induce agents with no perspective of trade to join. The cost may then be huge as the intermediary may have to pay a large population to attract a small one. An alternative interpretation is that the payment is in kind rather than monetary.

To achieve this goal, the intermediary may tie some good or service with registration so as to create a value to registration for consumers even if producers do not participate. This interpretation is particularly attractive in the context of online intermediation because information goods involve mostly a fixed production cost and no distribution cost. This point is emphasized in Bakos and Brynjolfsson (1999) to explain the emergence of large bundles.[25] What matters for us is that the intermediary will not be too concerned about the extra cost of subsidizing the good to consumers not interested in the intermediation activity.

Suppose that there is an overall population of consumers of size $N + 1$. The mass N consists of consumers who are not interested in intermediation, and face no registration costs. The mass 1 of the rest of consumers is as described before. Any subsidy to consumers would then lead the N consumers to join. Suppose that the intermediary is selling a good that can be bundled with participation. Let v be the utility gain obtained by a consumer when consuming the information good proposed by the intermediary, assumed to be the same for all. Suppose that the variable cost is nil. The intermediary must have some market power over the good, as otherwise the agents could obtain the full value with some competitor. Assume it is a monopoly, the profit from the sale of the good in case there is no bundling is thus $(N + 1)v$.

Suppose that the firm wants to provide the intermediation service but cannot set negative registration fees for the reason exposed already. The intermediary can decide to provide intermediation tied with the information good. Then at price (p, q), there will be a unique positive and active participation equilibrium if $q < F(v - p)\pi$. The total maximal profit is then

$$\max_{p,q,t} \ pN + pn + qm + mnP(t)t,$$

$$st \ 0 < q \le F(v - p)\pi \ \text{and} \ 0 \le p.$$

This will be profitable if it yields more profit than the sale of the product alone, where the price p has to be strictly lower than v. The condition is thus

$$(p - v)n + qm + mnP(t)t > N(v - p).$$

Result 10.8 Tie-in may help solve coordination failures generated by the two-sided nature of the market.

Turning to the case of competition, we have seen that the strategies discussed involve negative payments, in particular negative registration fees. These payments moreover are not due, for instance, to a cost normalization. Negativity of some payments is often embedded in the nature of the strategies. Again a possible interpretation is one where the intermediary offers a gift to consumers registering, or is tying in some good providing a positive value. These are two alternative commercial strategies that can be used to provide subsidies to consumers, depending on the nature of the good tied, and they affect competition in a different manner.

In one scenario, these operations are short-run commercial strategies targeted at some groups for some period of time. One may think here of advertising campaigns, special offers, limited-time gifts, discriminatory subsidies, etc. These fit well with the earlier story because such practices can be adjusted as fast as the prices. If we define the net price as $p - a$ where a is the acquisition cost and if a spent on a consumer yields a units of monetary-equivalent utility, we can interpret a negative price as $a > 0$ and $p = 0$. The platform would then choose both p

and a, or equivalently $p - a$. However, such short-run strategies have limited scope.

In another scenario, the intermediary is active on several products that are offered on a permanent basis. This is the case of portals, or of information sites (ZDNet). In this case, the previous analysis may not apply if the value of these additional services is large. A difference is that the choice of the bundle is made already when platforms decide on prices and cannot be adjusted in the short run. Remember that information goods have negligible variable costs, so that in the case of information goods the ratio of value to price may be large. The key difference when the tied services are valuable enough is that consumers may be willing to remain a client of a particular intermediary or seller, even if there is no intermediation value, just to consume the information goods. The previous analysis argues that one source of profit is that producers are not willing to pay anything if consumers leave the platform. Thus there is some profit qm that vanishes when the competing platform attracts consumers and this profit can not be appropriated by a competitor. This is no longer true with tying of valuable services.

Suppose that all agents receive an extra value v in addition to intermediation with any intermediary, with a cost γ for the platform. It is not clear that this will modify the nature of equilibrium prices and avoid negative prices. Consider the case with transaction fees. The profit of an active platform setting $Pt = S$ is

$$mnS + (p - \gamma)n + (q - \gamma)m$$

$$n = F(v - p); \quad m = H(v - q).$$

The zero profit result derived in the case of full nondistortionary taxation is still valid. Indeed setting $Pt = S$ eliminates the two-sided nature of the market, and agents simply would join the lowest registration platform so that the traditional undercutting Bertrand logic applies. Still prices will be positive only if γ is large enough, which is not the case for information goods.

Consider the case where there are no transaction registration fees. With the reasoning of section 5.2 on the divide-and-conquer strategy, the registration fee for producers must convince them to give up v thus (for fixed m and n):

Conquer: $q_2 = \pi + v + \inf\{0, q - v\}$.

Then, provided that $q < v$, this leads to the condition that the platform 1 profit is less than $(s - \pi)$. By symmetry, whenever $p < v$, we find that the active platform profit must be less than $(\pi - s)$. But $\min\{s - \pi, \pi - s\}$ is negative so that if both prices are below v, both registration fees need to be negative, otherwise the second platform has a profitable conquering strategy.

Indeed, as shown in Jullien (2000), if the two intermediaries tie the intermediation with other information goods, and these goods are valuable enough, the two-sided nature of the market intensifies competition. In particular, a (pure) equilibrium may not exist if the two intermediation platforms offer similar services. This suggests that intermediation markets may be unstable or "too contestable." Jullien (2000) then argues that the intermediaries can evade from competition by combining two strategies:

1. Product differentiation Intermediaries may differentiate the information goods they tie with the service. They then segment the intermediation market, focusing only on a subpopulation. This may involve strategic degradation of the quality of some services as a commitment not to compete for some subsegment of the population. Clearly, these strategies leading to a peaceful coexistence of differentiated platforms involve inefficiencies. In particular, platforms do not exploit all the potential gains from network effects.

2. Information sharing Differentiated intermediaries may soften competition by sharing their information and allowing their customers access to competitors' networks. Doing that, they reduce the importance of network effects at the platform level as they are transferred at the market level. The reason is that divide-and-conquer strategies rely on network effects within an intermediary network and they are a very powerful competitive tool. By eliminating the strategic attractiveness of divide-and-conquer strategies, information sharing, and more generally compatibility between network goods may soften competition. An example of this strategy is the increased cooperation of traditional stock markets, partly as a reaction to the emerging online electronic exchanges.

10.7 Conclusion

Infomediation requires that the various sides of the market agree on using the same service. Thus the intermediaries online can be seen as platforms on which trading partners meet and interact. Such platforms are subject to two-sided network externalities, a potential source of market failure. In such a context, traditional price analysis does not apply. Intermediaries should be seen as setting a price structure, and evaluating the impact of this price structure globally, accounting for indirect effects. The approach of the activity in terms of two-sided markets brings some preliminary conclusions.

Pricing should and will involve some form of cross-subsidy. The service provider will attract one side of the market with a low price in order to stimulate the participation of the other side. Typically, the low externality side of the market should be the target for subsidy.

Competition exacerbates the tendency to cross-subsidize as competitive strategies involve a divide-and-conquer dimension. While ex post concentration is likely to occur, competition should discipline the market to a larger extent than standard isotropic network effects. The contestable nature of such markets remains a debatable question as it seems to rely on extreme strategies that would be risky in a more uncertain context.

In such a context, an intermediary may engage in tying information goods for efficiency purposes, such as solving coordination problems.[26]

Multihoming may improve efficiency, although one should be concerned about the potential softening of competition that may result from systematic multihoming. In particular, mandatory access to each other's platforms may not always be in the best interest of consumers if it leads to higher prices.

Another conclusion is that platforms should try to intervene on the design of the trading process, raising the total surplus from the transactions operated on the platforms. This may involve direct interventions, or some indirect effect through prices.[27]

Two issues remain to be addressed as natural extensions of these conclusions. First, it is unclear whether the nature of market failures justifies some regulation, and which form it would take. Second, given that these markets are concentrated due to network effects, they should fall under the scrutiny of antitrust authorities. So far the implications of the type of cross-subsidy and tying occurring in these markets for the conduct of antitrust policy have not been properly addressed (see Evans 2003). At the least, it is important that antitrust authorities understand the economic rationale of these practices and their procompetitive effects.

Notes

The author thanks Carole Haritchabalet, Martin Peitz, Monika Schnitzer, and participants at the CESifo conference "Understanding the Digital Economy," and at the IDEI conference "The Economics of Electronic Communications Markets" for valuable comments.

Toulouse University (IDEI and GREMAQ-CNRS), email: bjullien@cict.fr.

1. See also the survey on electronic commerce in *The Economist* (February 2000).

2. Nextag, for instance, proposes a search engine to compare products and prices over all furnishers.

3. There are other externalities involved that are ignored in this chapter. In particular the terms of trade may be affected by the degree of concentration on each side of the market.

4. See Yanelle (1989).

5. See Ghemawat and Baird (1998). Amazon is discussed by Peitz and Waelbroeck in chapter 4, and by Dinlersoz and Pereira in chapter 9 of this book.

6. Amazon allows the use of an Amazon account to operate an online transaction without providing credit card information.

7. See Rochet and Tirole (2003).

8. See Katz and Shapiro (1985, 1986) and Farrell and Saloner (1985).

9. The alliance between Cornerbrand and Kazaa described by Peitz and Waelbroeck in chapter 4 of this book is a good example of such a strategy, as each side benefits from it.

10. Notice that consumers differ ex ante only by their opportunity cost c. The trading surplus may vary ex post (once the trading partner is found) but in expected terms, it is the same for all consumers ex ante.

11. A simple model goes as follows: At the time they choose to access the service, consumers do not know which product they will be willing to buy. They connect to the Web, and only then do consumers draw randomly single products that they wish to consume (their valuation being 0 for the others). At this stage they do not know yet what will be their precise valuation for the good nor its price. Then they must find whether the product is available, what its precise characteristics are, and what its price is. For this they have access to the search technology of the intermediary.

Once the match is done, the consumers observe their final valuation w for the good as well as the price quoted by the producer. The distribution of w determines a demand function $D(.)$ for the good that is assumed to be the same for all goods. Given that all consumers are alike at the time the producers decide on the price and that consumers learn the price and w only after the search process is completed, producers will choose the price $\hat{p}(t)$ net of t_P that maximizes $\hat{p}D(\hat{p} + t)$. Let λ be the probability that a match is performed when the pair is present; then the expected participation profit is $\pi(t) = \lambda\hat{p}(t)D(\hat{p}(t) + t)$, while $s(t)$ is equal to $\lambda \int_{\hat{p}(t)+t}^{\infty} D(w)\,dw$ and $P(t) = \lambda D(\hat{p}(t) + t)$.

12. See Ferrando, Gabsewicz, Laussel and Sonnac (2003), Anderson and Coate (2004), or Crampes, Haritchabalet, and Jullien (2004).

13. Notice that intermediation also may involve direct negative externalities. For instance, when sellers compete on the platform, the presence of an additional seller

increases the competitive pressure and reduces the expected profit of other sellers (see Baye and Morgan 2001, or Belleflamme and Toulemonde 2004).

14. Notice that a negative transaction fee may induce parties to claim false matches and collect the fees. We may conclude that the optimal transaction fee is zero in this case.

15. Rochet and Tirole (2003) focus on a situation where the volume of transaction V depends on both the total transaction fee and its distribution between the parties. They refer to this case as a two-sided usage externality. I shall not consider such externalities. The situation described in the present chapter corresponds according to their terminology to a one-sided usage interaction.

Still, by reducing the gains from trade, a tax on transactions also affects the participation levels. Thus the determination of the usage fee must account for a two-sided dimension "mediated" through the participation levels, but not for the relative intensity of usage by both sides.

16. Clearly, this result relies on the fact that the expected surplus is the same for all trading pairs. Otherwise welfare maximization would call to maximize the average welfare from trade given the participation levels, while profit maximization will account for the surplus of the marginal consumers and producers.

17. With risk averse participants, a positive transaction fee may help in providing some insurance to the participants.

18. Hagiu (2004) develops an argument along this line where transaction fees are negative. He then examines a sequential pricing and participation game (producers then consumers). He points to the fact that running a deficit on transactions allows the raising of the producers' registration fee, but it may hinder the incentives to attract consumers thereafter. The ability to commit on future prices for consumers then matters for the conclusion. Without such a commitment, transaction fees will be higher.

19. Their results, as with all results in this literature, require some restrictions on the way consumers and producers select their platform. While there are many alternatives discussed in the literature, they would all lead to the same conclusion for the competitive benchmark. Although important, these selection issues are rather conceptual and technical, so I leave them aside.

20. A similar argument would show that two intermediaries cannot be active.

21. Remember that there is at most one allocation where a single platform serves the market at any price structure. Therefore a consumer cannot expect to have more than m producers on a platform at the exhibited prices.

22. Jullien (2000) provides a treatment of a general competitive game between networks, allowing for asymmetric network effects and price discrimination.

23. Given the symmetric condition for q and p, if $\pi > s$, the prices are $p = s - \pi$, $q = \inf\{\pi, 2(\pi - s)\}$ leading to profit $\Pi = \inf\{s, \pi - s\} > 0$.

24. Passive expectations are not consistent with subgame perfection in a two-stage game where platforms set prices and then consumers and producers register. Notice, however, that it would be compatible with a Bayesian equilibrium of the same two-stage game where each side of the market sees only its prices but not the other side's prices, which seems to fit their equilibrium analysis.

25. A more general discussion of the tying of information goods is presented by Belleflamme in chapter 6 of this book, focusing on other aspects.

26. See Rochet and Tirole (2004b) for a similar view on tying between two payment card services.

27. See Damiano and Li (2003) for an application of this principle to assortative matching.

References

Anderson, S., and S. Coate (2004): "Market Provision of Broadcasting: A Welfare Analysis," forthcoming, *Review of Economic Studies*.

Ambrus, A., and R. Argenziano (2004): "Network Markets and Consumer Coordination," CESifo Working Paper 1317.

Armstrong, M. (2005): "Competition in Two-Sided Markets," mimeo, University College London.

Armstrong, M., and J. Wright (2004): "Two-Sided Markets, Competitive Bottlenecks and Exclusive Contracts," mimeo, University College London.

Bakos, Y., and E. Brynjolfsson (1999): "Bundling Information Goods," *Management Science*.

Baye, M. R., and J. Morgan (2001): "Information Gatekeepers on the Internet and the Competitiveness of Homogeneous Product Markets," *American Economic Review* 91, no. 3, 454–474.

Belleflamme, P., and E. Toulemonde (2004): "B2B Marketplaces: Emergence and Entry," CORE Discussion Paper 2004/78, Université Catholique de Louvain.

Caillaud, B., and B. Jullien (2001): "Competing Cybermediaries," *European Economic Review* (papers and proceedings) 45, 797–808.

——— (2003): "Chicken & Egg: Competition Among Intermediation Service Providers," *Rand Journal of Economics*, 34, 309–328.

Crampes, C., C. Haritchabalet, and B. Jullien (2004): "Competition with Advertising Resources," IDEI Working Paper.

Damiano, E., and H. Li (2003): "Price Discrimination in Matching Markets," mimeo, University of Toronto.

Evans, D. (2003): "The Antitrust Economics of Multi-Sided Platform Markets," *Yale Journal on Regulation*, 20: 325–382.

Farrell, J., and G. Saloner (1985): "Standardization, Compatibility and Innovation," *Rand Journal of Economics* 16, 70–83.

Ferrando, J., J. Gabsewicz, D. Laussel, and N. Sonnac (2003): "Two-Sided Network Effect and Competition: An Application to Media Industries," mimeo, CREST-LEI.

Gabszewicz, J., and X. Wauthy (2004): "Two-Sided Markets and Price Competition with Multi-homing," CORE Discussion Paper 2004/30, Université Catholique de Louvain.

Gaudeul, A., and B. Jullien (2001): "E-commerce: Quelques éléments d'économie industrielle," *Revue Économique* 52, 97–117.

Ghemawat, P., and B. Baird (1998): "Leadership Online (A): Barnes&Noble vs Amazon.com," Harvard Business School, Case Study 9-798-063.

Hagiu, A. (2004): "Optimal Pricing and Commitment in Two-Sided Markets," mimeo, Princeton University.

Innes, R., and R. Sexton (1993): "Customer Coalitions, Monopoly Price Discrimination and Generic Entry Deterrence," *European Economic Review* 37, 1569–1597.

Jullien, B. (2000): "Competing with Network Externalities and Price Discrimination," IDEI Working Paper.

Katz, M., and K. Shapiro (1985): "Network Externalities, Competition and Compatibility," *American Economic Review* 75, 424–440.

Katz, M., and K. Shapiro (1986): "Technology Adoption in the Presence of Network Externalities," *Journal of Political Economy* 94, 822–841.

Rochet, J. C., and J. Tirole (2003): "Platform Competition in Two-Sided Markets," *Journal of the European Economic Association* 1, 990–1029.

Rochet, J. C., and J. Tirole (2004a): "Two-Sided Market: An Overview," IDEI Working Paper.

Rochet, J. C., and J. Tirole (2004b): "Tying in Two-Sided Markets and the Honor-all-Cards Rule," IDEI Working Paper.

Wright, J. (2003): "Optimal Card Payment System," *European Economic Review* 47, 587–617.

Yanelle, M. O. (1989): "On the Theory of Intermediation," dissertation, University Bonn.

Contributors

Paul Belleflamme
Université Catholique de Louvain

Jay Pil Choi
Michigan State University

Emin M. Dinlersoz
University of Houston

David S. Evans
LECG LLC

Chaim Fershtman
Tel Aviv University

Neil Gandal
Tel Aviv University

Amit Gayer
University of Haifa

Andrei Hagiu
Research Institute for the
Ministry of Economy, Trade and
Industry, Japan

Gerhard Illing
Ludwig Maximilian University of
Munich

Bruno Jullien
Université des Sciences Sociales
de Toulouse

Eirik Gaard Kristiansen
Norwegian School of Economics
and Business Administration

Jae Nahm
Hong Kong University of Science
and Technology

Martin Peitz
International University in
Germany

Pedro Pereira
Portuguese Competition
Authority

Stan J. Liebowitz
University of Texas at Dallas

Richard Schmalensee
Sloan School of Management,
Massachusetts Institute of
Technology

Oz Shy
University of Haifa

Patrick Waelbroeck
Université Libre de Bruxelles

Index